IMAGES
of America

PECOS

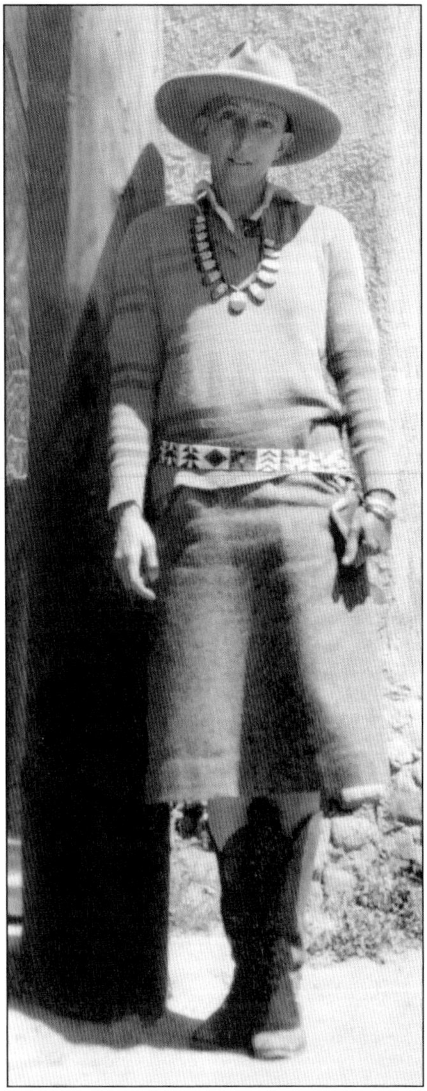

Edith Gladys Jenkyns, known as "Jenks," was born on June 3, 1892, in Burley, England. A trained nurse in England, after immigrating to America in 1915, she became the nanny for the Yallalee and Hamilton families, first at Valley Ranch in 1916 and then at Mountain View Ranch when the families moved there in 1917 for the summer months (see chapter four). In the winter, the families resided at Bishop's Lodge, outside of Santa Fe (see Arcadia Publishing's Images of America: *Santa Fe's Historic Hotels*). In the 1920s, she was employed as a "courier," or tour guide, for the Indian Detour Transportation Co. In the 1930s, she became manager of that company, based out of the La Fonda Hotel in Santa Fe. She never married, and she died in Santa Fe in January 1969. See chapter eight for more on the Indian Detour. (Courtesy of Merideth Hmura, No. 1499.)

ON THE COVER: In this 1926 photograph, an Indian Detour car and bus have stopped to give some tourists, or "dudes," as the tour company called them, a look at the Pecos ruins (see chapters two and eight). These tours were an integral part of the Atchison, Topeka & Santa Fe (AT&SF) Railway and the Fred Harvey Company's introduction of the Southwest to adventuresome travelers. On the grill of the car are the words "Packard Harveycar." This is a rare image from a group of lantern slides in the collection of Diane Drobka. (Courtesy of Diane Drobka.)

IMAGES
of America

PECOS

Paul R. Secord

ARCADIA
PUBLISHING

ISBN 978-1-4671-3237-4

Published by Arcadia Publishing
Charleston, South Carolina

Printed in the United States of America

Library of Congress Control Number: 2014937885

For all general information, please contact Arcadia Publishing:
Telephone 843-853-2070
Fax 843-853-0044
E-mail sales@arcadiapublishing.com
For customer service and orders:
Toll-Free 1-888-313-2665

Visit us on the Internet at www.arcadiapublishing.com

To those passing through Pecos on any day, past, present, or future: Native Americans, explorers, adventurers, outlaws, traders, soldiers, farmers, ranchers, innkeepers, dudes, retailers, miners, archaeologists, forest workers, hatchery workers, National Park Service staff, retirees, Hollywood stars, village and valley denizens, tourists, and any other groups I might have missed.

Contents

Acknowledgments

Many people and organizations made this book possible. Here is a partial list: my wife, Marcia, for her proofreading, comments, counsel, and making several key contacts; Jennifer Coile, Bill Baxter, and Gordon Bronitsky, PhD, for critical proofreading and editing; Rick Hendricks, PhD, state historian; Pecos National Historical Park, in particular Christine Beekman and Jeremy Moss for their comments; Merideth Hmura for comments, proofing, and access to photographs from the Matie R. Viles Collection; Michael J. Trinklein for his map of the state of Montezuma; Joe Mildenberger for his artwork of the Yellowstone Saloon; and Mayfield Marshall for his automobile identification skills.

The images in this volume appear courtesy of: Nancy Tucker (NT), Diane Drobka (DD), Alice and Bill McSweeny (AM), Leon McDuff (LM), Ed Irvin (EI), Joanna and Tito Herrera (J&TH), Katherine Summers Price (KSP), Salli Slaughter (SS), Merideth Hmura (MH), the New Mexico State Records Center and Archives (NMSRCA), the New Mexico Center for Southwest Research (CSWR), the Pecos National Historical Park (PNHP), the US Historic American Building Survey (HABS), the US National Archives and Records Administration (USNA), and the author's collection (AC).

I would also like to thank the staff at Arcadia Publishing for their rapid responses to all my questions and for making it easy to bring this project in ahead of schedule. Lastly, a most heartfelt thanks to friends and associates, without whom this book would not exist.

Introduction

There is no greater range of history in New Mexico than that found within the 15 miles surrounding the village of Pecos in Santa Fe and San Miguel County. This book explores the last 1,000 years of that history, expressed by many cultures and events, including Native Americans, Spanish explorers, a Civil War battle, the Santa Fe Trail, railroads, and Route 66, as well as miners, saloon keepers, archaeologists, tourists, important architects, and even Hollywood stars.

The US National Park Service preserves several prehistoric and historic Pueblo villages and Spanish ruins as part of Pecos National Historical Park. Pioneering archaeologist Alfred Kidder carried out the first extensive archaeological explorations of the Pecos area early in the 20th century. The ruins of Pecos Pueblo were important landmarks and a stopping point on the Santa Fe Trail. There is a connection to the modern Towa-speaking Pueblo of Jemez, 70 miles to the west, where the last inhabitants of Pecos Pueblo, also Towa speakers, took final refuge when they abandoned their pueblo in 1838.

Glorieta is the site of the most important Civil War engagement in the West. The outcome guaranteed that the New Mexico Territory remained part of the Union. A small community developed around the Glorieta railroad station in 1879.

Until the mine closed in May 1939, Tererro was a center for metal mining in northern New Mexico. Tererro was also the starting point of what was once the longest ore-transportation aerial tramway in North America, carrying ore over mountains and canyons to a large mill just outside the village of Pecos.

The village of Pecos, located in the center of the Pecos Valley, is the commercial center of the region, with a post office since 1883. Until 1937, Route 66 passed through the village. The valley also contains Fir Tree House, the only complete Frank Lloyd Wright house in New Mexico. Just north of the village of Pecos is the Lisboa Springs Fish Hatchery, the oldest in the state.

Genízaros were principally of Native American heritage, although without specific tribal affiliations, having been assimilated into New Mexico's Spanish culture. In about 1800, they formed the core population of several fortified villages along the Pecos River, which served as a buffer between raiding Plains Indians and the Rio Grande valley.

Cattle ranches and sheep grazing were once mainstays of the Pecos economy. Pecos has also long been a center for tourism, serving as a main destination on Fred Harvey's Indian Detour in the 1920s and 1930s, with a lunch stop at the Valley Ranch Apache Inn. The region once had a number of dude ranches with famous guests, including the silent movie star cowboy Tom Mix.

Hollywood came to Pecos when rodeo promoter "Tex" Austin's ranch house, designed in 1925 by John Gaw Meem, became the summer home for many years of "Buddy" Fogelson and his wife, actress Greer Garson. Actress Jane Fonda also maintains a ranch in the area.

The Pecos area was the focus of one day on the initial 1925 three-day Indian Detour route: a trip in specially designed Packard Eight touring cars and buses under the auspices of the AT&SF Railway and the Fred Harvey Company that continued through the 1930s. This included visits to a number of the places presented in this book.

For hundreds of years, Pecos was a regional cultural center. It was the site of one of the largest prehistoric and historic Pueblo communities in the Southwest, a key early Spanish settlement, and an important cultural crossroads at the edge of the Great Plains. The Santa Fe Trail passed through the region, followed by the railroad and, for a brief period, Route 66. Pecos is an epicenter for many of the myths and stories associated with New Mexico. The rest of this introduction focuses on a discussion of some of these myths.

Several Pueblo Indian legends are associated with the Aztec emperor Montezuma. Many of these have Montezuma either (a) born at Pecos; (b) leaving Pecos on the back of an eagle; but, (c) before leaving, lighting a sacred fire that must not be allowed to go out; (d) founding the Aztec capital Tenochtitlan when the eagle, after catching a rattlesnake, alighted on a cactus plant; and (e) vowing to return to liberate New Mexico from oppressors.

There were two real Montezumas in history: Montezuma I (c. 1398–1469), the fifth Aztec emperor, who oversaw a major expansion of Tenochtitlan (now Mexico City); and Montezuma II (c. 1466–June 29, 1520), the ninth and last Aztec emperor, who was killed during the Spanish conquest of Mexico.

While the origins of the many Montezuma stories in New Mexico remain enigmatic, and all of them are undocumented, they have continually been reinvented through the centuries, speaking to different cultural traumas. Many possible origins exist for stories about Aztec emperor Montezuma in New Mexico.

Accounts of Montezuma I may have been popular in Mexico before the European conquest and found their way to New Mexico long before Europeans entered the Southwest.

In 1540–1541, Francisco Vásquez de Coronado led the first European expedition into what is now New Mexico. The expedition consisted of about 400 Spaniards and as many as 1,500 natives of Mexican tribes. Some of these *indios amigos* stayed in New Mexico after the Spaniards left and were absorbed into Pueblo society. Other Mexican natives were part of the permanent settlement of New Mexico by Juan de Oñate, starting in 1598. Many of these native peoples were Tlaxcalans, the traditional enemies of the Aztecs.

Montezuma stories might trace their origins in New Mexico to 17th- and 18th-century Spanish colonists or their Mexican Indian servants. Many Pueblo stories equate Montezuma with native gods in a contest with the Catholic God, sometimes conflated with the Pueblo hero Poseyemu, or even Jesus Christ.

There are reports of a document called "History of Montezuma," written in Mexico City, which purportedly substantiates Mexican title to the New Mexico region from the Pueblo Indian point of view. However, this propaganda piece apparently backfired. The legends did not support Mexican claims to New Mexico, as they had Montezuma leaving the Pueblos (Pecos), prophesying a conquering race (Spaniards), and returning with a liberating "white" race coming from the east (Americans).

William H. Prescott's work *A History of the Conquest of Mexico* was published in 1843 and received wide circulation. This work describes the Aztec civilization and discusses Montezuma. It was well known to educated Anglos in New Mexico, such as military officers. New Mexican stories of connections with the Aztecs would have resonated in light of this first comprehensive history of the Mexican conquest, which came out just before the 1846–1848 Mexican border campaign and the resulting American acquisition of New Mexico.

Some myths suggest the Aztecs are originally from the Pueblo Southwest. This is the myth of Aztlán, expressed by William Ritch's 1885 promotional book *Aztlán: The History, Resources and Attractions of New Mexico* and adopted by the Chicano movement in the late 1960s.

To this day, Matachines dancers at Pueblos and Hispanic communities enact a "conquest dance," with the chief characters including El Monarca, the monarch Montezuma, his main generals, and Malintzin, the Indian mistress of Hernán Cortés.

The Montezuma stories are often associated with a "sacred fire" supposedly maintained by the inhabitants of Pecos Pueblo. The embers of the fire were said to be tended in a ceremonial chamber (kiva) or in a secret cave. There are caves in the vicinity of Pecos that are known to have been used by Native Americans since prehistoric times. The caves are not open to access by the public, as they are still used by Native Americans.

Special fires and their ashes are associated with Pueblo rituals. Pueblo ceremonial chambers, called kivas, always have a fire pit. A kiva is usually, but not always, a round subterranean room with access restricted to initiated members. They also function something like men's clubhouses.

Over 20 kivas are known at Pecos Pueblo. Excavations at a locale inside a house blocking where the fire was said to have been kept revealed no evidence of such a fire.

The earliest recorded mention of the fire dates from a September 24, 1847, article in the *Santa Fe Republican* about an 1835 visit to the "furnace of Montezuma" at Pecos.

A cinder said to be from "Montezuma's fire" may well have been the first souvenir purchased at Pecos. In September 1839, an old shepherd told a Montezuma story to journalists Matthew C. Field and David C. Waldo while they were having supper at the foot of the altar inside the ruins of the Pecos church. The shepherd said that the following morning he would show them the cave where the sacred fire had been kept, but, not having time for the excursion, they paid the shepherd a "few bits of silver" for the aforementioned cinder and continued on their journey.

Marta Weigle and Peter White, in their excellent book *The Lore of New Mexico*, quoted historian John L. Kessel's description of how Quetzalcoatl, a Mesoamerican deity in the form of a feathered serpent, slithered his way up to New Mexico in prehistoric times. This creature transmogrified to become the Awanyu in the Southwest. He lost his feathers on his trip north, grew a horn, and has a dog-like head with teeth, along with the tail of a rattlesnake.

Depictions of Awanyus are common throughout the Southwest. There are rock art figures in close proximity to Pecos, although none are known within the boundaries of Pecos Historical Park and all are on restricted-access properties.

There are also stories of the people at Pecos keeping a very large rattlesnake either in a kiva or, more probably, in a cave. None of these have been substantiated by eyewitness testimony. The longest documented western rattlesnake was just over seven and a half feet long.

In the 1920s, an older worker on Alfred Kidder's Pecos archaeological excavations identified a specific kiva as being the one where a giant snake was kept. However, this kiva was not excavated and is now completely buried. In addition, most stories have the snake kept in a cave rather than a kiva.

So, myths abound that include variants of a Montezuma story coupled with a sacred fire and a giant snake. In her famous 1927 novel *Death Comes for the Archbishop*, Willa Cather drew on these accounts, describing a Pecos Indian leading Bishop Latour to take shelter from a storm in a sacred cave. Later, Latour hears parts of the Montezuma legend, including the part about a giant snake. In addition, Elsie Clews Parson, in her 1925 study *The Pueblo of Jemez*, stated, "There is considerable probability that the [Jemez] Snake society is of Pecos origin."

In 1863 and 1888, proposals were made to change the name of New Mexico to Montezuma, while, in 1903, Arizona was added to the proposed state of Montezuma, forming a super-state. This idea was submitted to a popular vote in 1906, only to be soundly defeated in Arizona, although approved in New Mexico.

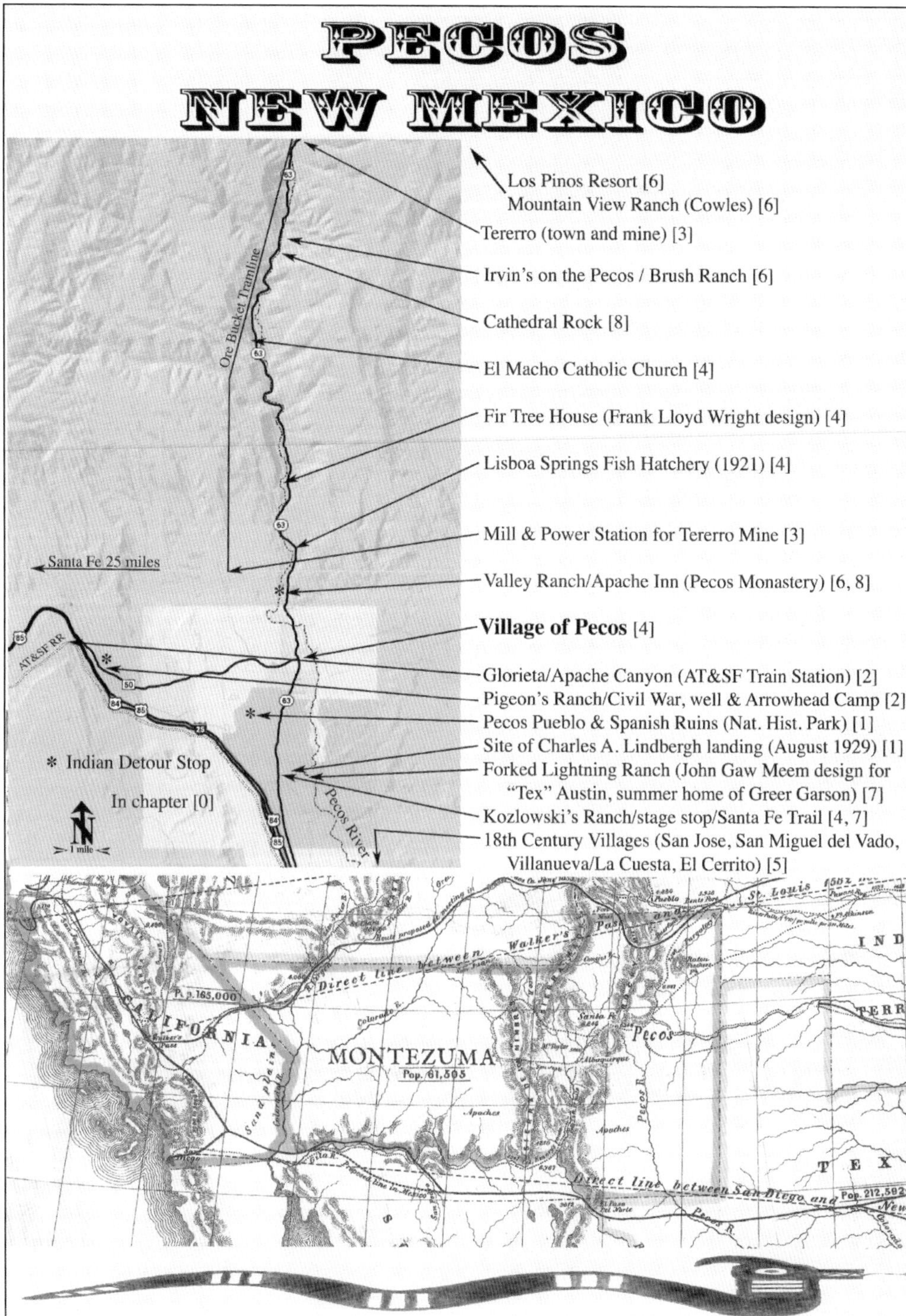

The above image was prepared by Paul R. Secord in January 2014. The map of the state of Montezuma is from Michael J. Trinklein's *Lost States*, published by Quirk Books in 2010. The plumed serpent is from the author's collection.

One

Indians and Spanish

Human habitation of the Pecos area goes back as far as any place in the Americas. There is evidence in the region of Clovis Culture hunters (10,000-plus to 5,500 years ago), followed by Archaic Period hunter-gatherers (5,500 to 800 years ago), early Puebloan farmers (1100 to 1300 AD), and "Classic"-period Pueblo peoples, as applied at Pecos, from 1325 to 1838 AD.

The proper Towa name for Pecos is Cicuyé. Pecos is the Keres-language name for this pueblo, used by a group of pueblos to the west and most often used by the Spanish. Pecos was first and foremost a significant Native American farming village inhabited by Towa speakers, a Kiowa-Tanoan language now spoken today only at Jemez Pueblo. Pecos Pueblo, along with several others in the area, is located at an elevation of nearly 7,000 feet. All are in a pass near the Pecos River separated from the other pueblos along the Rio Grande by the southern foothills of the Sangre de Cristo Mountains and from the Plains Indians to the east by the Tecolote Mountains. From prehistoric into historic times, there were a number of very large Native American pueblos, occupied primarily by Tano speakers in the Galisteo Basin to the south.

For many years, Pecos was the site of trade fairs where nomads from the Plains brought slaves, buffalo hides, flint, and shells to trade with the pueblos for pottery, crops, textiles, and turquoise. These trade fairs continued well into historic times.

Pecos Pueblo was first visited by Europeans, members of the Francisco Vásquez de Coronado expedition, in 1540–1541. The first Spanish church at Pecos Pueblo is generally attributed to Fray Pedro Zambrano Ortiz in about 1619 and was built on an isolated site northeast of the main pueblo. It was abandoned in 1625. A series of three churches and two *conventos* have been identified as having stood at the site of the present ruins of the 18th-century church complex.

While Pecos was generally sympathetic to the Spaniards, it was also deeply factionalized, a factor that contributed to its demise. In the early 1700s, raiders became an increasing problem for the residents of Pecos. They were mostly Comanches from the east, and even Navajos from the west, who forced the Pecos Apache allies off the plains and into the mountains. Smallpox and other diseases also drastically reduced local populations and disrupted the Pueblo culture. By 1838, the last 17 native residents left Pecos.

Pecos Pueblo and many nearby archaeological sites have been the subjects of extensive archaeological exploration and excavations since the early part of the 20th century.

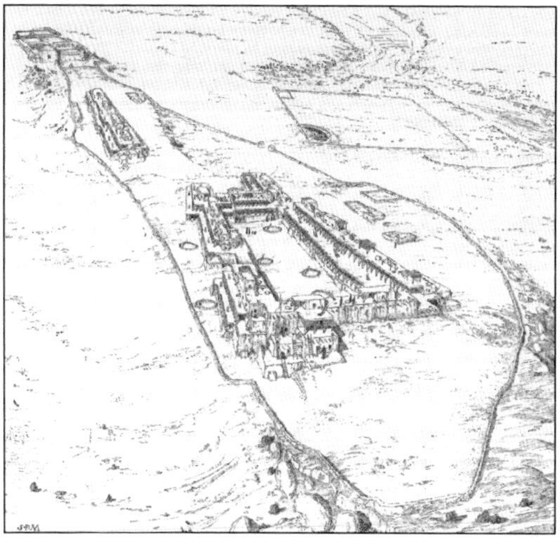

These illustrations show Pecos as it appeared in 1700. The pueblo was a multistory structure on a low ridge built around a central plaza. Note the round kivas. Beyond the main building is a rectangular house block, and beyond that is the church complex. A low wall encircled the habitation areas. (AC.)

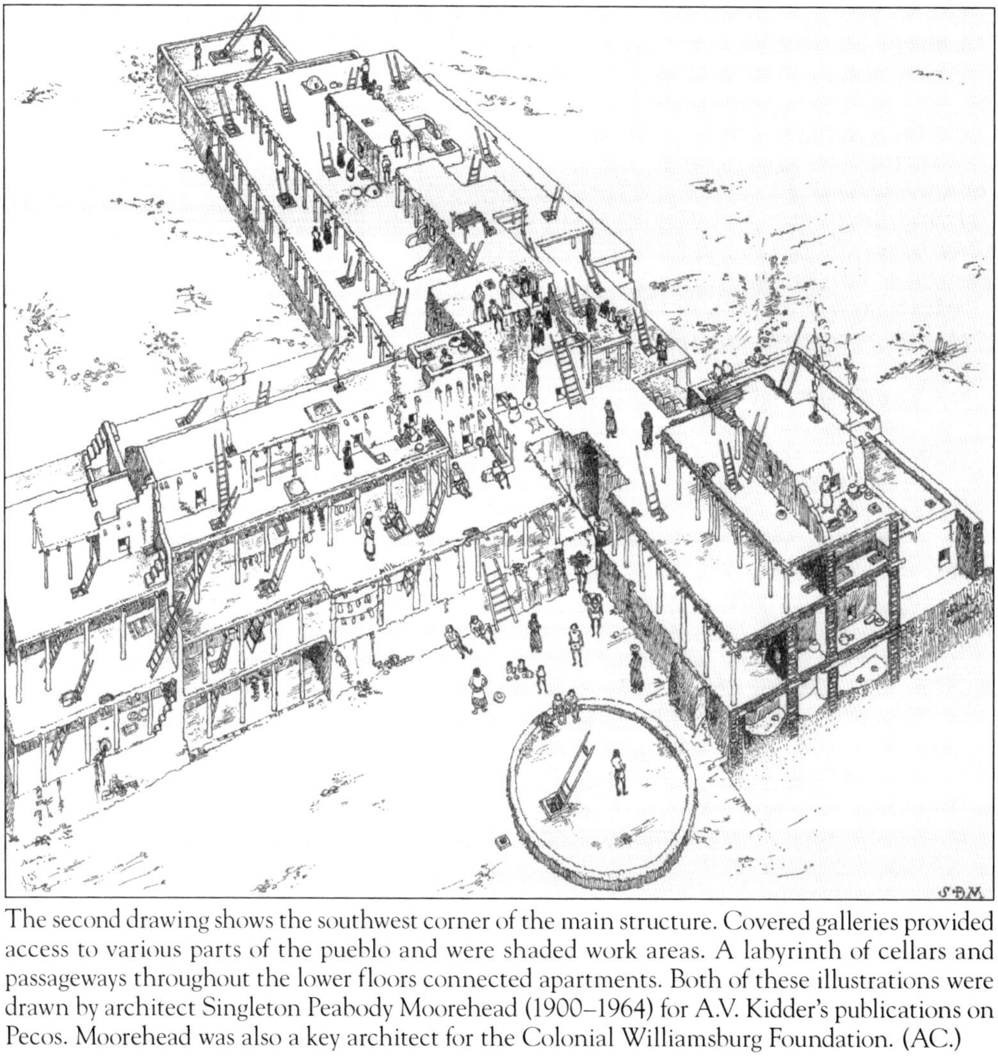

The second drawing shows the southwest corner of the main structure. Covered galleries provided access to various parts of the pueblo and were shaded work areas. A labyrinth of cellars and passageways throughout the lower floors connected apartments. Both of these illustrations were drawn by architect Singleton Peabody Moorehead (1900–1964) for A.V. Kidder's publications on Pecos. Moorehead was also a key architect for the Colonial Williamsburg Foundation. (AC.)

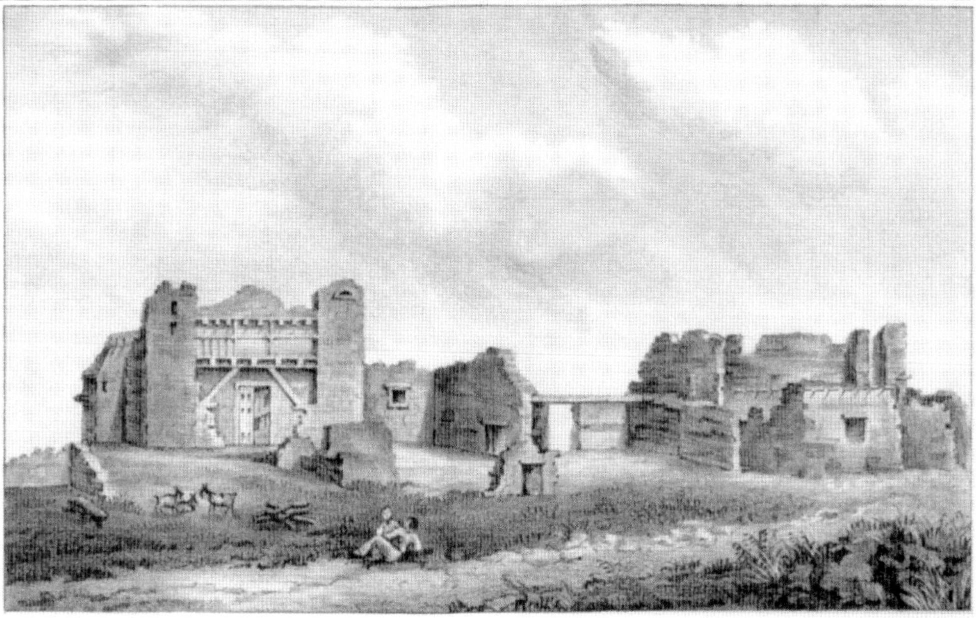

RUINS OF PECOS CATHO CHURCH

Lith by E. Weber & Co. Balto.

The lithographs reproduced on this page show the Pecos church complex; with the image below, although it is identified as the "Ruins of Pecos Aztek Church," it is actually the remains of the main pueblo, from approximately the same location as the room block cutout illustration on the preceding page. This is how Pecos appeared on August 16, 1846, during the US military expedition of Col. Stephen Watts Kearny (1794–1848) from Fort Leavenworth, Kansas, to San Diego, California, during the Mexico border campaign. Both of these lithographs were drawn by John Mix Stanley (1814–1872), a draftsman for the Corps of Topographical Engineers who recorded the Kearny expedition. They are reproduced in the 1848 publication *Notes of a Military Reconnoissance* [sic] by William H. Emory (1811–1887). (Both, AC.)

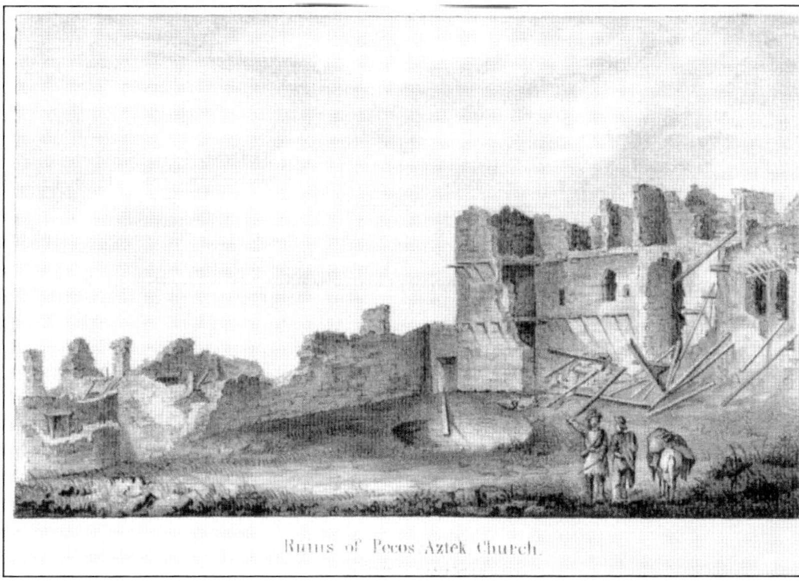

Ruins of Pecos Aztek Church.

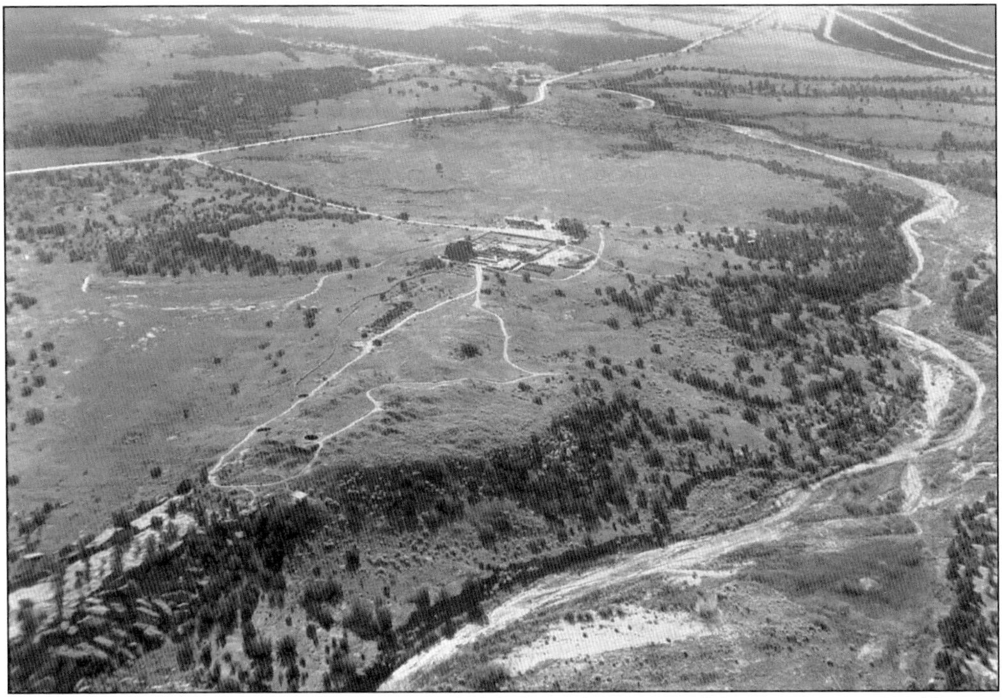

The photograph above is an aerial view, probably from the 1960s, of the entire Pecos Pueblo site. In the house block mounds, several round kivas are visible, as are the church complex ruins. Wagon ruts of the Santa Fe Trail are visible from the National Park Service building beyond the church ruin to the bend in the road. The photograph below is an early view of the church complex ruins looking southeast. It was taken in the late 19th century. The pond is a remnant of an extensive Pueblo water catchment system. The main settlement at Pecos was begun around 1300, with major additions in about 1450. During that time, people from many other settlements in the Pecos Valley relocated to the main Pecos Pueblo site. (Above, PNHP No. 1229-3; below, No. 1229-6.)

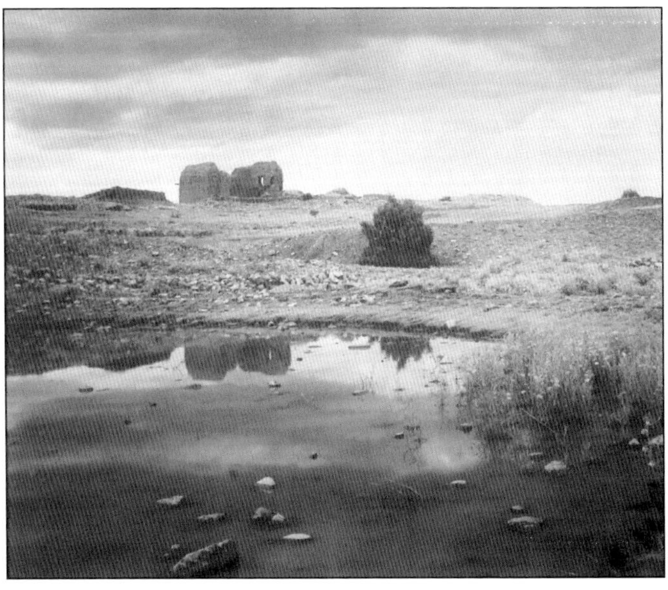

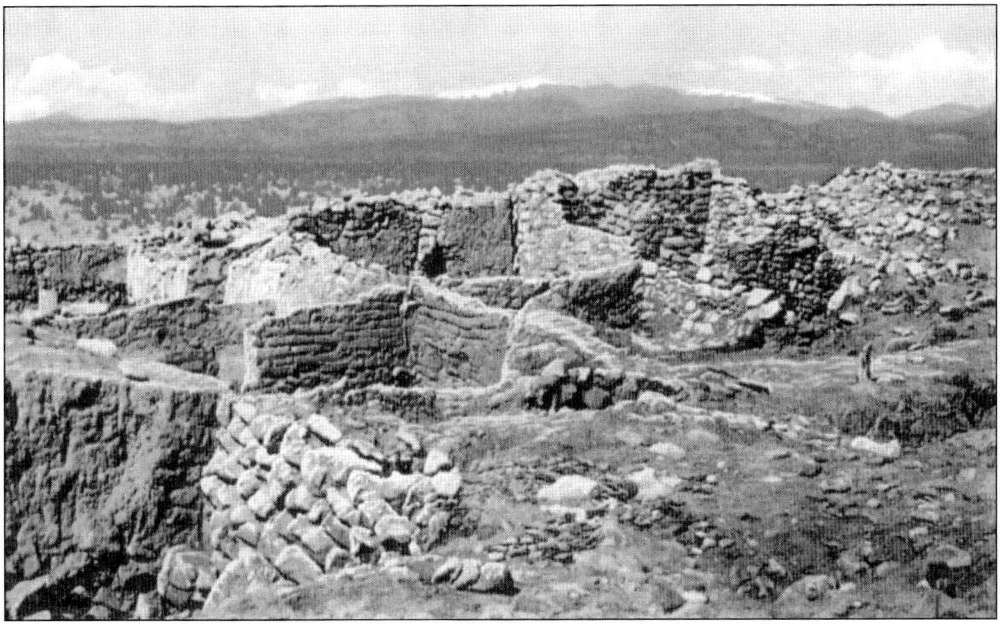

The postcard image above, probably from the 1930s, shows the excavated north pueblo, work that was done by A.V. Kidder in the early 1920s. The photograph below, taken about 1922, shows excavations of the far northern portion of the main house block. Glorieta Creek is on the right, and a portion of the perimeter wall surrounding Pecos is clearly visible. (Above, NT; below, CSWR.)

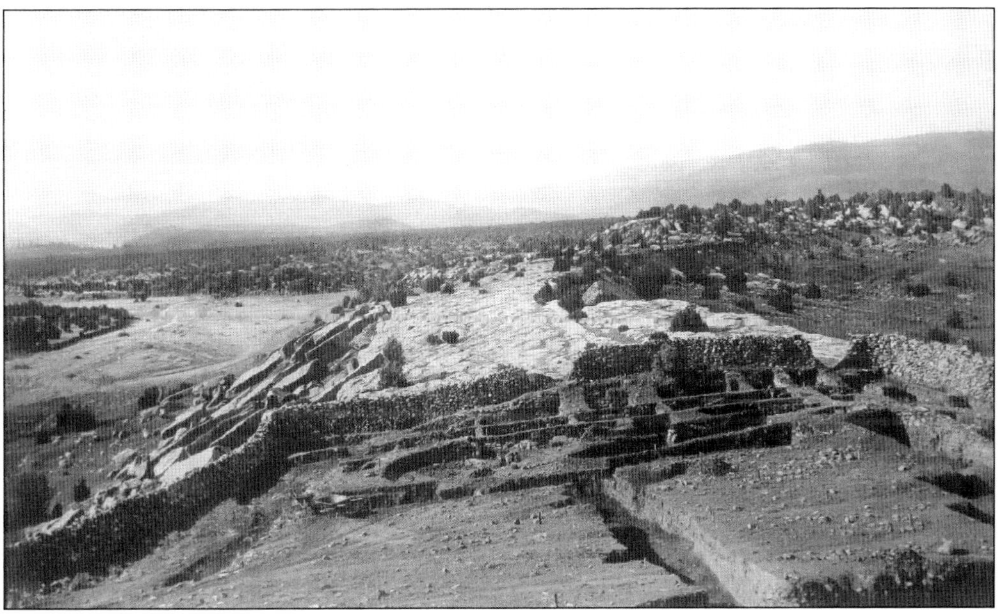

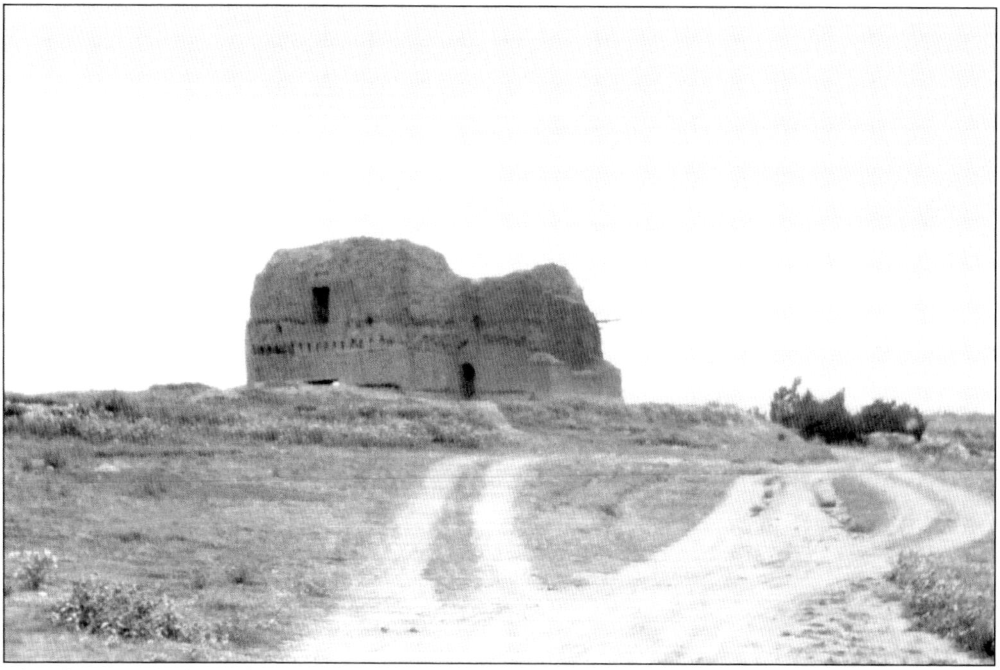

The photograph above shows the Pecos Church at the time of a visit by Adolph Francis Alphonse Bandelier (1840–1914), the first professional to work on historical sites in the American Southwest. Bandelier initially saw Pecos looking out the window of the train on his first trip to New Mexico in August 1880. Then and there, he likely decided to make Pecos his first intensive exploration of a Pueblo ruin. The photograph below was taken in the summer of 1911 by Jesse Nusbaum, the first archaeologist for the National Park Service, during a field trip to Pecos with famous Southwestern archaeologists Kenneth M. Chapman (1875–1968) and A.V. Kidder. (Above, MH No. 1506; below, PNHP No. 1449-1.)

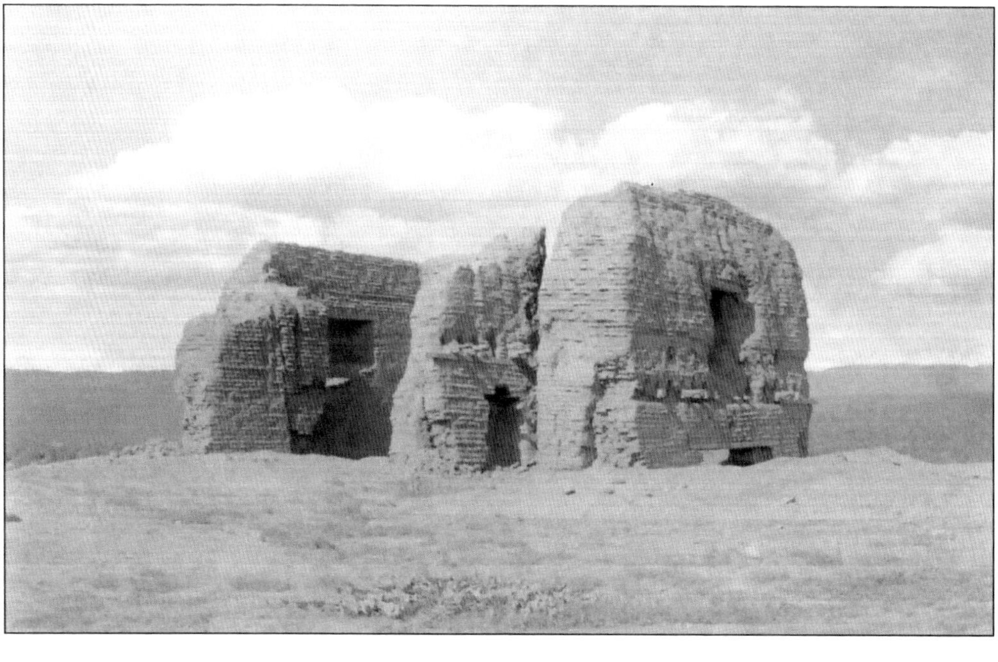

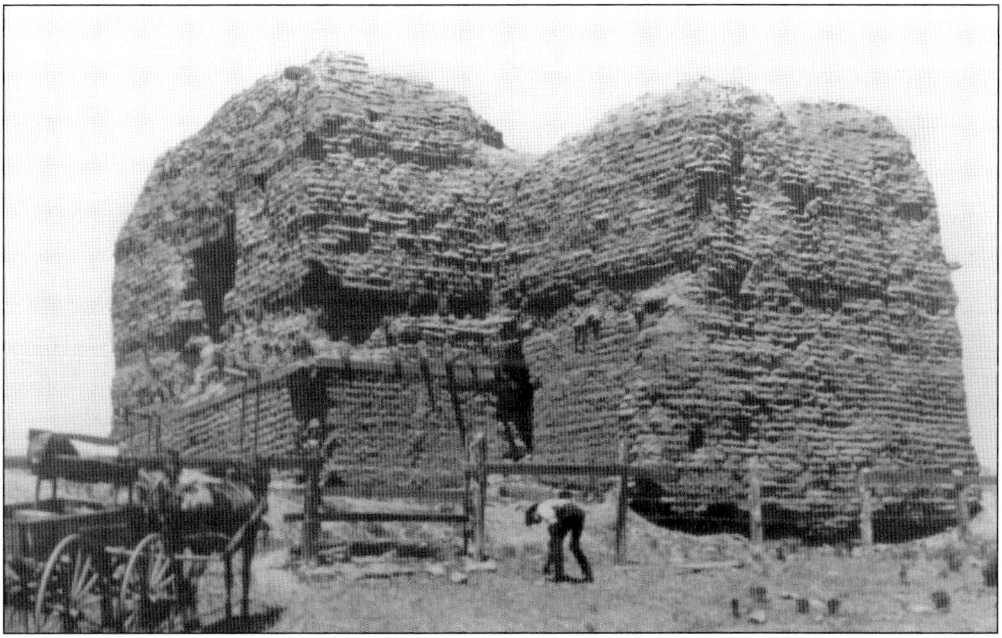

Both of these photographs show the remains of the 18th-century Pecos Church between 1910 and 1915. The last of four churches at Pecos, it was completed in 1717. It was called Iglesia Nuestra Señora de los Ángeles Porciúncula and was constructed on top of the rubble of the razed 17th-century church in a cruciform shape with an open transept. The walls were red adobe, and there were two bell towers flanking the door, making a shallow narthex that held a balcony. It had a flat roof of squared ponderosa pine beams resting on carved corbels of juniper or pine. A clerestory window was covered with sheet mica. There were five steps up to the altar. (Above, PNHP No. 2383; below, NT.)

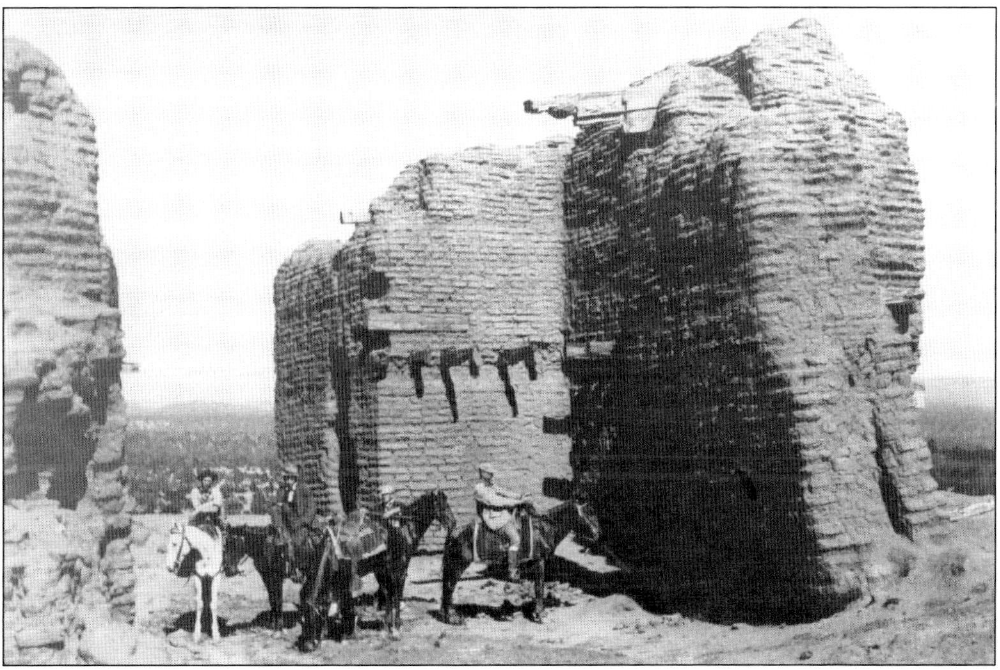

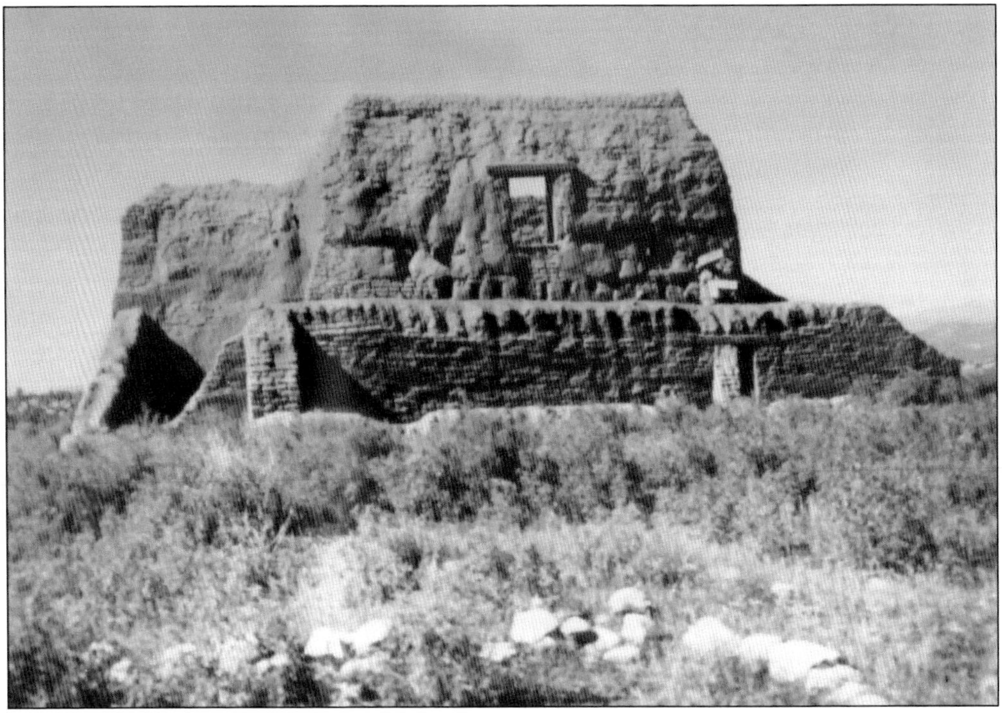

In 1915, Jesse Nusbaum partially excavated the 18th-century church and rebuilt portions of the rear wall of the sanctuary. He then stabilized the walls and rebuilt the interior arches. Prior to Nusbaum's work, the ruins had suffered greatly from the removal of structural beams for reuse by local ranchers, other wooden components for firewood, and carved beams and corbels cut out for sale as relics. One such carved beam was on display for many years at the Harvey House in Las Vegas, New Mexico. The photograph above shows the church prior to Nusbaum's work, while the lower shows work in progress in 1915. Re-excavations of Spanish buildings were undertaken in the late 1930s by John Corbett and J.W. Hendron. Further work was also done in the 1960s. (Above, NMSRCA; below, PNHP No. 1449-3.)

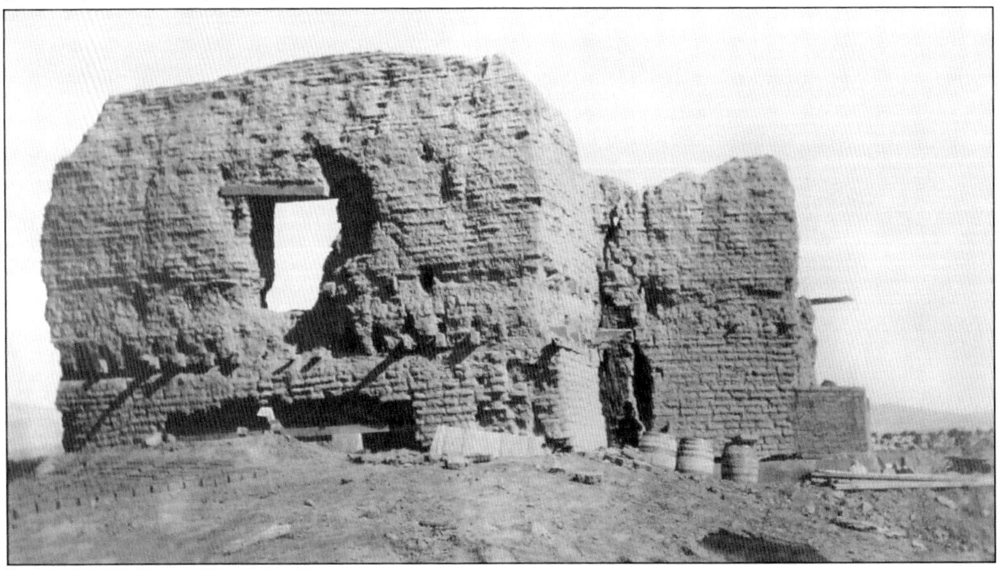

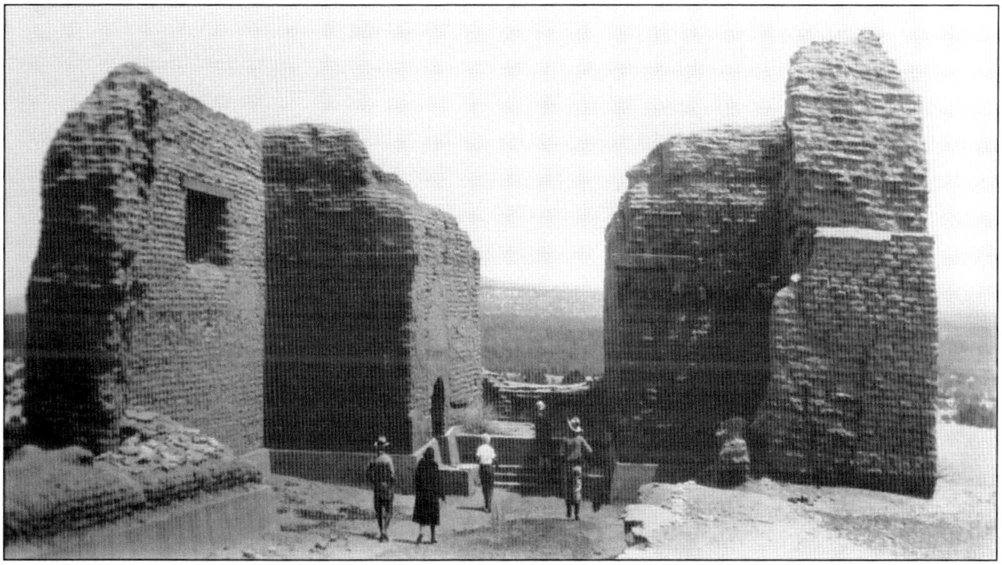

These photographs show work on the church complex completed by Nusbaum in 1915. The concrete reinforcements proved to do more harm than good, causing moisture damage at the wall bases. As a result, they were removed in the 1930s and replaced with 15,000 new adobe bricks to build up the walls. Repair and replacement of adobe bricks with chemically treated adobe to further preserve and stabilize the building continues to this day. In the 1960s, foundations of the 17th-century church were discovered and stabilized. By the 1970s, work was completed on the church complex. Additional rooms within the convento were also excavated and preserved. Further work was done in the 1960s by Jane M. Pinkley and Alden Hayes. (Above, NMSRCA; below, PNHP No. 3332.)

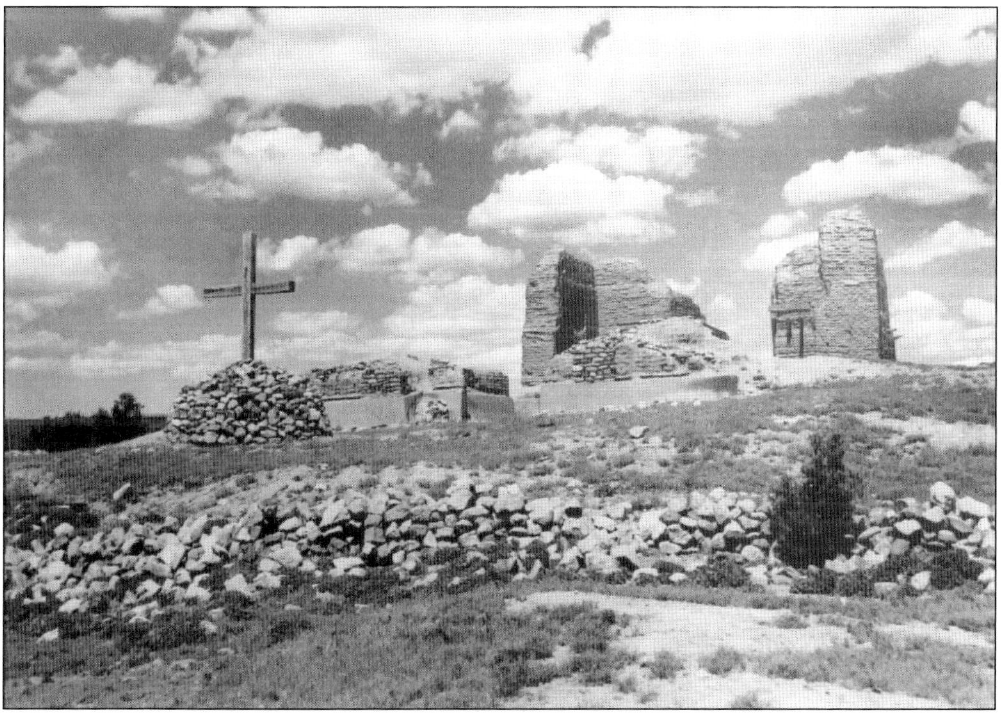

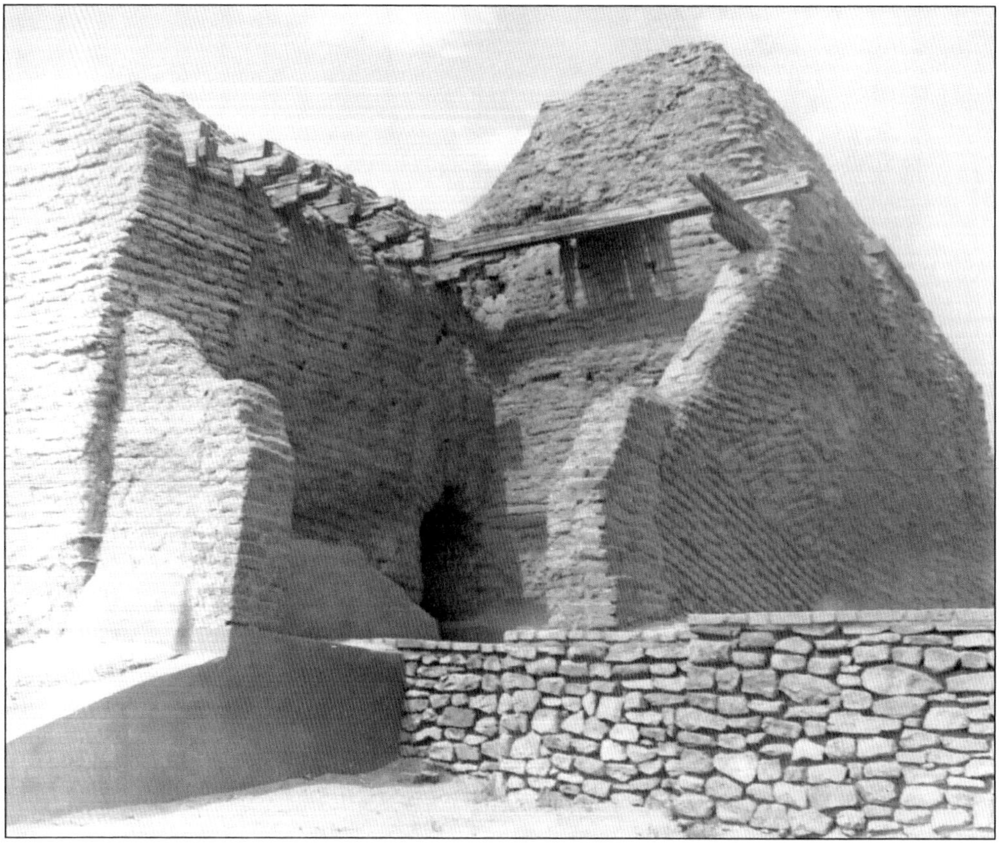

The altar of the 18th-century church is flanked on both sides by arched doorways. These two arches are the only two such features known from Spanish church interiors in New Mexico. Arches are an architectural feature common to California's later Franciscan missions. The diagonal placing of abode bricks is structural rather than decorative. It is assumed that the "new" church was designed and begun by Fray Antonio Aparico in mid-1714 and completed by Fray Carlos Delgado and Fray Jeronimo de Linan in mid-1717. Aparico designed the church to fit neatly into the prior chapel built in 1694 by Fray Diego de Zeinos. This followed the destruction of an earlier church during the Pueblo Revolt of 1680, during which time the Native Americans expelled the Spanish from the Southwest for a period of 12 years. (Both, CSWR.)

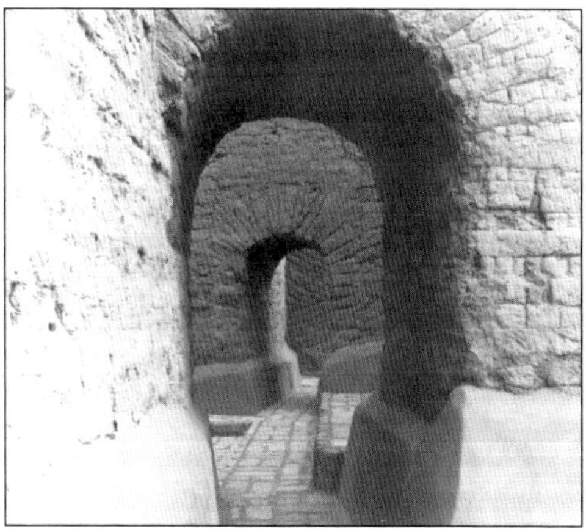

The photograph at right is an early view, perhaps from the 1870s, of the interior of the church ruin. It shows a number of ceiling beams and corbels still in existence. In 1776, Fray Francisco Atanasio Dominguez stated that he had observed the name of a Franciscan friar, "Frater Carolus," carved into one of the vigas of the nave. This is Fray Carlos Jose Delgado, who was stationed at Pecos from about August to October 1717. Apparently, he oversaw construction at the time of the final roofing. The photograph below shows sketches of several roof corbels from the Pecos Church reused in the church at the Hispanic village of Lower Colonias, located about six miles southeast of Pecos. (Right, CSWR; below, PNHP No. E26, "Cultural Resources Inventory.")

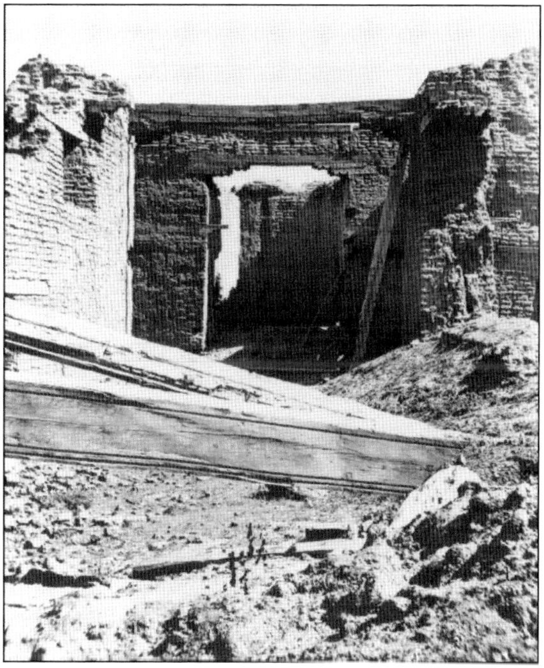

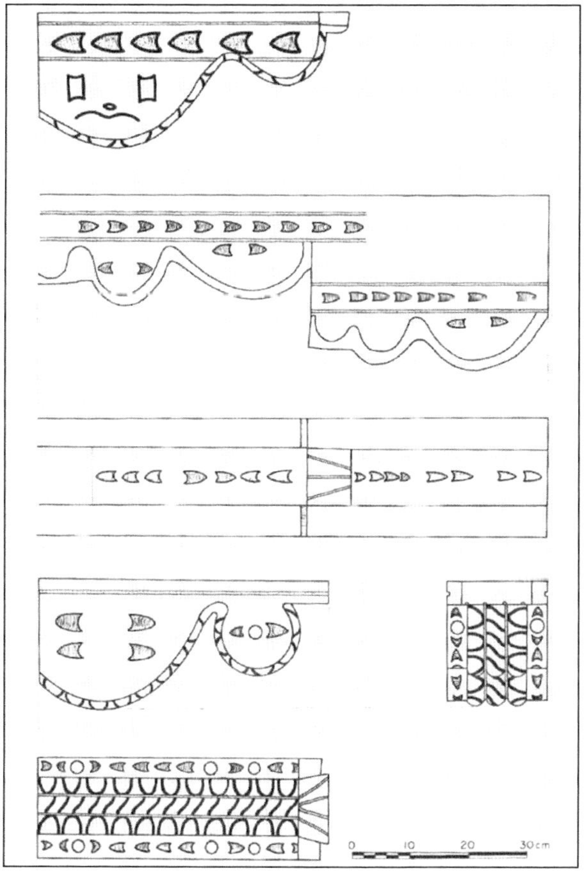

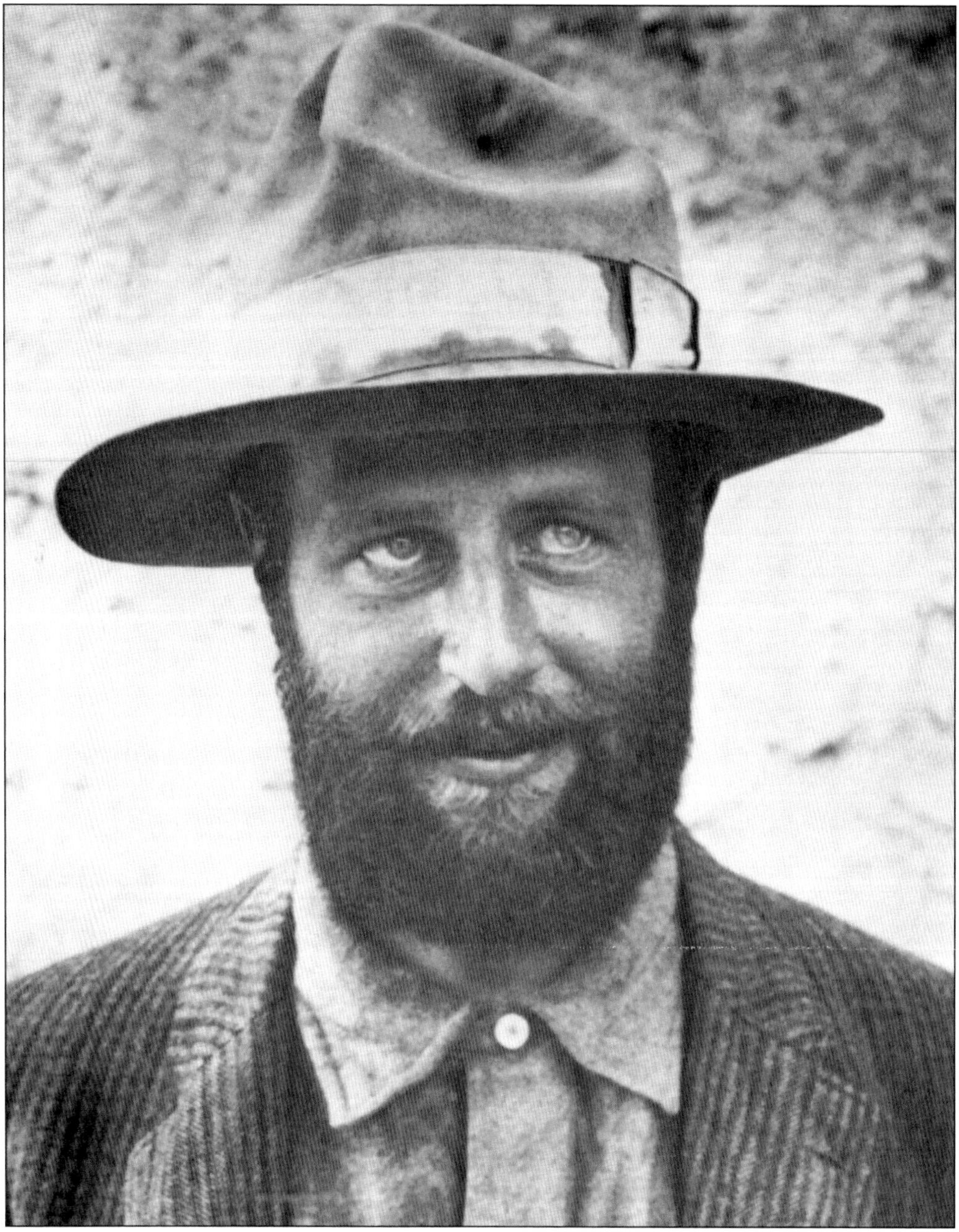

Alfred Vincent "A.V." Kidder (1885–1963) is a seminal figure in Southwestern and Mesoamerican archaeology. He received his PhD from Harvard University in 1914, the sixth archaeology degree awarded from there. Kidder first experienced the Southwest in the late spring of 1907, when he accepted a job on an archaeological survey in the area. In 1915, he began extensive fieldwork at Pecos, initially sponsored by the R.S. Peabody Foundation of Phillips Academy in Andover, Massachusetts. This work continued, except for a break during World War I, until a final season in 1929. Kidder's work at Pecos was instrumental in developing a Southwestern cultural sequence and chronology. It was also the first large-scale and thoroughly systematic stratigraphic operation in American archaeology. (PNHP.)

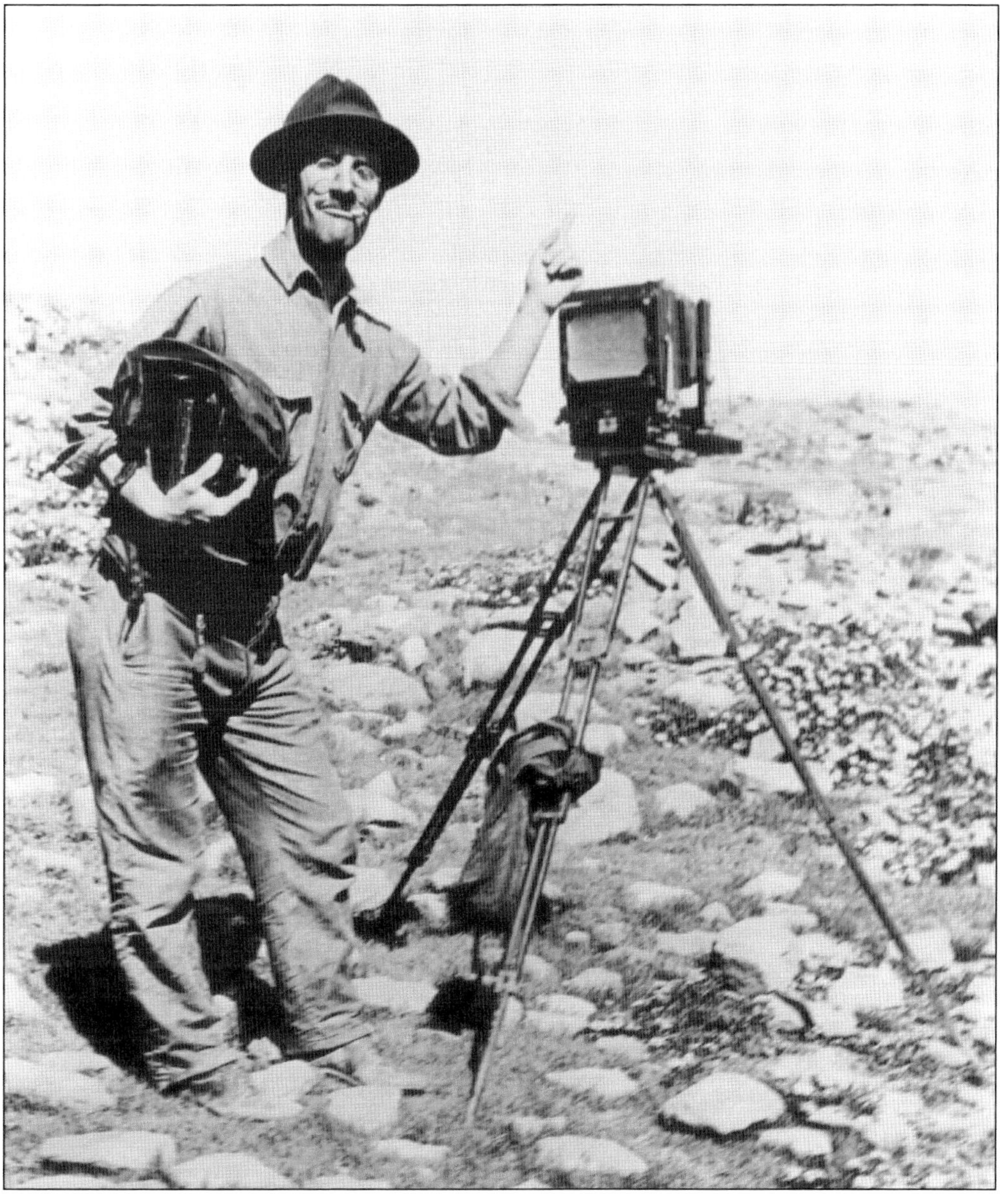

In 1909, Jesse Logan Nusbaum (1887–1957) became the first employee hired by Dr. Edgar L. Hewitt at the Museum of New Mexico. In 1911, he accompanied Kidder on a trip to Pecos and took a number of photographs; this image probably dates from that trip. Following his work at Pecos in 1915, he later became superintendent of Mesa Verde National Park. (PNHP No. 4322.)

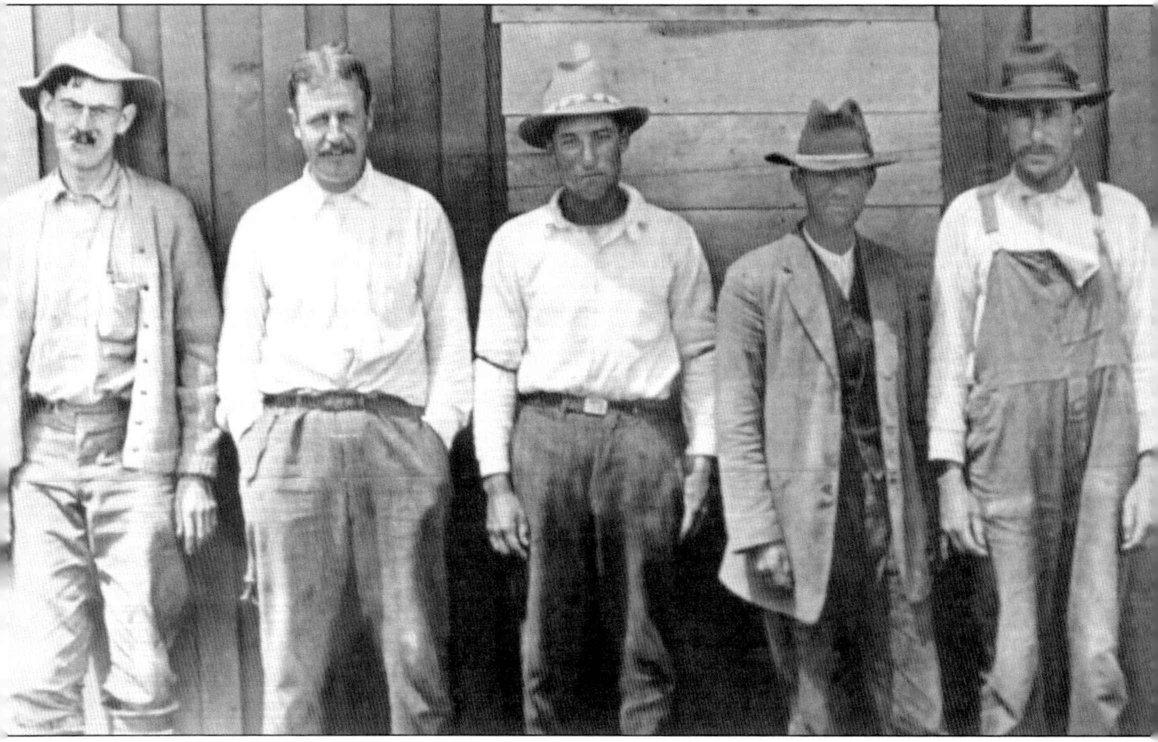

Kidder was never a formal teacher or professor; however, as head of the Pecos field camp, he helped develop a corps of archaeologists who received their first systematic training at Pecos. Many of these men became leaders in the field for decades afterward. In this photograph, from left to right, are C.E. Guthe, Kidder, George C. Vaillant, Martin Varela, and Muriano Quintana. Guthe worked on Mayan codices (books). Vaillant did stratigraphic analyses in Mexico inspired by his work at Pecos. Varela and Quintana were local residents of the Pecos Valley. In addition, Kidder's wife, Madeline, worked alongside her husband and was also an accomplished archaeologist. (PNHP No. 1228.)

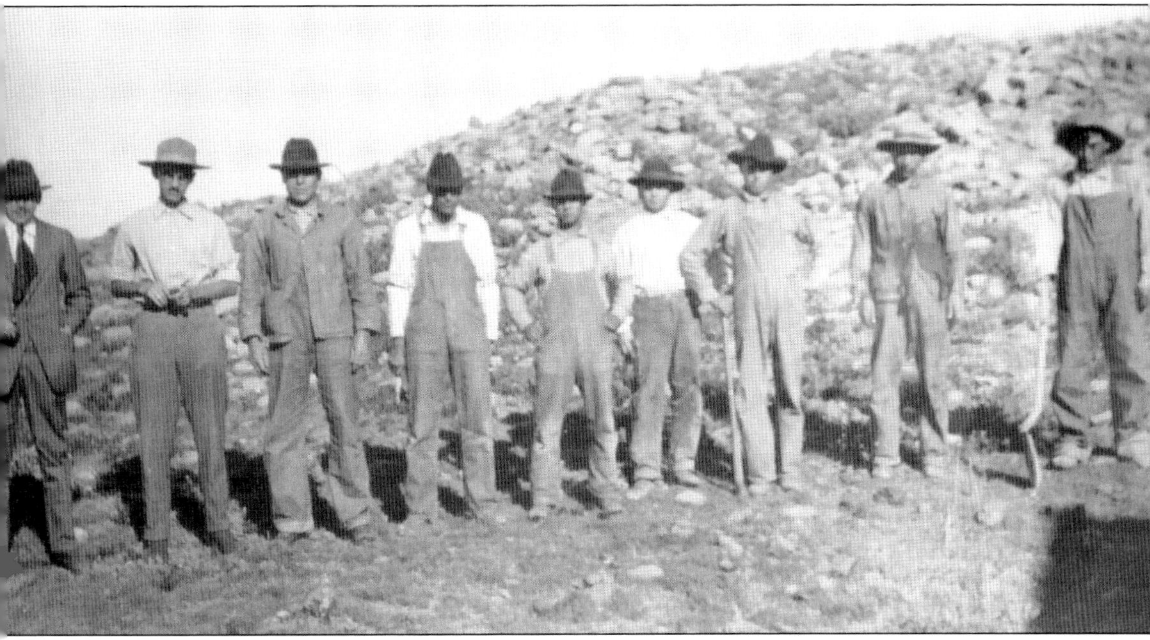

In this photograph are Kidder and C.E. Guthe (far left), accompanied by seven local workmen. The background shows the Pecos Church ruin. Kidder's team undertook excavations not only at the Pueblo ruins of Pecos but also at the Forked Lightning ruin, an earlier Pueblo site just south of Pecos. In addition, the team engaged in extensive reconnaissance work throughout the Pecos Valley. (PNHP No. 1229.)

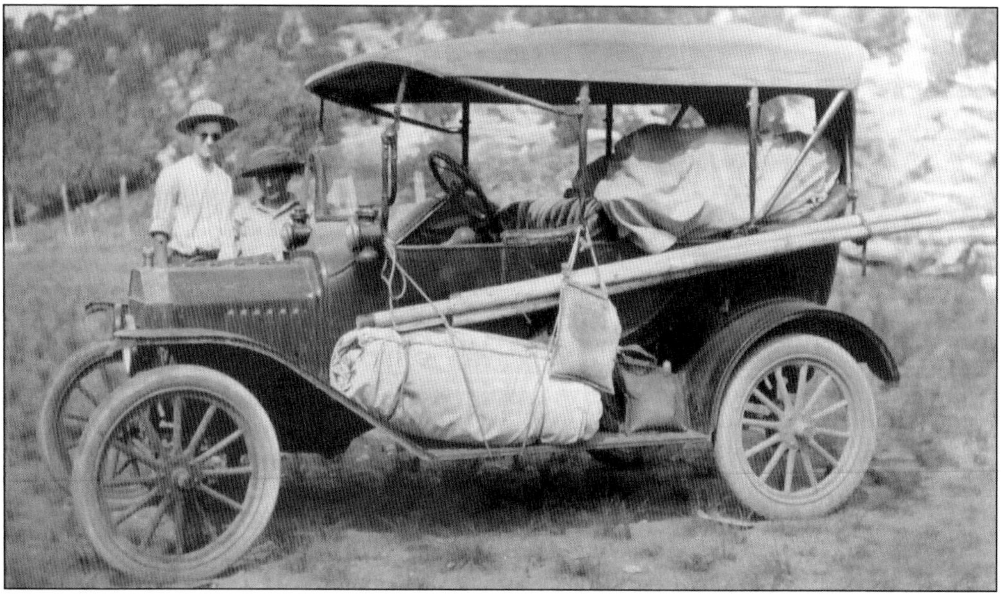

"Old Blue" was Kidder's trusty 1911 Ford Model T. In the photograph above, a new-looking "Old Blue"—or perhaps this is "Black," the other expedition Model T—is heading off on a camping and exploration trip. The photograph below is unquestionably of "Old Blue," shown in full work mode at the Pecos excavations. The box on the front fender reads "A.V. Kidder, Andover, Mass.," the crate in the back reads, "Peabody Museum," and the man at the wheel is clearly Kidder. (Above, PNHP No. 1227-3; below, No. 1227-8.)

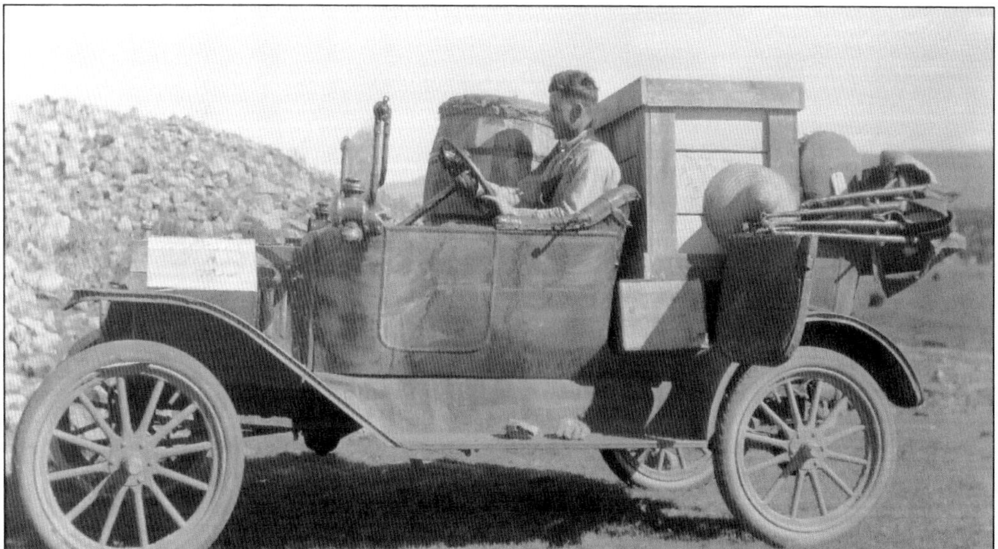

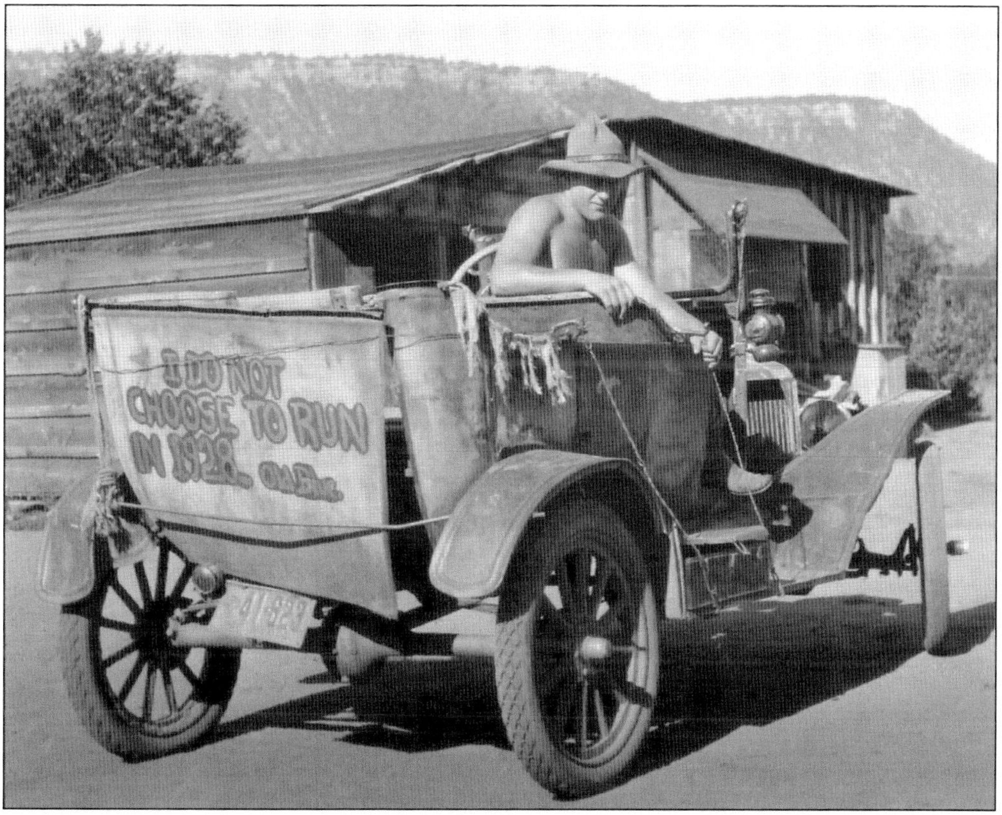

In the photograph above, the inscription on the back of a tired "Old Blue" states, "I do not choose to run in 1928 – Old Blue." This was the year Herbert Hoover beat Al Smith for president, the last election for 24 years in which a Republican won the White House. However, the comment by "Old Blue" probably has more to do with its condition after years of service than with politics. The photograph below, from 1929, shows "Old Blue" with a number of missing parts, including its top, hood, and rear fenders. At this point, it was almost an archaeological artifact in its own right, but it still had a trip to Mexico in its future. (Above, PNHP No. 1227-6; below, No. 1227-2.)

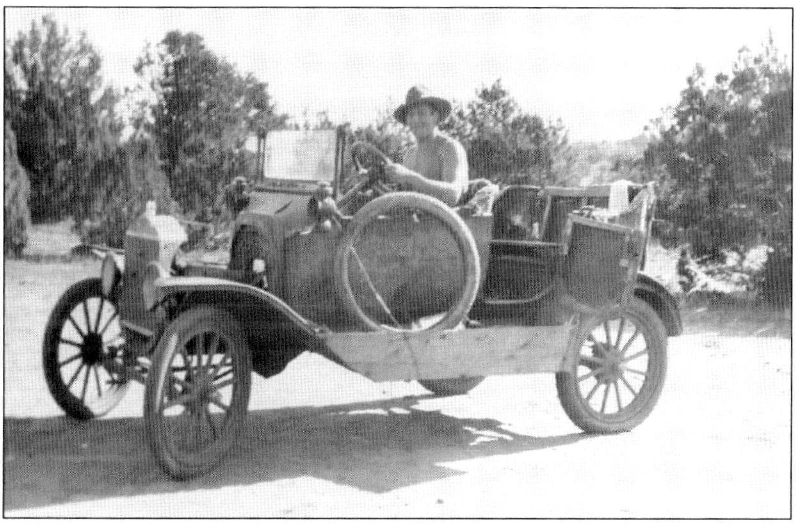

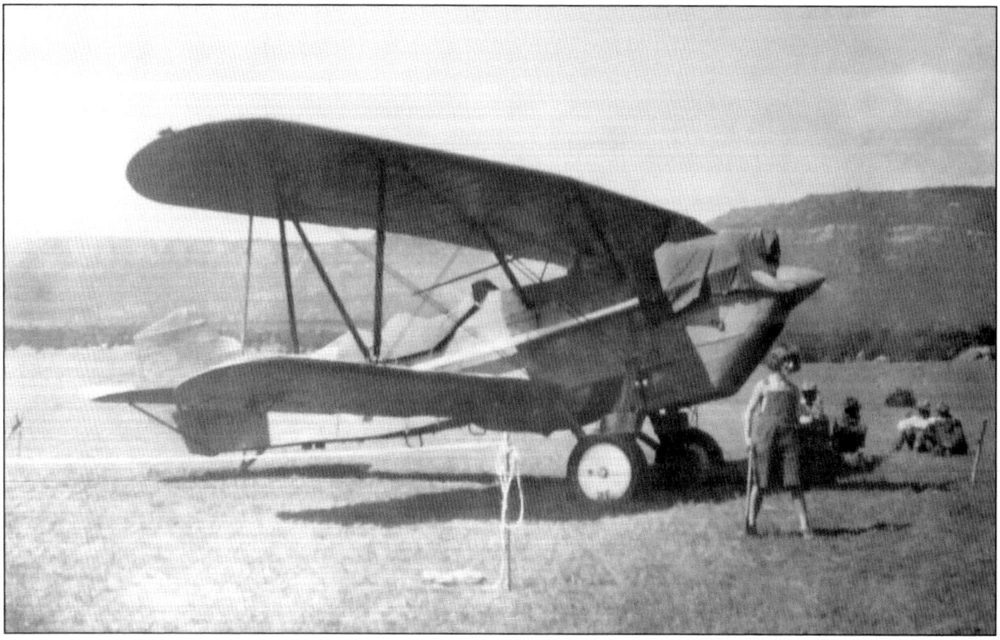

Charles A. Lindbergh, while flying along the coast of the Yucatan in Mexico in 1929, noticed the Mayan ruins. Struck by the potential value of aerial photography to archaeology, he telephoned Dr. Charles G. Abbot, secretary of the Smithsonian Institution, who put him in touch with J.C. Merriam, president of the Carnegie Institution. At Merriam's request, A.V. Kidder, then in his last season working at Pecos, made a list of areas for Lindbergh to photograph. In August 1929, Lindbergh landed his "Lindbergh Special" Curtiss Falcon mail plane in a grassy field at Tex Austin's Forked Lightning Ranch, a couple miles east of the Pecos ruins. (Above, PNHP No. 14; below, PNHP.)

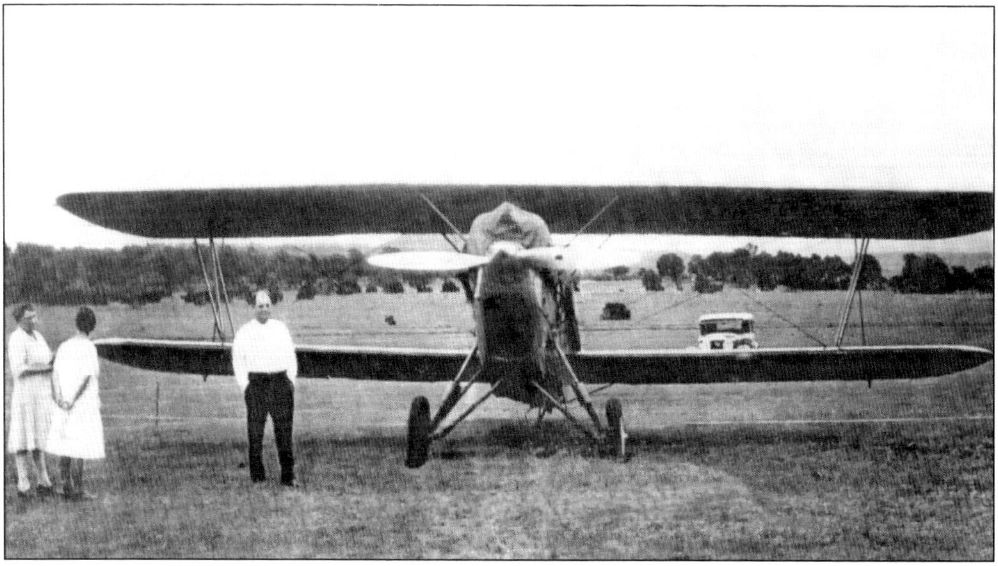

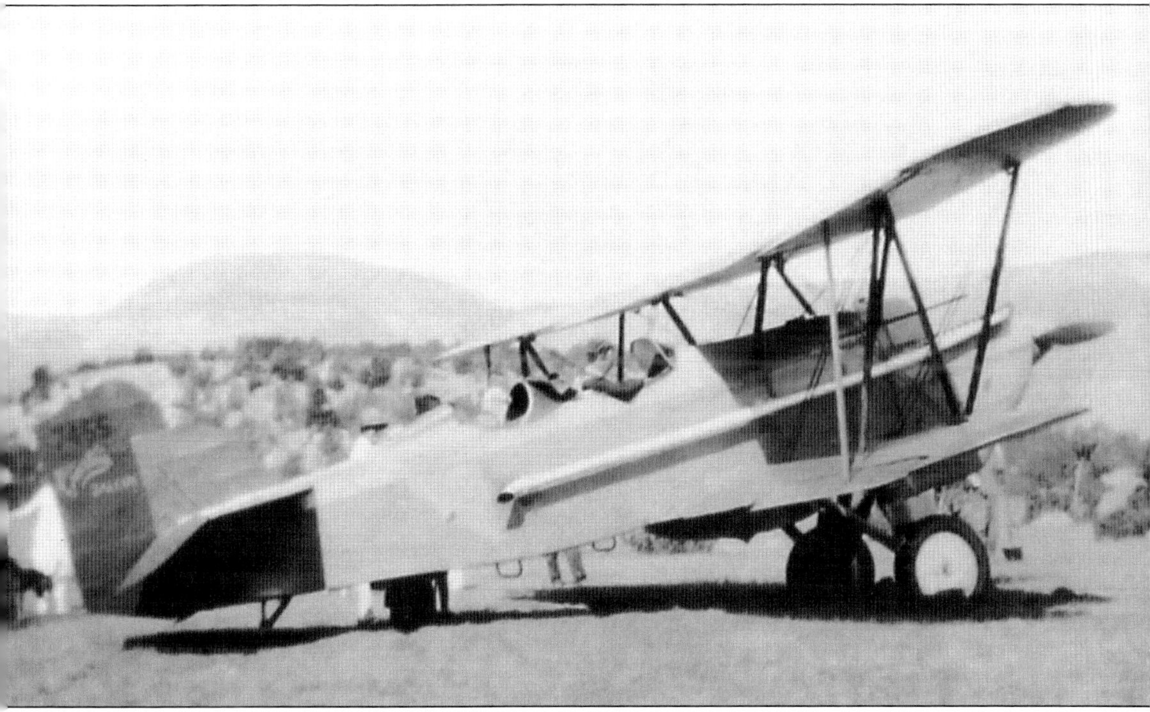

Lindbergh and his wife, Anne Morrow Lindbergh—who took the actual photographs, as Lindbergh himself was busy flying the plane—made over 100 photographs of sites in New Mexico and Arizona. The archaeological survey was a side venture for Lindbergh, who at the time was conducting a survey for the Transcontinental Air Transport Company (or T-A-T, which became TWA in 1930) to design a nationwide air network to obtain airmail contracts. Because the Pecos landing field was short, Lindbergh had to keep the plane light to allow for takeoff, requiring him to fly to the T-A-T field in Albuquerque each morning to top up his fuel tanks. (PNHP.)

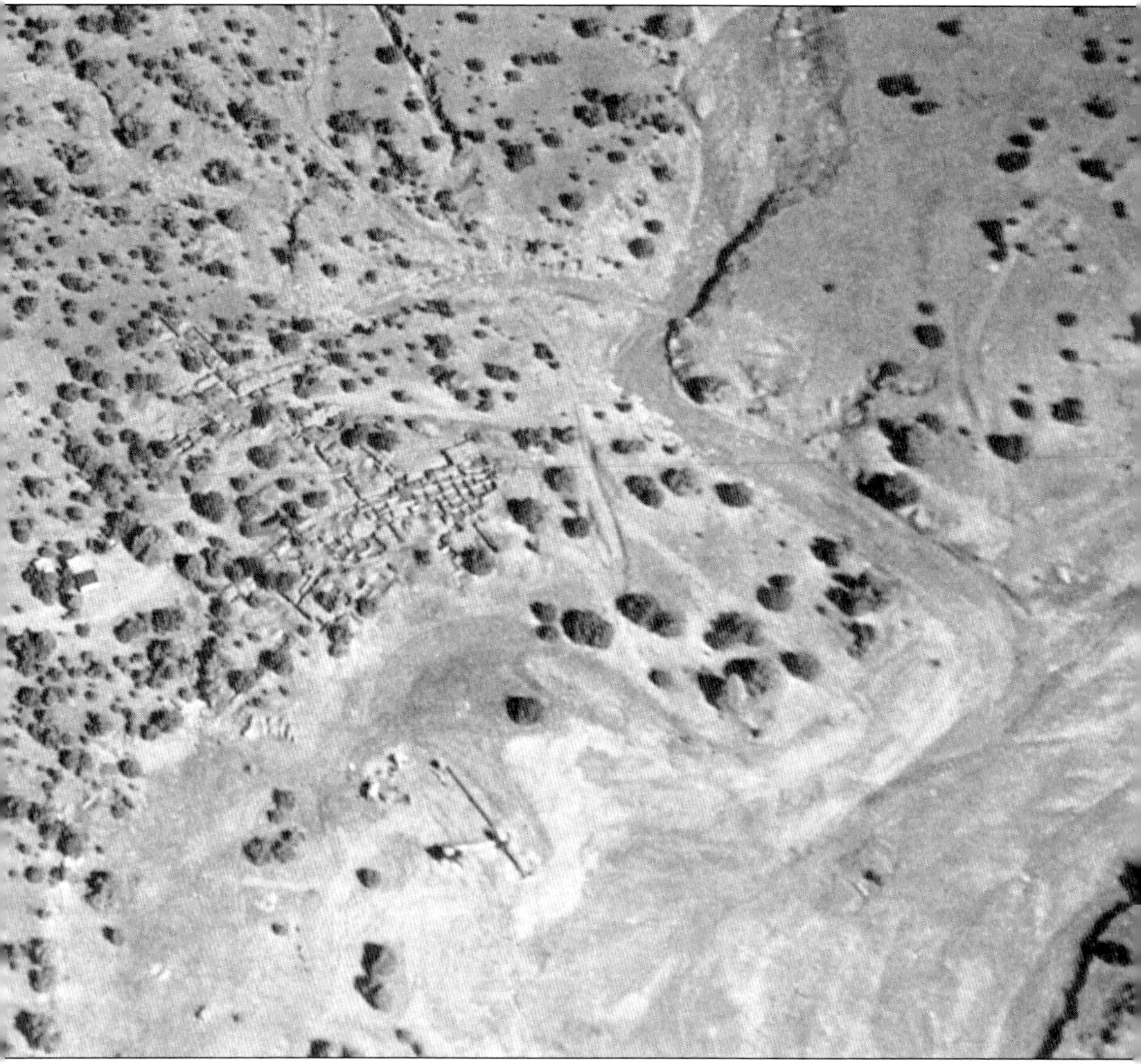

While not the first aerial archaeology photographs in America, the Lindbergh photographs were the first of the Southwest, and they are still used today to assess the condition of archaeological sites. They are also proving to be especially useful for the assessment of changing ecological conditions. This is a photograph of the Forked Lightning ruin, near Pecos. (PNHP.)

Two

Glorieta and War

Glorieta means "bower" or "arbor" in Spanish. It is also used to denote a road intersection. Which definition applies in this case is not known. The current village of Glorieta, six miles west of the village of Pecos, was founded in 1879 and has had a post office since 1880, when the New Mexico & Southern Pacific Railroad (later the Atchison, Topeka & Santa Fe [AT&SF] Railway and now the Burlington Northern Santa Fe [BNSF] Railroad) established a railroad station at the pass through the Sangre de Cristo Mountains leading to Santa Fe. The railroad still moves freight and Amtrak passengers along the original 1879 right-of-way.

While the train no longer stops at Glorieta, the original AT&SF train station still exists. It is used as the local post office. As a regional railroad station, Glorieta was the terminus for cattle drives, wool, and lumber, as well as the loading site for ore concentrates from the Pecos mines.

Glorieta Pass has been the principal route into the Santa Fe area from time immemorial, first for Native Americans and later for Spanish and Americans along the Santa Fe Trail. However, Glorieta Pass is primarily known as the site of the most important Civil War battle fought in the Southwest. The battle took place over a period of three days in March 1862. While the Confederates initially held the upper hand, they were forced to retreat due to the destruction of their supply train. It marked the end of the Confederate expansion into the western United States.

Since 1993, portions of the battlefield site, designated as a National Historic Landmark, have been managed under the jurisdiction of the National Park Service, Pecos National Historical Park.

During the 1920s and 1930s, the Pigeon's Ranch area of Glorieta, famous as an important component of the Civil War battle, was a major "tourist trap." It included Civil War locales such as Artillery Hill, Sharpshooters Ridge, the main battle lines, and the Union field hospital, as well as several mostly apocryphal sites, such as the "Oldest Well."

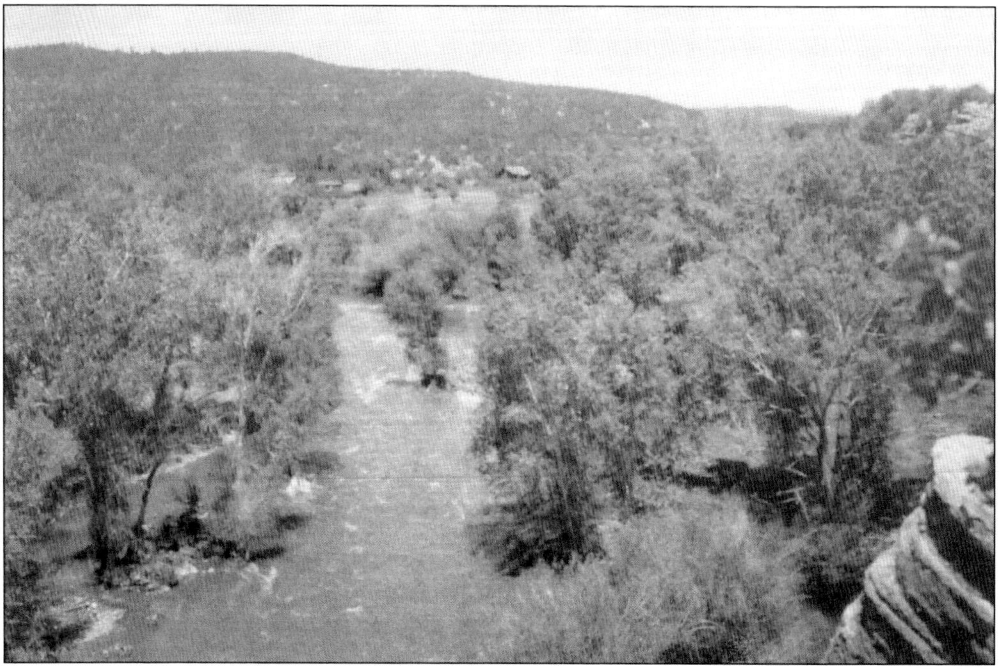

The view above shows Glorieta Pass as it would have looked prior to the Civil War. The vantage point is northwest of Pigeon's Ranch, looking to the northwest. The buildings in the background are where Interstate 25 now passes through Glorieta. The destruction of Glorieta Civil War sites by the road's construction reinvigorated a movement that led to the current preservation of the battlefield. The photograph below shows Pigeon's Ranch (described on page 36) as it would have appeared in about 1860. This was an important stop on the Santa Fe Trail and was later a stage stop between Las Vegas, New Mexico, and Santa Fe. Eventually, it became a "tourist trap" on Route 66. (Both, NT.)

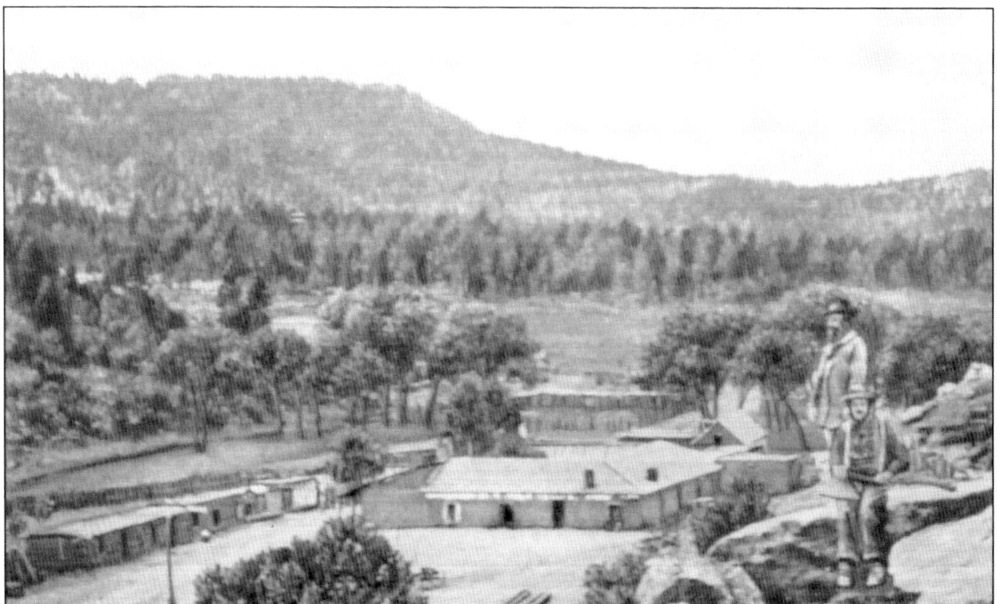

The woodcut at right, by Ben McCullough, is purported to be of a typical Texas Ranger that appeared in *Harper's Weekly* on July 6, 1861. A copy of this illustration in Benson Lossing's 1868 *Pictorial History of the Civil War* is identified as "one of Sibley's Texas Rangers." Each ranger, riding a mustang, is said to have been armed with a pair of Navy Colt revolvers, a .52-caliber Sharps rifle, a tomahawk, a Texan Bowie knife, and a lasso. Note the bottle; is it whiskey or water? The photograph below is identified on the reverse as "George Hibbard and compadres on the spot where Clark shot the commander of Sibley's forces. Glorieta, New Mexico, June 1880." More specifically, this is the spot where Maj. John Shropshire, commanding officer of the Confederate Texas Mounted Volunteers, was shot between the eyes. (Right, AC; below, PNHP No. 4715.)

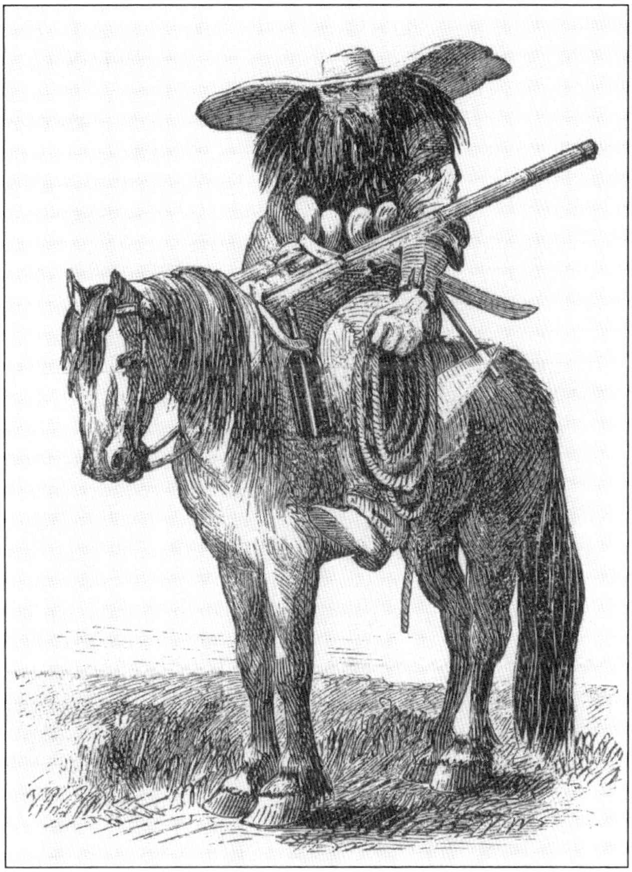

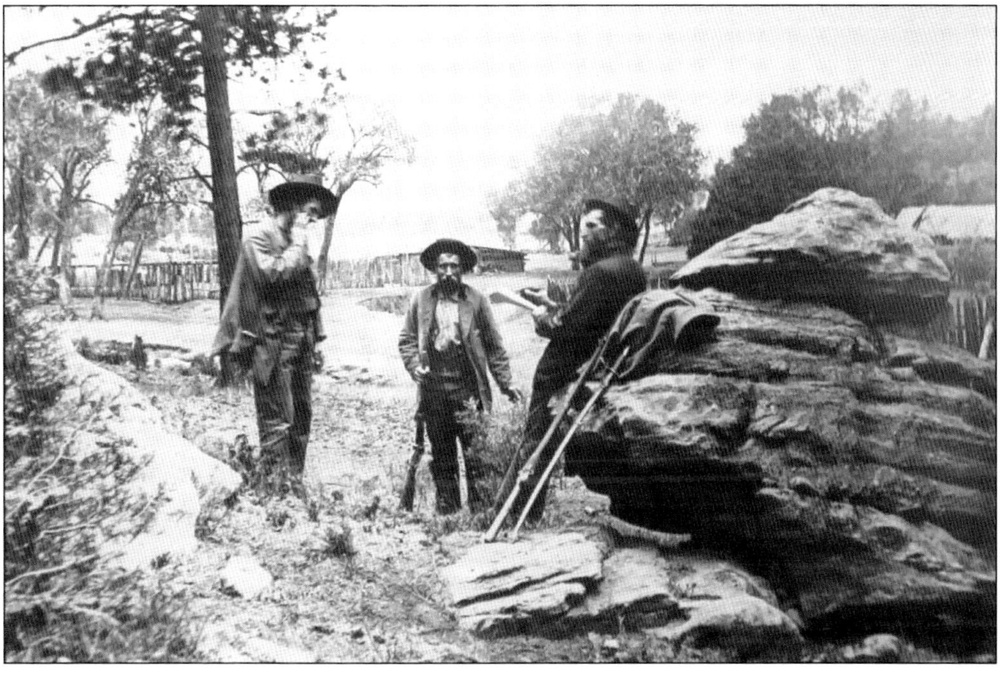

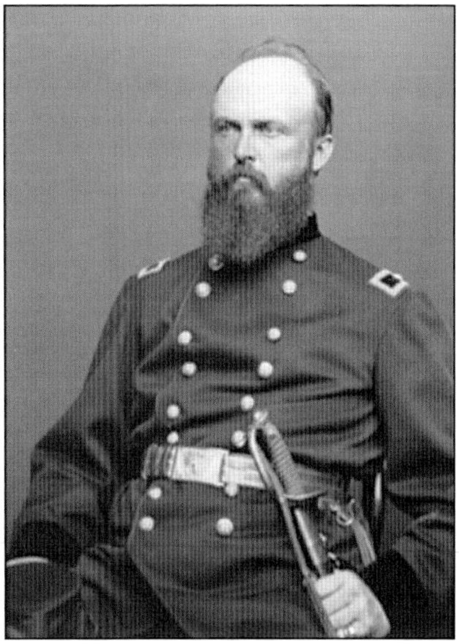

The individuals on this page are the key Union commanders during the Battle of Glorieta Pass: Col. John Potts Slough (1829–1867, left) and Maj. John M. Chivington (1821–1894, below). Slough, of the 1st Colorado Infantry, moved his men to Fort Union, north of Las Vegas, New Mexico, when he heard of Confederate advances from Texas into New Mexico. He disobeyed orders to stay at Fort Union and marched to Glorieta Pass to engage the enemy. The Confederates might have easily won had Chivington's scouts not found the Confederate supply train, which was then destroyed. However, at Pigeon's Ranch, Alexandre Valle said of Chivington, as he galloped through a hail of bullets, "E poot 'iz 'ead down and foight loike a mahd bull." Following the engagement, the Confederates went to Santa Fe and, after hearing of a large buildup of Union forces, began a long retreat back to Texas. (Both, USNA.)

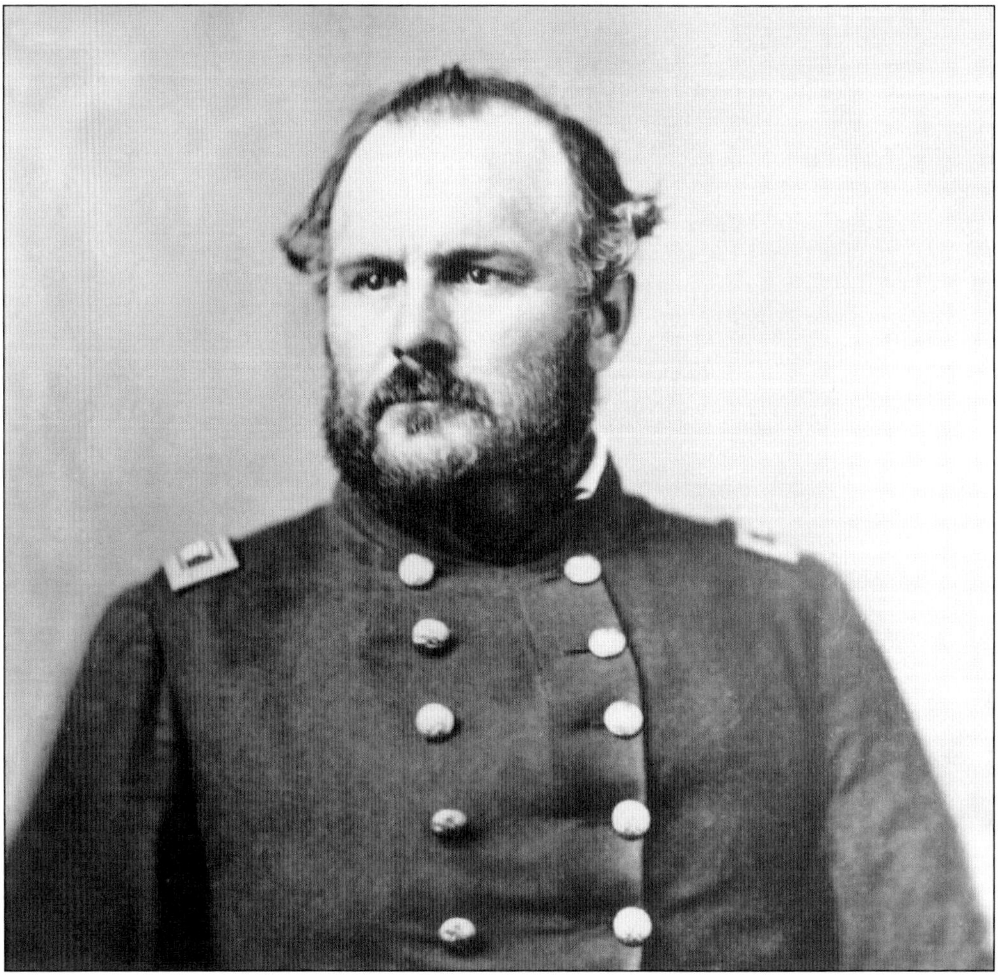

Seen here are two leading Confederate officers: Gen. Henry Hopkins Sibley (1816–1886, right) and Lt. Col. William Read Scurry (1821–1864, below). Sibley was born in Louisiana and was admitted at age 17 to the US Military Academy at West Point. He formed the Army of New Mexico in eastern Texas in 1861 with the idea of capturing the large Union supply depot on the Santa Fe Trail at Fort Union and controlling access to the goldfields of California and Colorado. However, he was a hard drinker, called by his soldiers a "walking whiskey keg." Scurry led several successful engagements against the Union forces at Glorieta and, after a rough start, was ultimately successful in pushing back the Union forces at Pigeon's Ranch. At first, both sides thought they had won the battle. (Both, USNA.)

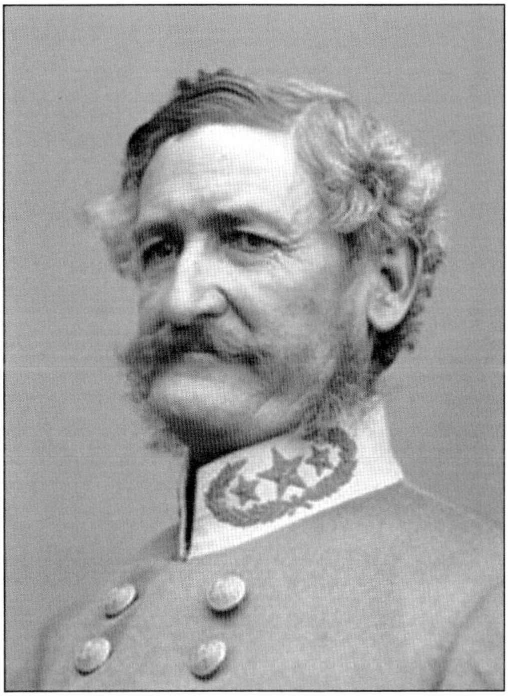

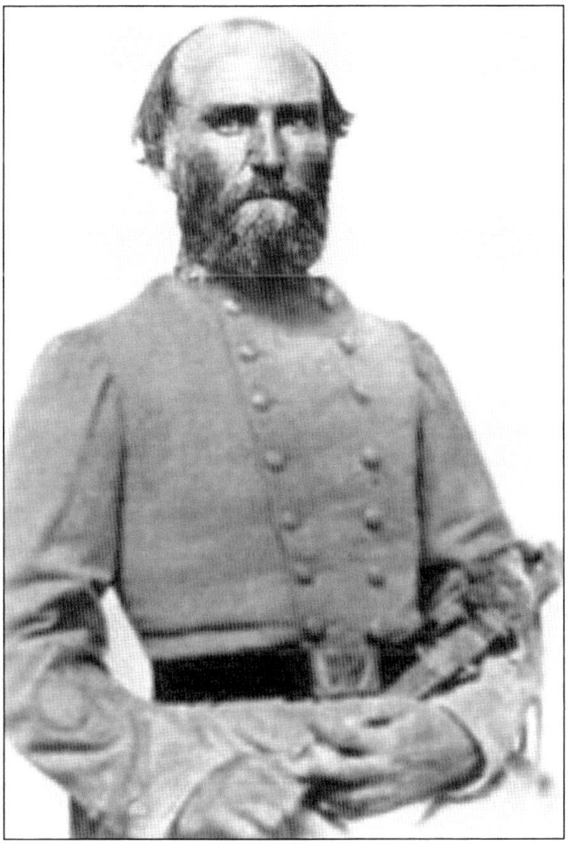

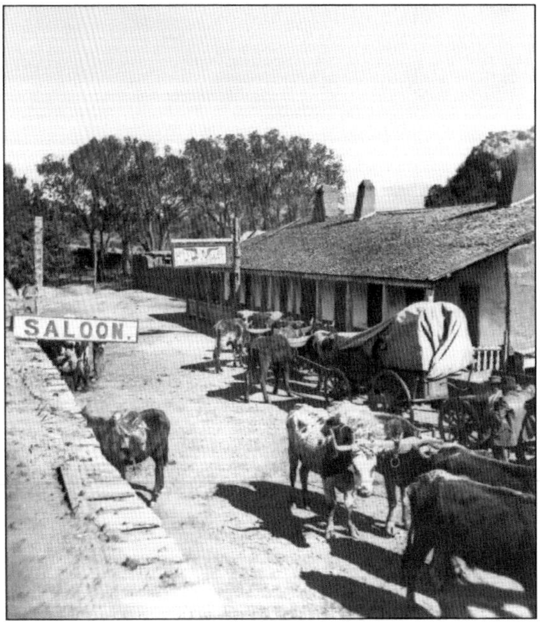

At the summit of Glorieta Pass is Pigeon's Ranch. Alexandre Valle, a Frenchman, along with his New Mexico–born wife, Carmen, established a ranch and travel stop about 1850 at a site adjacent to the main road between Santa Fe and Pecos. He may have been called "Pigeon" because of his amusing style of dancing, or perhaps because his mother married a man named Pigeon. By the 1860s, he had developed a complex of several buildings. A protected area with double corrals and stalls provided security for loaded wagons and resting places for the animals. The photograph at left was taken in June 1880, when Pigeon's Ranch was owned and operated by George Herbert. Shown are freight wagons and a saloon catering to teamsters and railway workers. (PNHP No. 4124.)

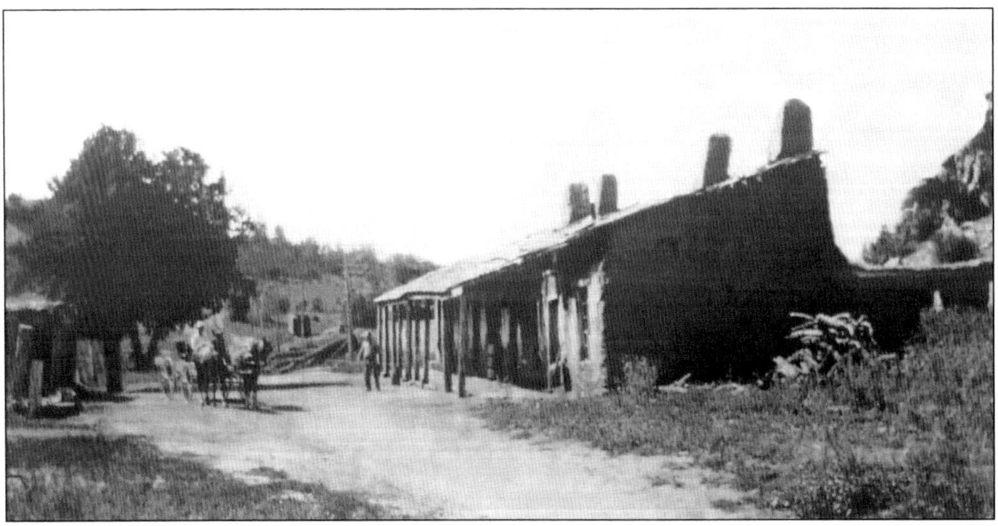

By the time this photograph was taken in about 1890, Pigeon's Ranch was semi-abandoned and falling into ruin. (NMSRCA.)

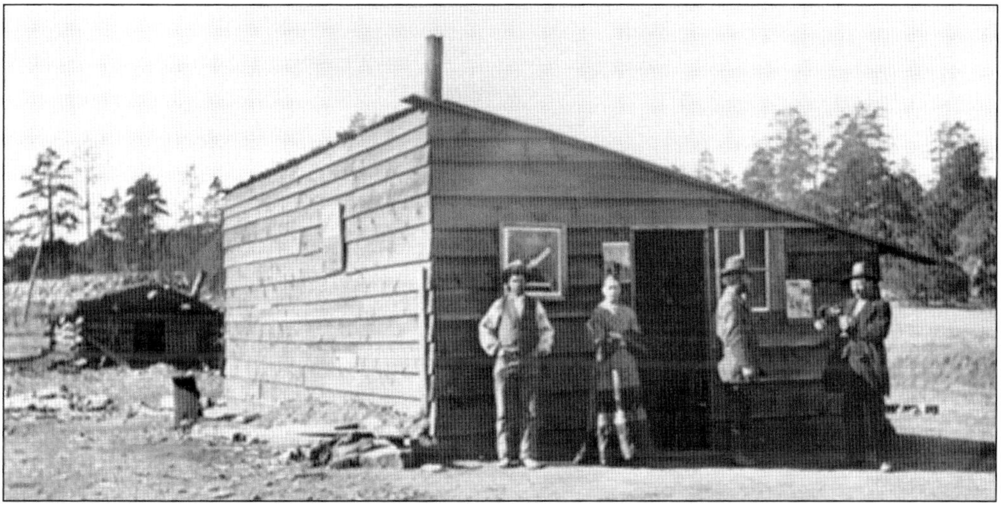

The railroad coming through the Pecos region in 1879 brought a huge influx of workers, which in turn brought camp followers. Seen here some time after 1880 is the rather grandiosely named Metropolitan Saloon, a one-room, clapboard-sided building with a stove in Glorieta. The log cabin in the background was typical of mountain dwellings in the area. (NT.)

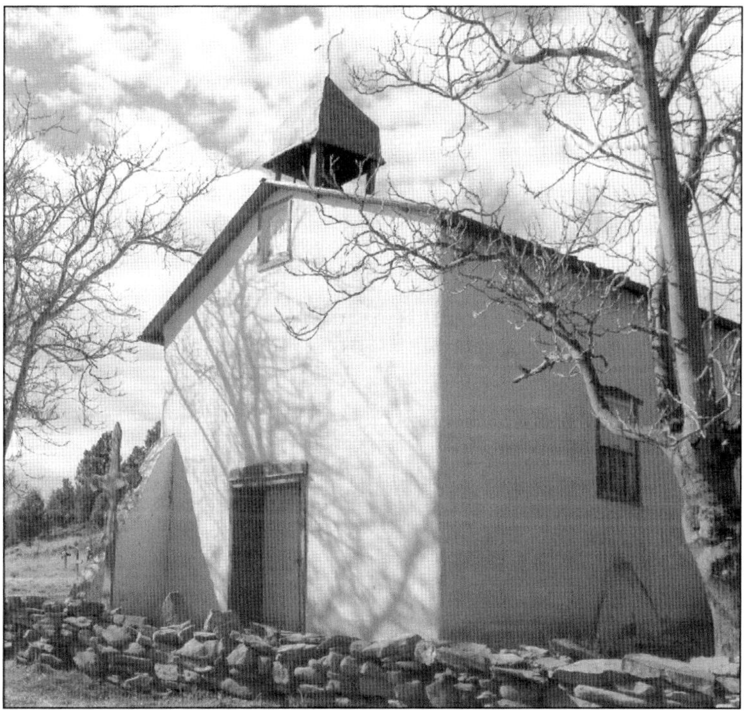

A few miles southwest of Glorieta, near the entrance to Apache Canyon (see page 42), at a settlement called Canoncito is the chapel of Nuestra Señora de la Luz, built about 1890. This is where the old Santa Fe Trail descended from the summit of Glorieta Pass towards Santa Fe. The chapel represents a continuation of 17th-century Spanish Colonial–style churches. (AC.)

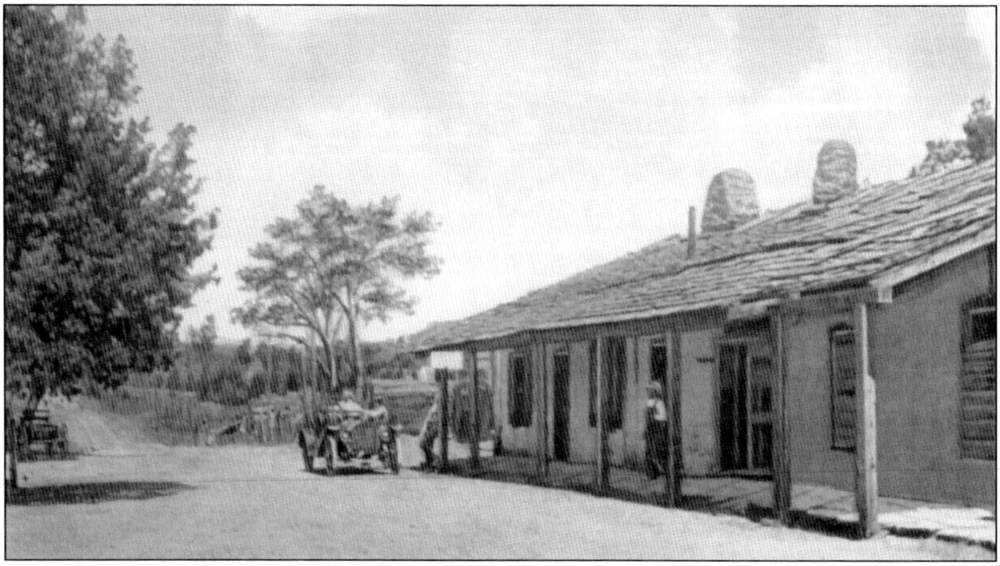

By the early 1900s, Pigeon's Ranch had fallen into disrepair, as seen in the photograph above. However, it continued as a dwelling, post office, and store. It is likely that materials salvaged from the site were used to construct the El Ortiz Harvey House Hotel, at Lamy, New Mexico, which was demolished in 1943. A 1910 proposal to make the Glorieta Pass battlefield site a state park probably saved Pigeon's Ranch from total destruction. The photograph below was taken in 1935, at the height of Tom Greer's "tourist trap." Greer was a Pecos cowboy who bought Pigeon's Ranch in 1926. He cleaned it up and romanticized it, adding gun ports for effect. With Route 66 running by his front door, he converted Pigeon's Ranch into a roadside attraction. By 1928, there was a "museum," a restaurant, and a curio store. (Above, PNHP No. 4107; below, 4110.)

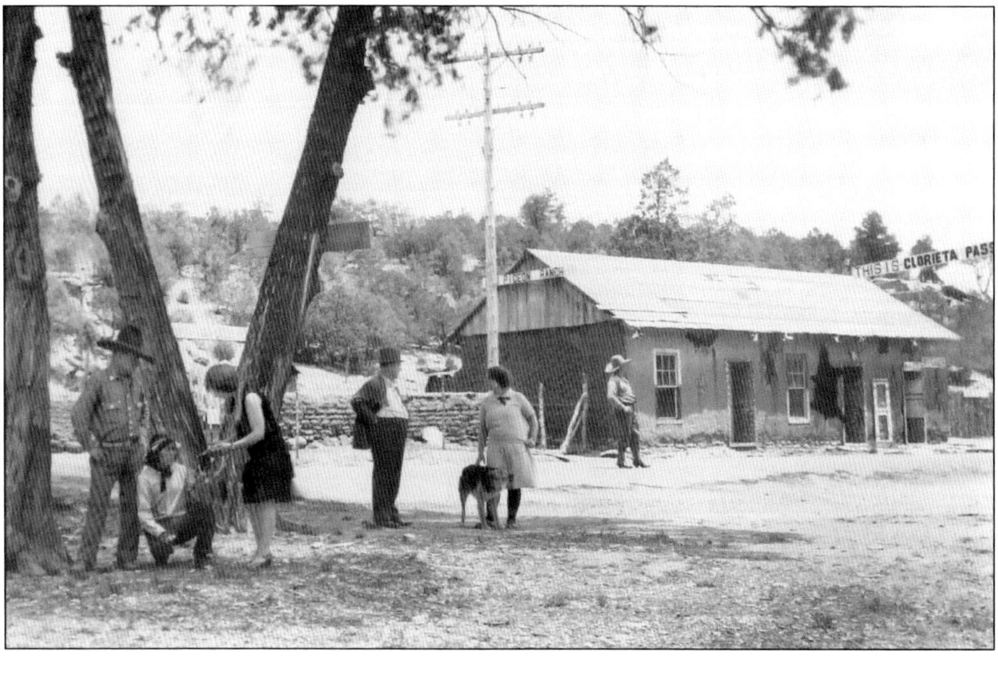

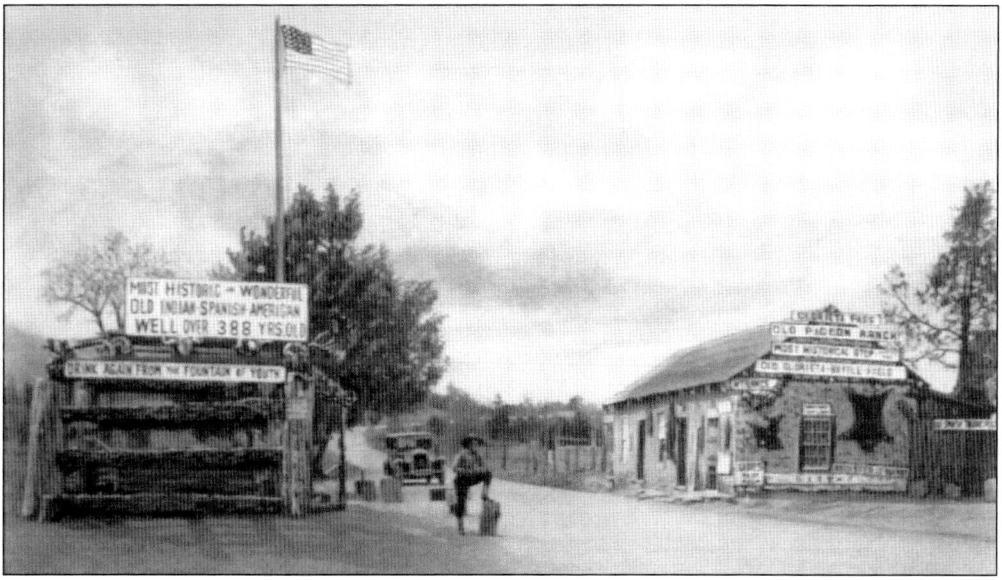

Greer, taking full advantage of his remote Route 66 location, opened a gas station and garage in the late 1920s and sold water from the "Oldest Well," across the road. He covered the exterior of his buildings with crudely painted signs advertising the "old cave," "old post office," "old walls," and "old Spanish fort," all of which were parts of or remnants of the original Pigeon's Ranch compound. (NT.)

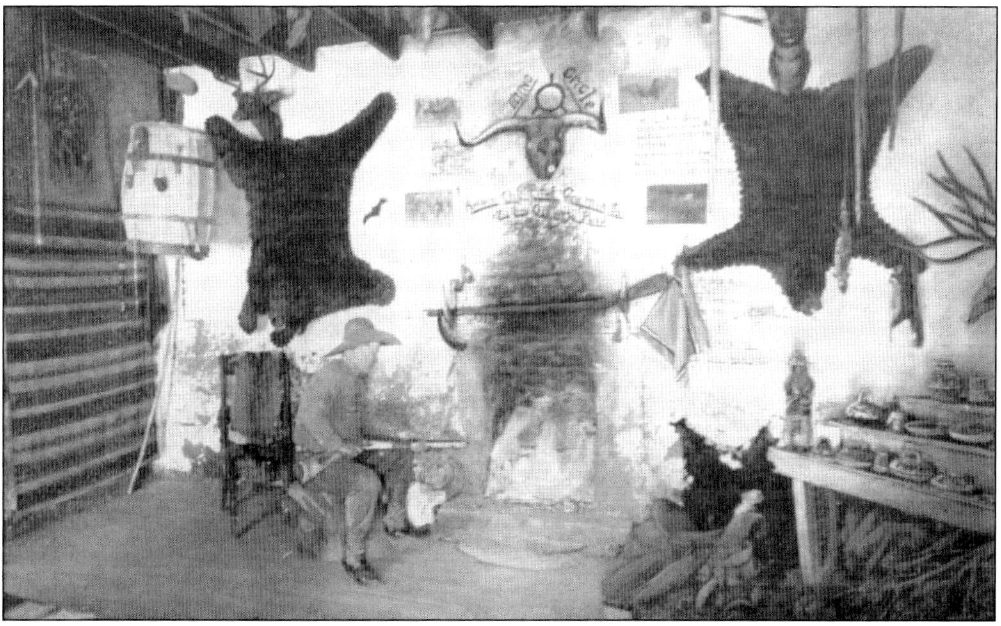

The only early interior photograph of the main Pigeon's Ranch building was taken in 1929 during Greer's operation. This photograph shows plastered walls and a fireplace. The plaster has been marked up with sayings, poetry, brands, and an odd assortment of stories written in black paint or charcoal. Remnants of this decoration remain inside the building to this day. Greer also covered the walls with artifacts, skins, antlers, and skulls. (NT.)

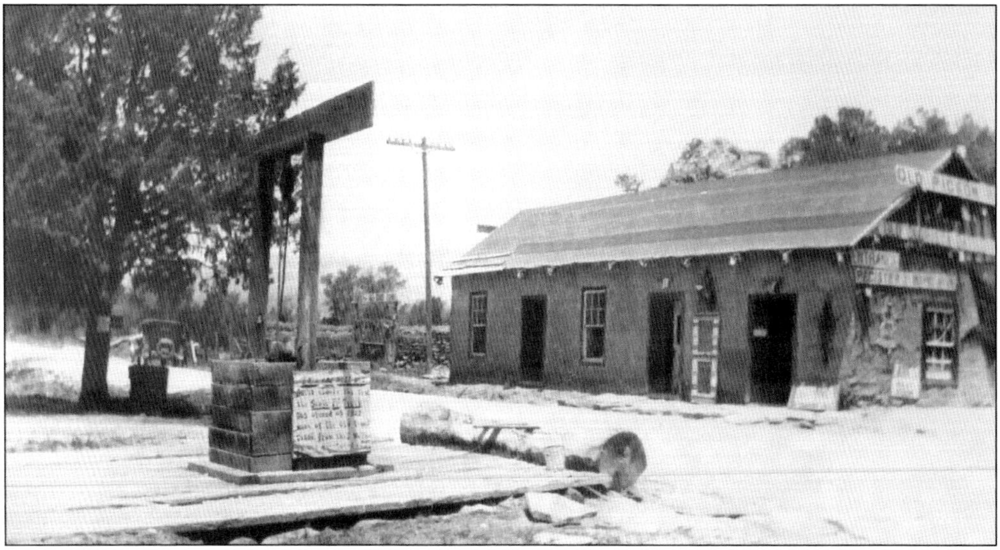

In the mid-1920s, the "Oldest Well," across the road from Pigeon's Ranch, was advertised by Tom Greer all along the highway to Santa Fe as being of great antiquity. However, the old-timers in the area smiled with derision at Greer's "from mouth to ear" tall tale. In fact, the well was originally dug for Alexandre Valle and probably finished in 1858. Local resident Octaviano Segua reported that he had heard firsthand from Valle that the well was dug to obtain clean water for his ranch because herds of cattle and sheep were polluting their prior water source, the little stream close to the well. Another elderly resident, Teodasio Ortiz, remembered that the well was dug by Luis Moya, Rafael Lucero, and Antonio Gabaldon. The well was greatly enlarged by railroad workers during the drought of 1904 and further "enhanced" by Greer. (Above, NT; below, PNHP No. 4104.)

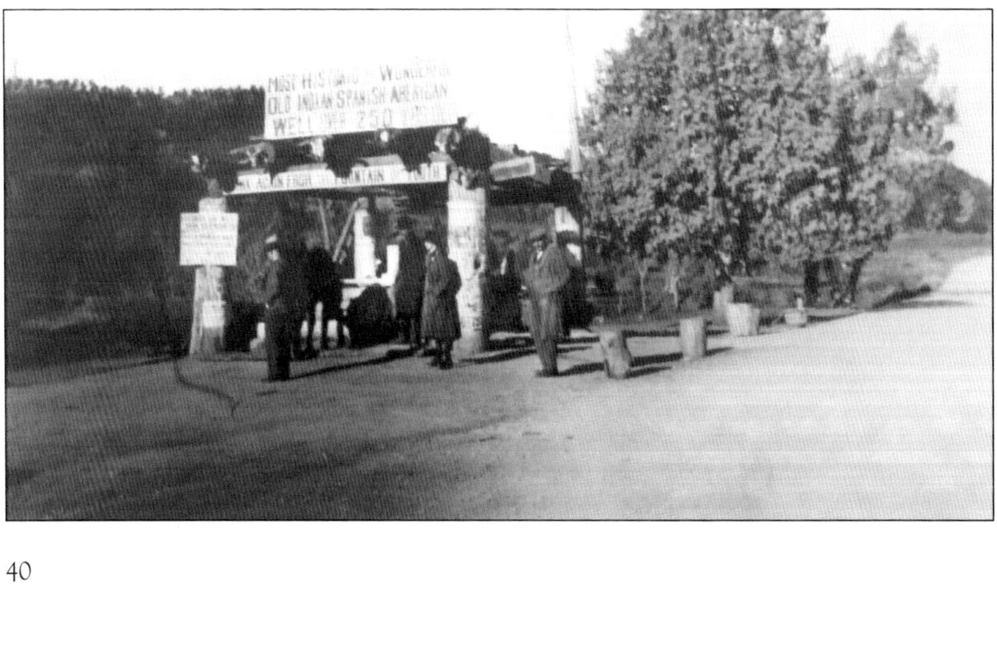

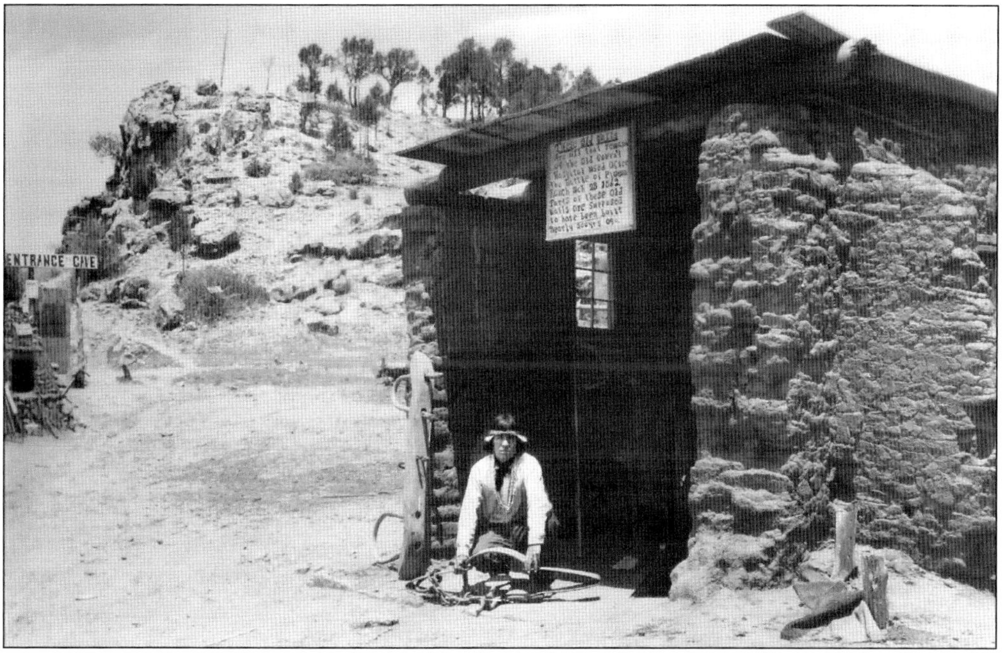

This photograph was taken in 1935 of the remains of the original building that apparently served as the Confederate field hospital for the wounded following the engagement at Pigeon's Ranch. In June 1987, excavation for a house foundation near this site turned up a mass grave containing 31 Confederate soldiers, three of whom were identified. The bodies were removed and buried at the National Cemetery in Santa Fe. (PNHP No. 4109.)

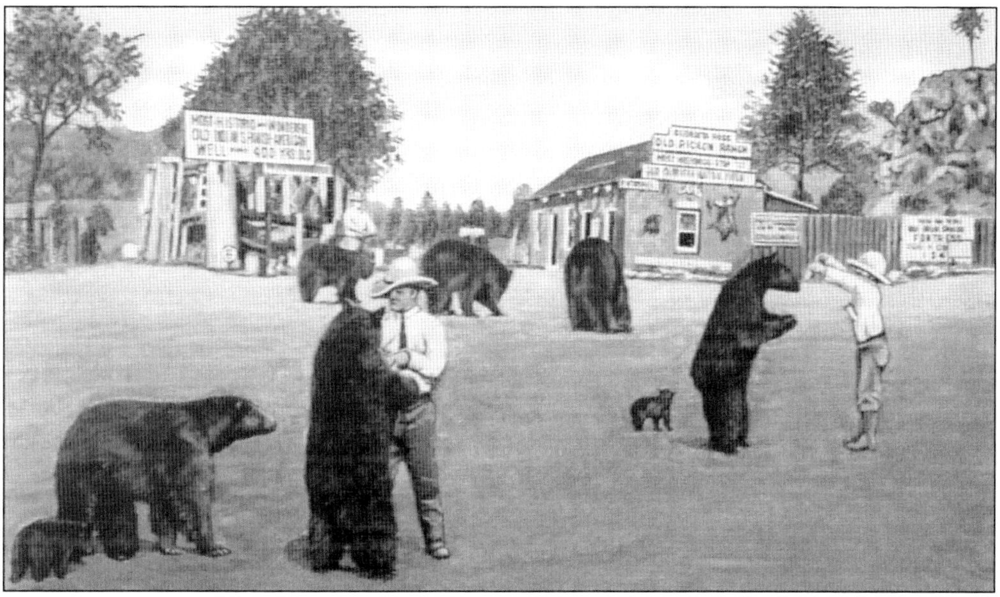

Greer would do just about anything to attract a tourist buck. Bears were also part of his roadside attraction. One particularly ornery black bear harassed visitors and apparently gave Greer some trouble. In 1937, Route 66 was rerouted from Santa Fe and no longer passed through Glorieta Pass. That, coupled with travel restrictions during World War II and the realignment of Highway 85 in the early 1950s, put an end to Greer's roadside attraction. (NT.)

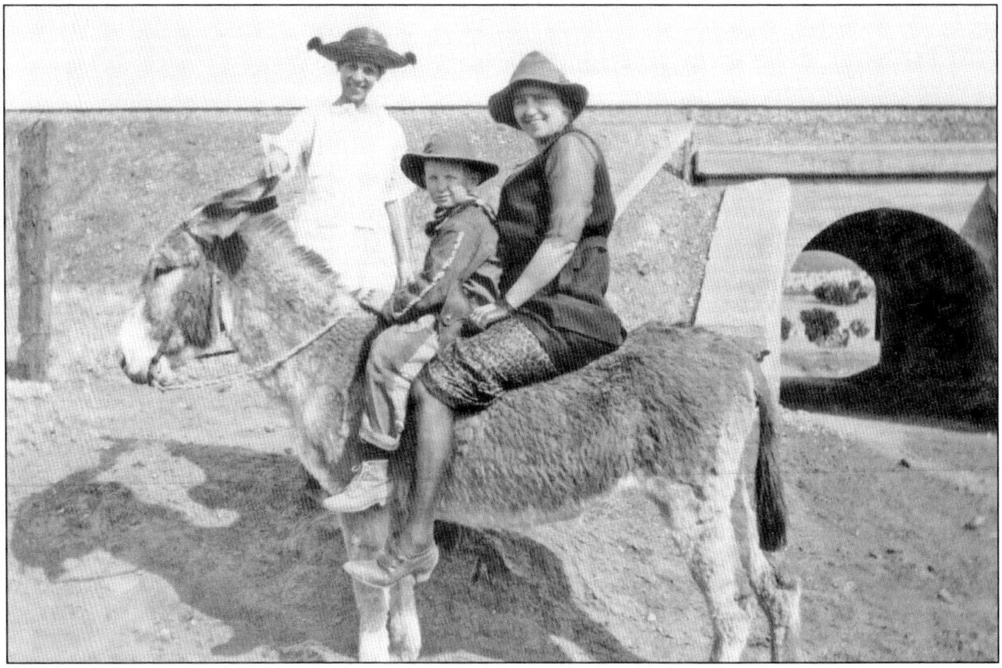

Here are Si Slaughter, wearing a cavalry uniform, and his mother (the standing woman is unidentified) on a noble steed near Apache Canyon west of Glorieta. This was the scene of the first action of the Civil War battle when on March 26, 1862, an advance Union force of 418 men under Major Chivington came face to face with the Confederates under the command of Maj. Charles L. Pyron. The Texans were forced to retreat after a dramatic charge by the Colorado cavalry, who jumped their horses over a deep arroyo. Apache Canyon later became the route of the AT&SF Railroad between Glorieta and Lamy. The railroad cuts through the narrow gorge as it leaves the mountains and heads west towards the Rio Grande valley. (Above, SS; below, DD.)

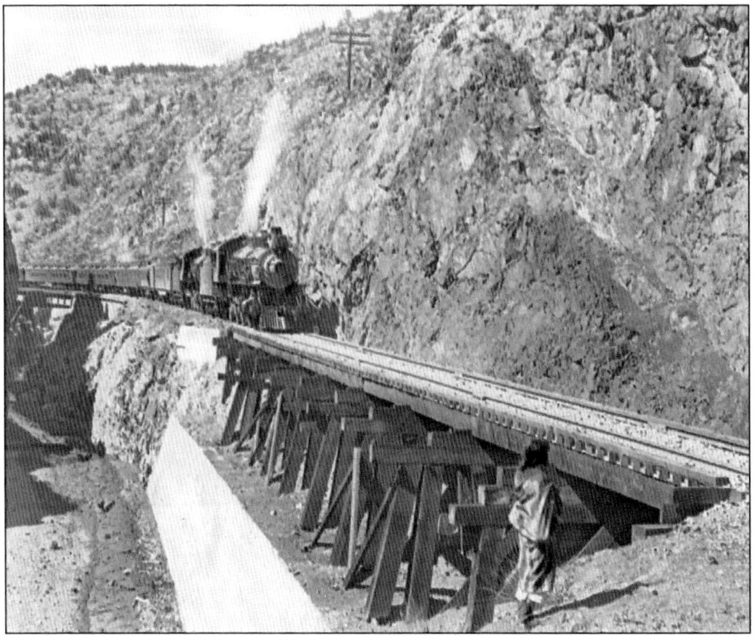

Just southeast of Pigeon's Ranch on Route 66 was Arrowhead Camp. All that remains today is the main building remodeled as a residence and a few ruined cabins, managed by the National Park Service and closed to the public. There were once several log cabins, a gas station, and a store (see Arcadia Publishing's *Route 66 in New Mexico*, page 33). This motor court was established in 1927 by Thad "Si" Slaughter (1885–1944) and his wife, Emma (1885–1943). Thad had been a railroad telegrapher who signed off as "Si," the shortest Morse code he could use; his son was officially named Si (1914–1997). At right is Emma "stepping out," and below is the family (Thad and Si standing, Emma facing the photographer, the man in cap and the other woman unidentified) having a picnic at nearby Arrowhead Pueblo Indian ruin, for which Arrowhead Camp was named. (Both, SS.)

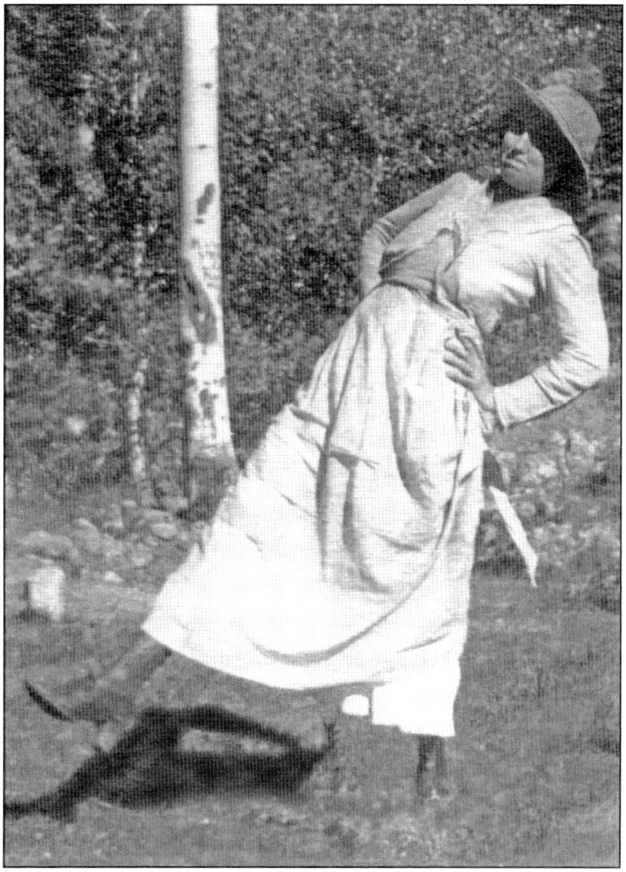

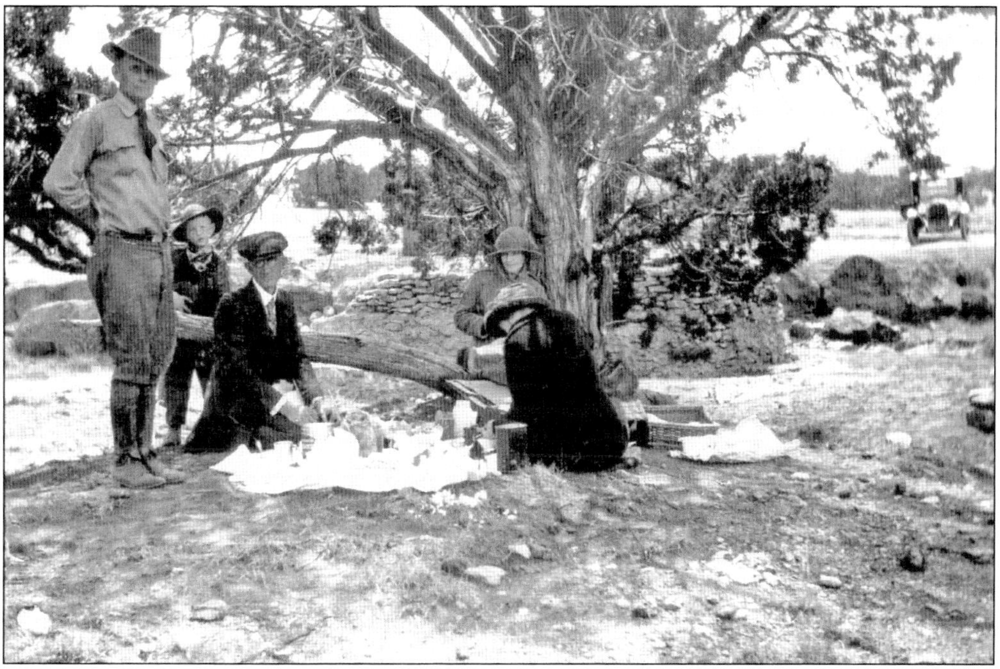

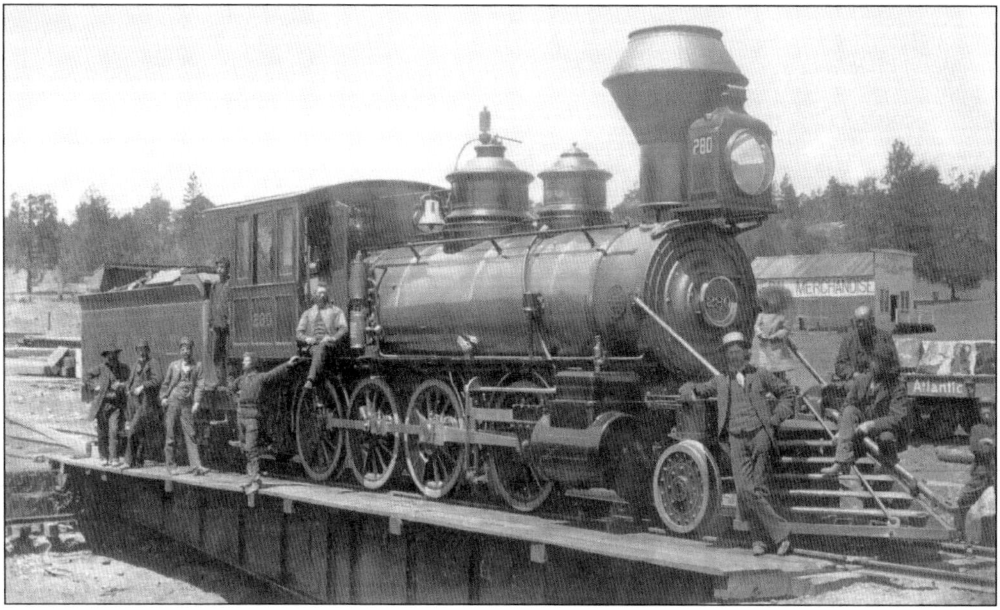

AT&SF Locomotive No. 280 is seen here at the summit of Glorieta Pass about 1890. It was a 2-8-0 Consolidation-type locomotive built by the Baldwin Locomotive Works. The sign on the front of the general mercantile store in the background identifies it as "A.W. Haskell, est. 189[?] Drygoods and Groceries, Hardware." The locomotive is on a turntable so that its direction can be reversed. A similar steam engine is on display at the Kansas Museum of History. (AC.)

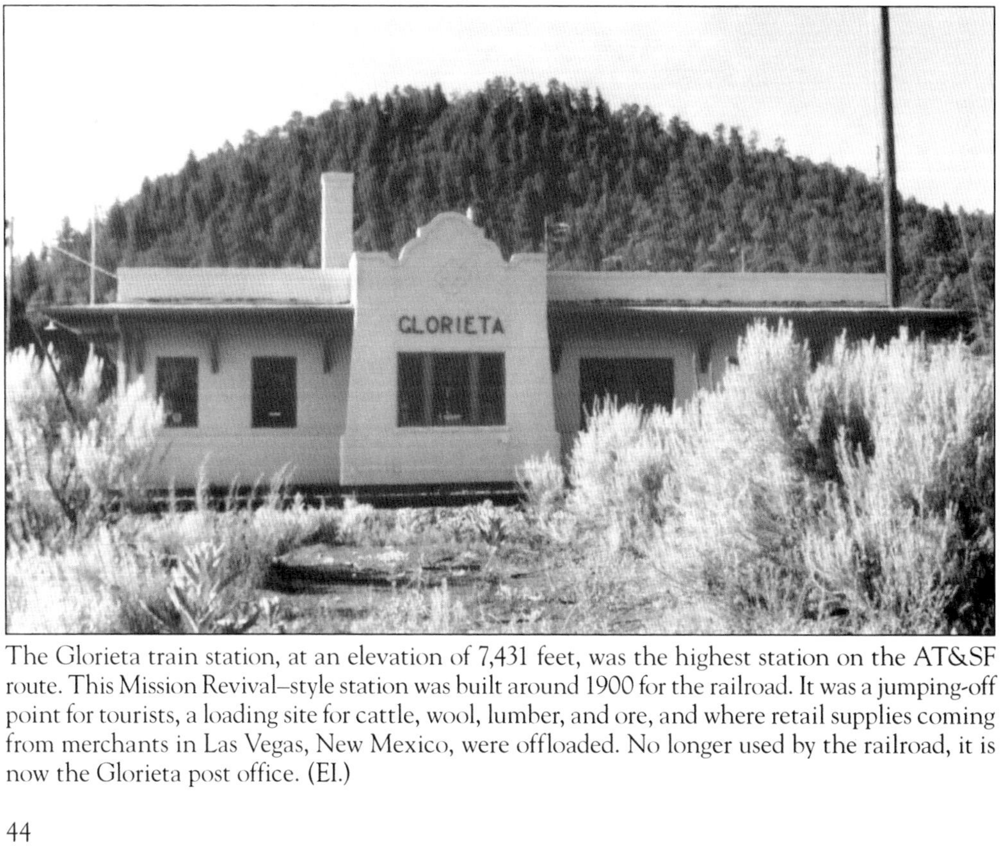

The Glorieta train station, at an elevation of 7,431 feet, was the highest station on the AT&SF route. This Mission Revival–style station was built around 1900 for the railroad. It was a jumping-off point for tourists, a loading site for cattle, wool, lumber, and ore, and where retail supplies coming from merchants in Las Vegas, New Mexico, were offloaded. No longer used by the railroad, it is now the Glorieta post office. (EI.)

Three

Tererro and Mines

The Pecos Mining District is located up the Pecos River Canyon at the mouth of Willow Creek. Mineral deposits were discovered there in 1882, and it was originally known as the Hamilton Mine of the Pecos River Mining Co. The deposits were oxides of lead, zinc, and copper. Initially, small amounts of high-grade copper ore from near the surface were hauled by wagon to Glorieta for shipment to a smelter in El Paso. In 1916, a New York company, Goodrich-Lockhart, began a program of prospecting and development. In 1925, it sold the mine interest to the American Metal Co., Ltd. (AMCO).

AMCO operated the mine from 1927 until 1939, when ore reserves played out. The ore fed to the mill was typically 15.4 percent zinc, 4.9 percent lead, 0.8 percent copper, 113 parts per million (ppm) silver, and 3.4 ppm gold.

Ore was transported from the mine to a mill by a 12-mile-long aerial tramway, the longest such tramway in North America. The mill was located at Alamitos, a few miles northeast of Glorieta, the nearest railroad station.

A company town called Tererro was built in the Pecos River Canyon adjacent to the mine. It had a post office, two markets, a hospital, a school, a restaurant, a jail, a barbershop, a golf course, and even a red-light district, known as "Chihuahua." It also had one of the best baseball teams in the state.

For the entire 14 years of its existence, the town and mine were ably managed by Joseph Tousely Matson (1881–1978). Providing steady employment for an average of 600 people throughout much of the Great Depression, the operation often had the largest payroll in the state.

With the closing of the Pecos Mine, San Miguel County lost its place as a major producer of metals. All that remains today of the mine, mill, and town are the post office and a small market.

Most of the photographs and much of the information in this chapter was graciously provided by Leon McDuff, born in 1921, who grew up in Tererro and whose 1993 book *Tererro* is the definitive work on the mines and the town.

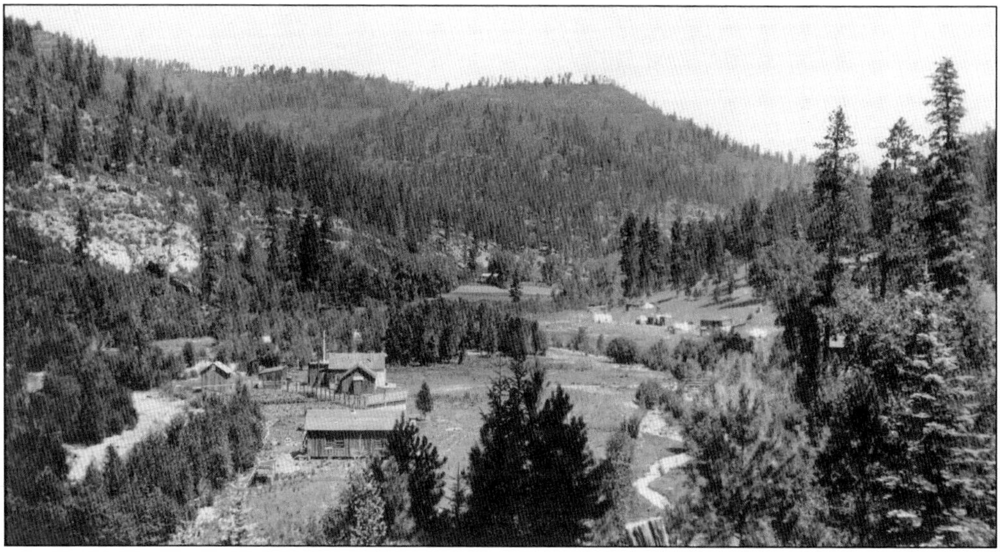

Here are two early views of the area at the confluence of the Pecos River and Willow Creek. The 1925 photograph above shows that only a few lived in the area. The photograph below shows Tererro well under construction in about 1926. This view is looking up Willow Creek where it crosses the main road. The mine complex is out of the picture to the right, up 134 steep steps and 11 landings. Buildings in the photographs include mine offices, the doctor's office, and a number of houses. There are also large piles of firewood. (Above, MH No. 463; below, CSWR.)

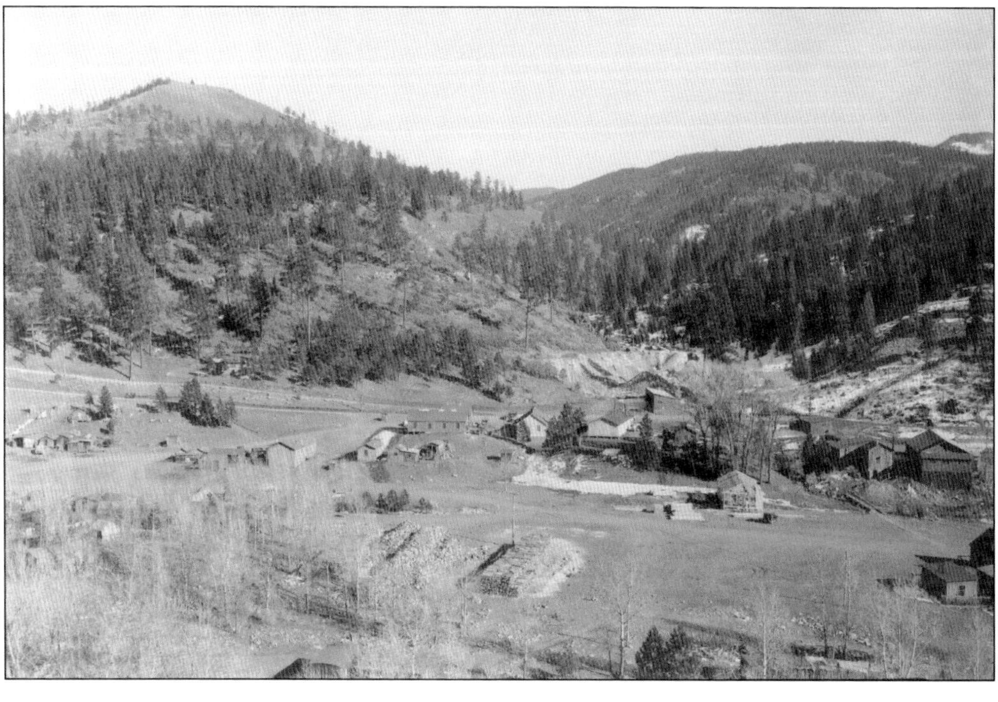

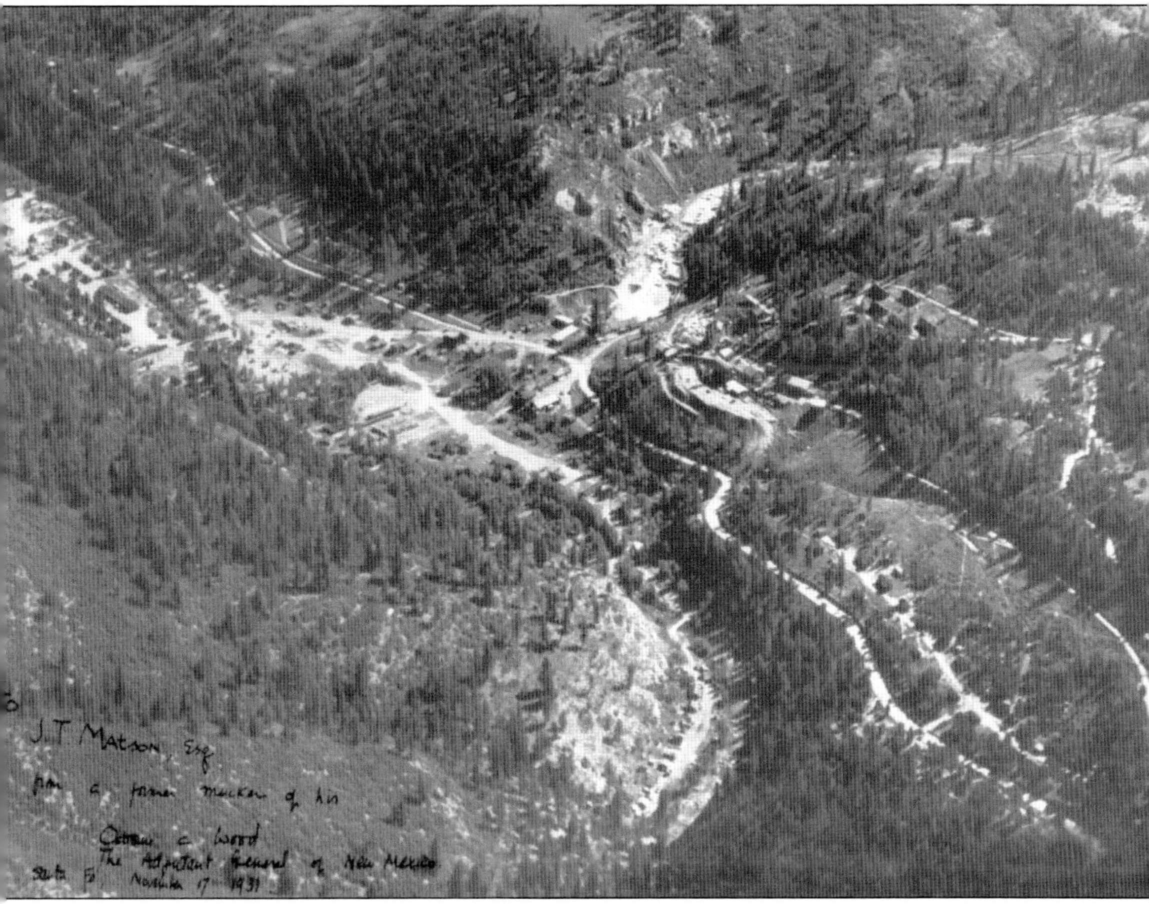

This aerial photograph was taken on a summer morning in 1931 by Osborne C. Wood (1897–1950), adjutant general of the New Mexico National Guard and the son of Gen. Leonard Wood (1860–1927). General Wood stipulated in his will that in order for his son to inherit his sizable wealth, the son would have to spend a year working at hard labor, having concluded that his son's life had been too cushy. Osborne, an Army lieutenant colonel, had met Joseph Matson, an Army captain and later the manager of Tererro Mine, in France during World War I. When Osborne learned that Matson was a mine manager, he requested a job as a mucker (a mine laborer who removes ore and waste rock by hand; the hardest job in a mine). He took a leave as the head of the New Mexico National Guard and worked as a mucker for all of 1929. (LM.)

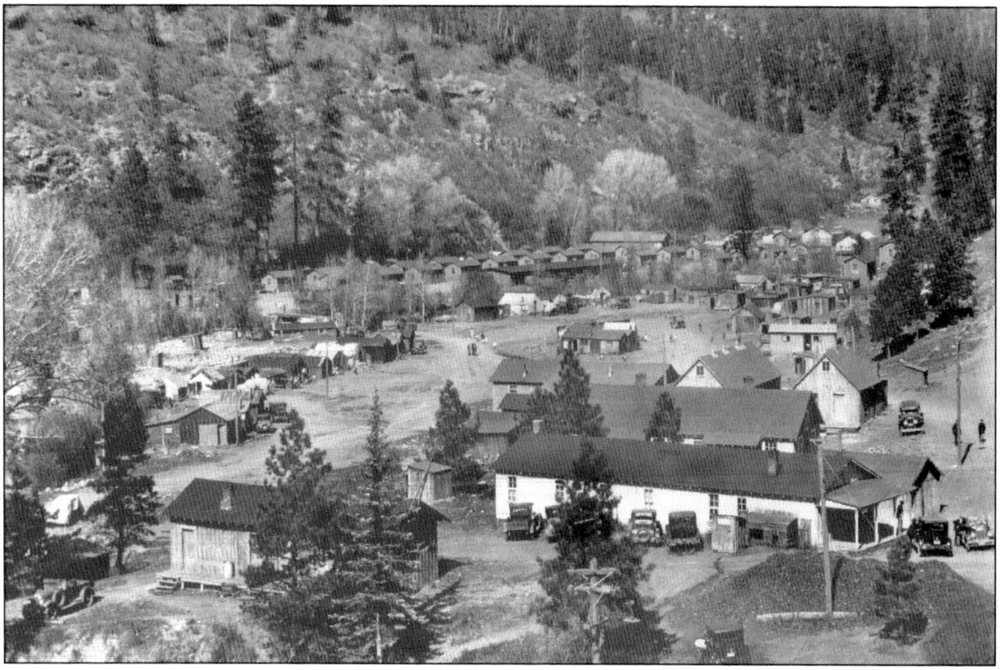

Both of these photographs show Tererro in its heyday, around 1930. Note the line of "married housing" in the background; bachelors lived in dorms that were also visible. Buildings shown also include the sheriff's office, the barbershop, offices, the jail, and the doctor's office. The name "Tererro" was thought to mean "deer-lick," a bog near the town where salt deposited after water evaporated, attracting deer. That is what the locals called it. It was also a place they tossed their trash. Tererro is actually a misspelling of the Spanish word for "dump" (*terrero*). The other option for the town name was Amco, after the mining company. (Both, LM.)

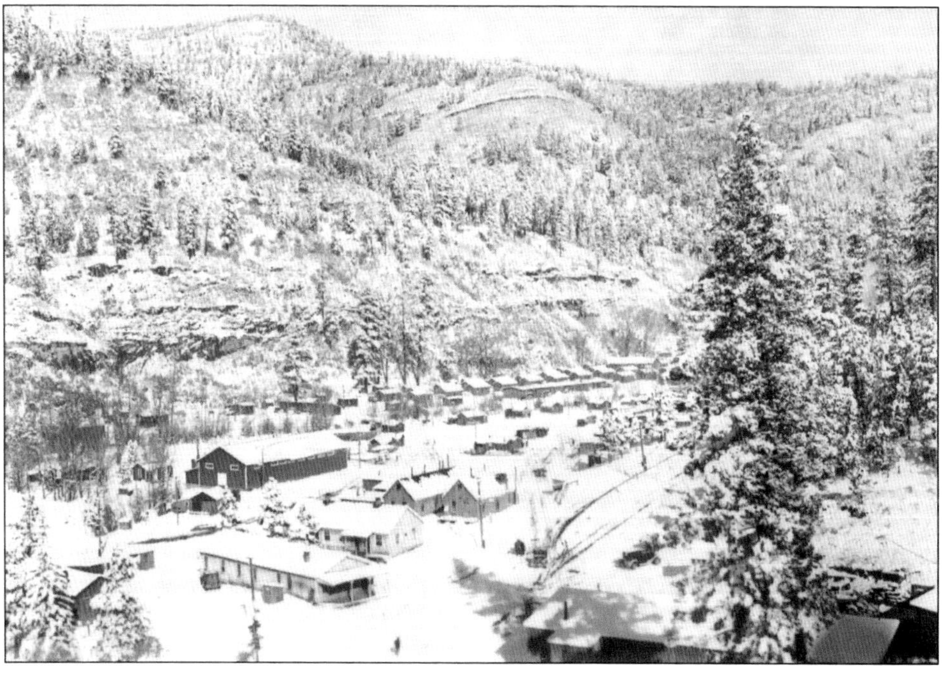

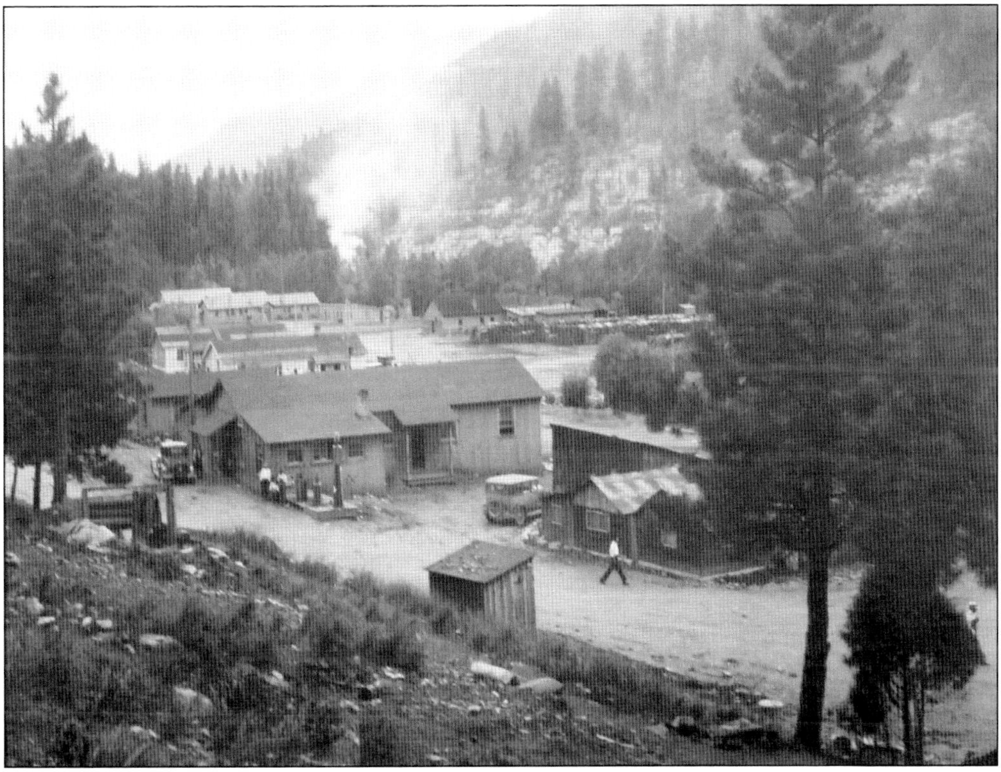

This portion of Tererro was adjacent to the main road between the village of Pecos and Cowles, several miles up the canyon at the end of the road. Judging from the automobiles, this photograph was taken in the mid-1930s. Note the gas pump and garage in the foreground, as well as many cords of firewood stacked in the background. Most heating and cooking was done with wood. (NT.)

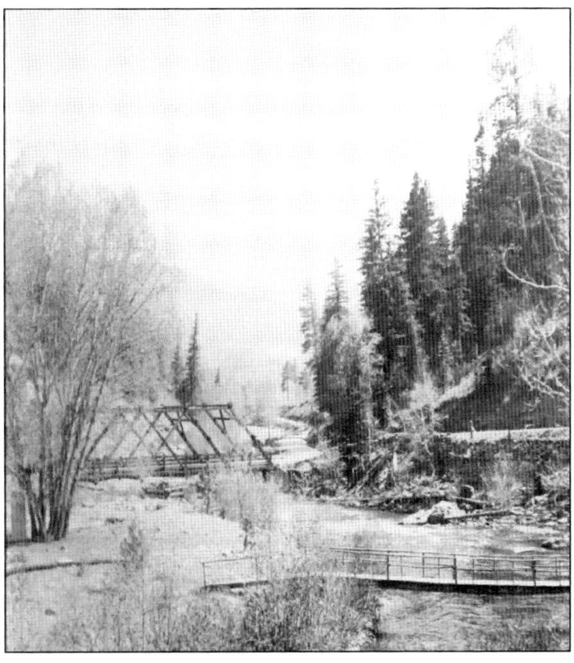

Leon McDuff's father was the third employee hired by AMCO. He was a carpenter and was taken on as a construction supervisor. His initial job was to oversee construction of four heavy-timber truss bridges across the Pecos River. This is the first bridge he built, the first structure constructed by AMCO, and the only AMCO structure still standing today. It was listed in the National Register of Historical Places in 1997. (NT.)

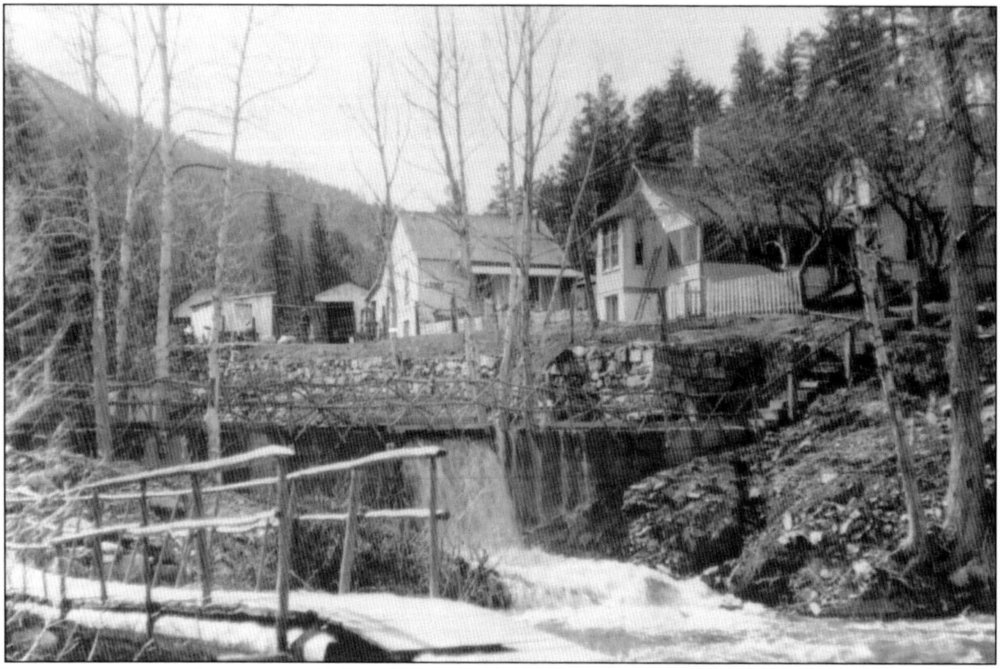

This photograph shows part of the Simmons Ranch complex in 1925, before it was purchased by AMCO and became the town hospital. The location is at the far southern end of AMCO property, just a little north of the bridge on the previous page. A little farther west were other Simmons buildings that became a dairy operated by H. Riley Littrell and his family, who provided dairy products to the town. (LM.)

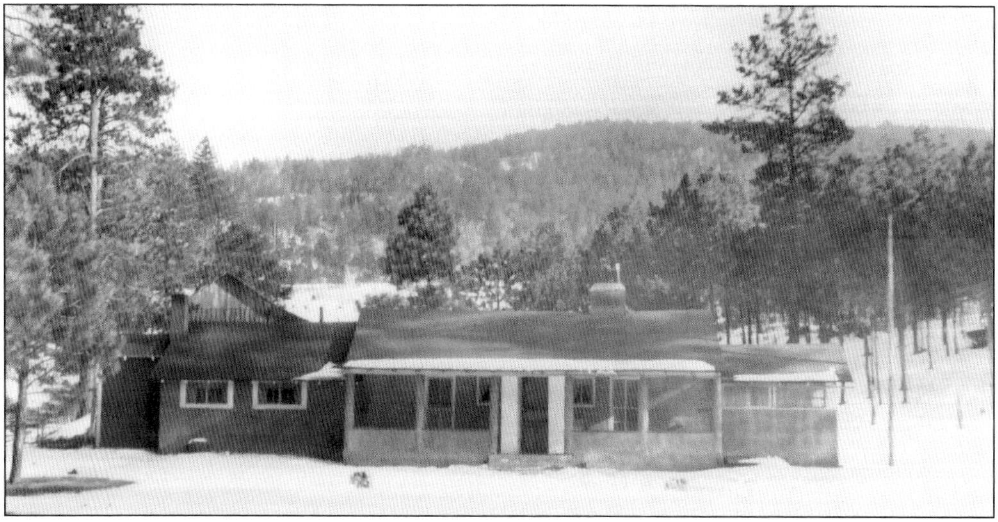

East of the mine was the home of mine manager Joseph "Joe" Tousely Matson (1881–1978), his wife, Frances, and their daughter Alice and son Joe Jr. Matson was well liked and was called "The Skipper." There was a guesthouse, as well as rooms for two servants: a housekeeper/cook and a handyman (Louise and Milton Henson). Milton was the nephew of Matthew Henson, the black sailor who had accompanied Admiral Perry to the North Pole. It was one of only three houses in town with indoor plumbing, the others being the Matson guesthouse and Dr. Warren George Smith's house. (LM.)

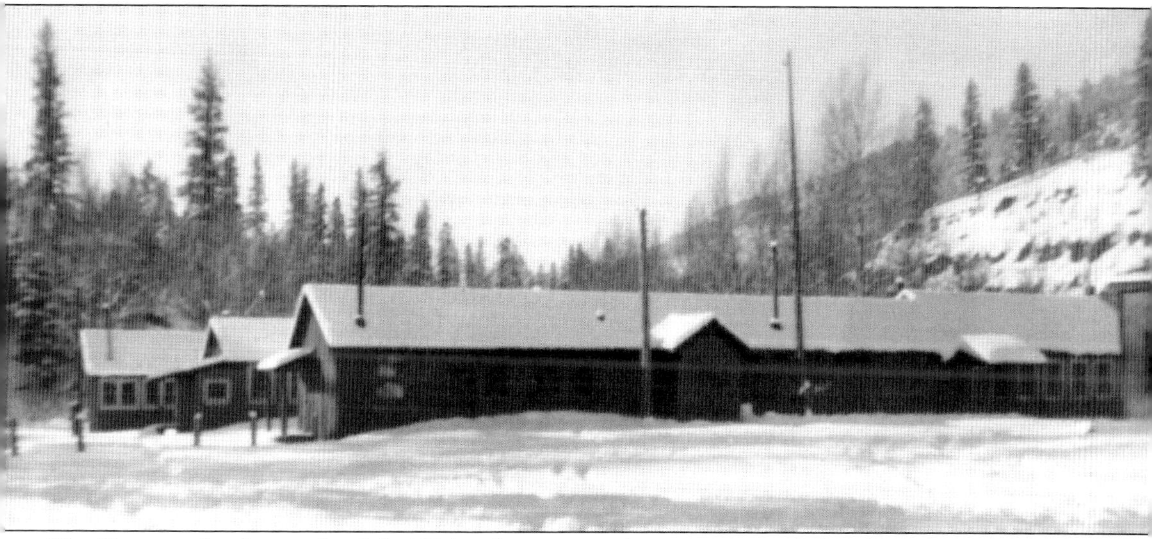

The Tererro school started in July 1926 with one room but soon expanded to three, having in a few months grown from 31 to 95 students. The county was asked to provide a third teacher, but it would only do so if there was an average class size of 32 or more. They said they would provide a teacher for a class of only 31, but that the mine would have to pay the teacher's salary. To solve the problem, Matson decided to allow any child at least five years of age to start school in the first grade. This added four students, Leon McDuff, Joe Matson Jr., Jane MacDonald, and Dick Smith, bringing the total to 99 students. This photograph shows the school in 1937. On the last day of the Tererro school, May 26, 1939, there were 358 students and 14 teachers. (LM.)

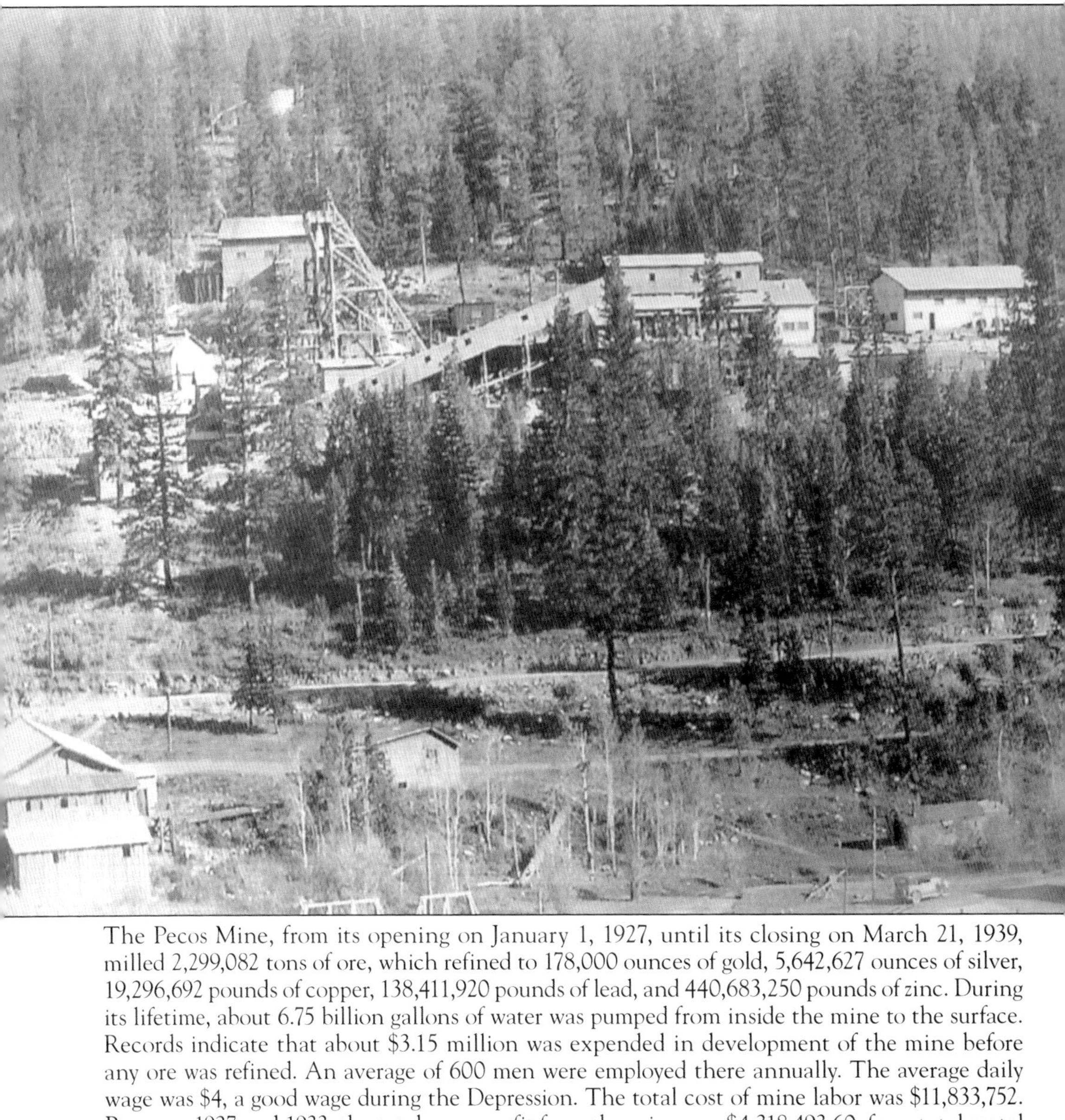

The Pecos Mine, from its opening on January 1, 1927, until its closing on March 21, 1939, milled 2,299,082 tons of ore, which refined to 178,000 ounces of gold, 5,642,627 ounces of silver, 19,296,692 pounds of copper, 138,411,920 pounds of lead, and 440,683,250 pounds of zinc. During its lifetime, about 6.75 billion gallons of water was pumped from inside the mine to the surface. Records indicate that about $3.15 million was expended in development of the mine before any ore was refined. An average of 600 men were employed there annually. The average daily wage was $4, a good wage during the Depression. The total cost of mine labor was $11,833,752. Between 1927 and 1933, the total gross profit from the mine was $4,318,493.60, from total metal sales of $39,644,376.01. For a number of years, the mine was the single largest employer and had the largest payroll in the state of New Mexico. (LM.)

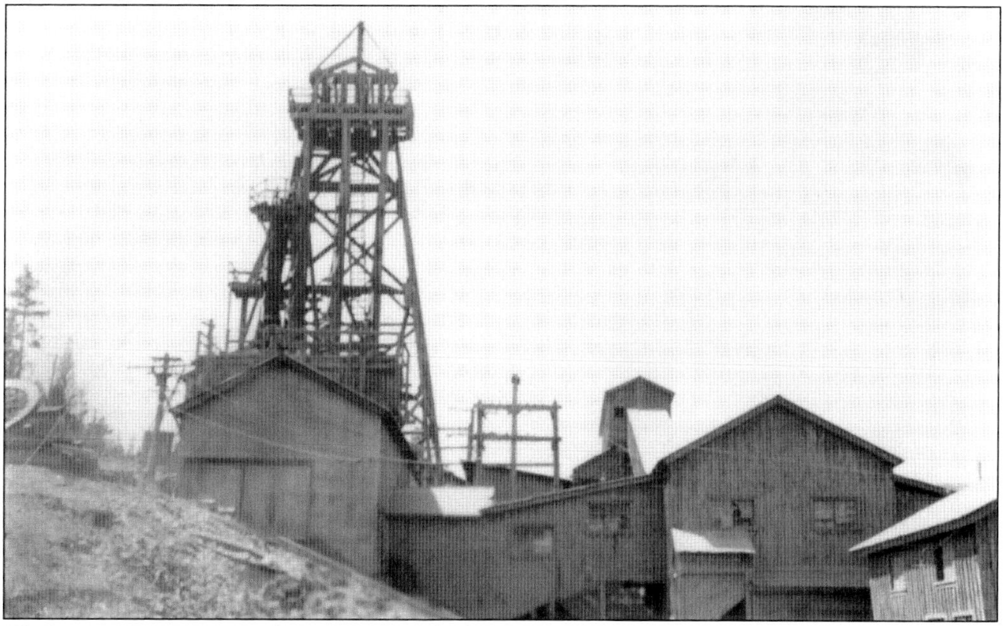

The Pecos Mine contained two major ore bodies, named the Katydid and the Evangeline. A third ore body that failed to produce was called the Katydidn't. The main vertical shaft into the mine, below the hoisting frame shown in this photograph (there were two shafts), eventually reached a depth of 1,750 feet below the surface, although little ore was found below 1,200 feet. An 85-pound jack hammer was the most common tool in the mine. Usually, digging a six-foot depth into the rock required 8 hours to drill, load, clear, and blast; 24 hours to shovel; and another 6 hours to install timbers, rail, guides, and pumps. (LM.)

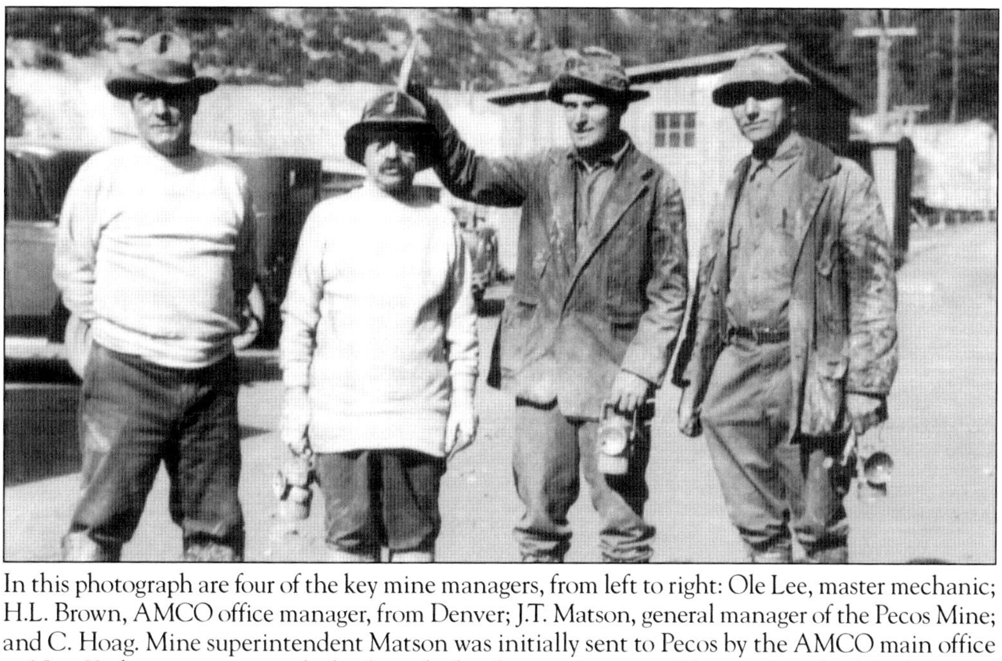

In this photograph are four of the key mine managers, from left to right: Ole Lee, master mechanic; H.L. Brown, AMCO office manager, from Denver; J.T. Matson, general manager of the Pecos Mine; and C. Hoag. Mine superintendent Matson was initially sent to Pecos by the AMCO main office in New York to investigate a lack of timely development reports. The situation he found was not good, so the manager at the time was fired and Matson was placed in charge. (LM.)

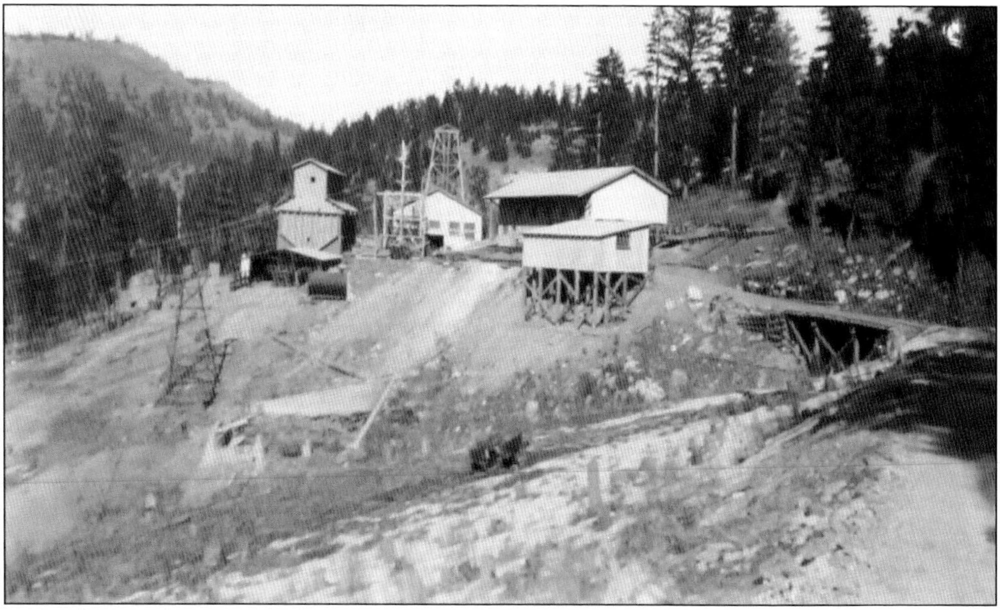

Both of these photographs show the mine complex as viewed from the north. The photograph above is from the mid-1920s, while the photograph below shows the mine as fully developed in the late 1930s. The aerial bucket tram to carry ore to the mill is clearly visible in both photographs. Note also the stockpile of pipe used in dewatering the mine. Water was a continual problem underground. At deep levels, water could shoot out from a bore hole at pressures exceeding 150 pounds per square inch. As a result, constant pumping was required. When the mine was shut and equipment removed, miners were told to try and salvage the lower pumps but to stop working and leave if the water got up to their waists. The lower-level pumps are still down there today. (Both, LM.)

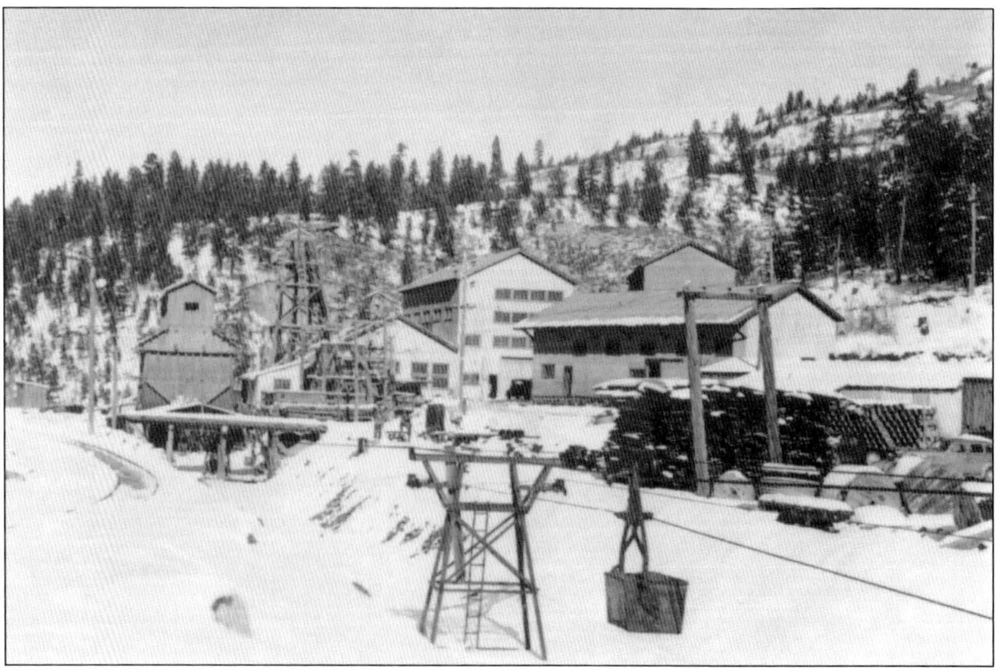

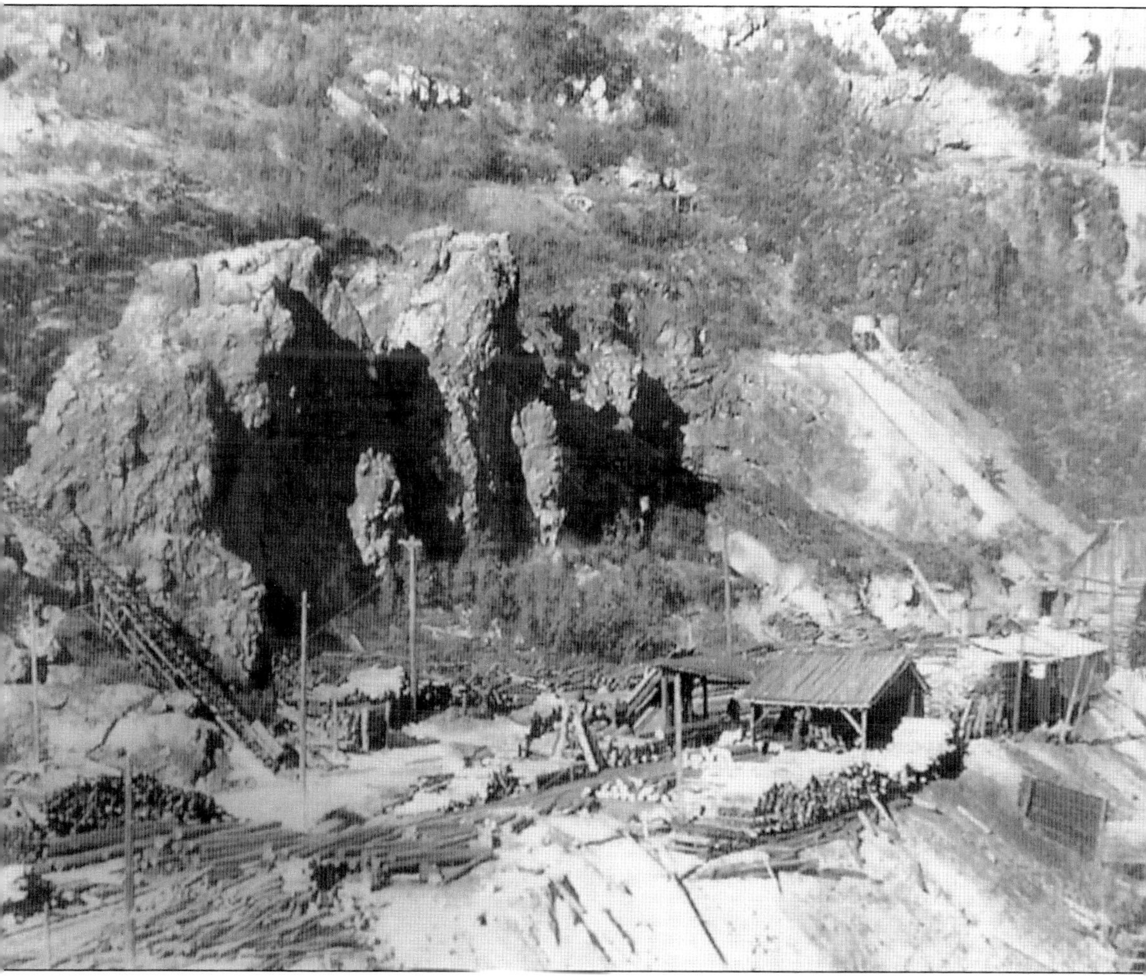

Where there is a mine in the mountains, there will also be a sawmill. At Tererro, in addition to providing lumber for the town, the mine itself required vast amounts of lumber for timber bracing, to prevent rock falls and cave-ins. Here is the mine sawmill at one of its locations, having to be moved as timber supplies dwindled at a particular location. The pile of lumber in the middle foreground is mine timber of one of several types: "square-set," "gob fence," "raise timber," or "drift set," depending on their application in the mine. The mine also had a full blacksmith shop. A "drill doctor" visited all working places every day to make repairs and keep track of the machines. An average of 360 pieces of steel were sharpened each day by one drill sharpener and two assistants. (LM.)

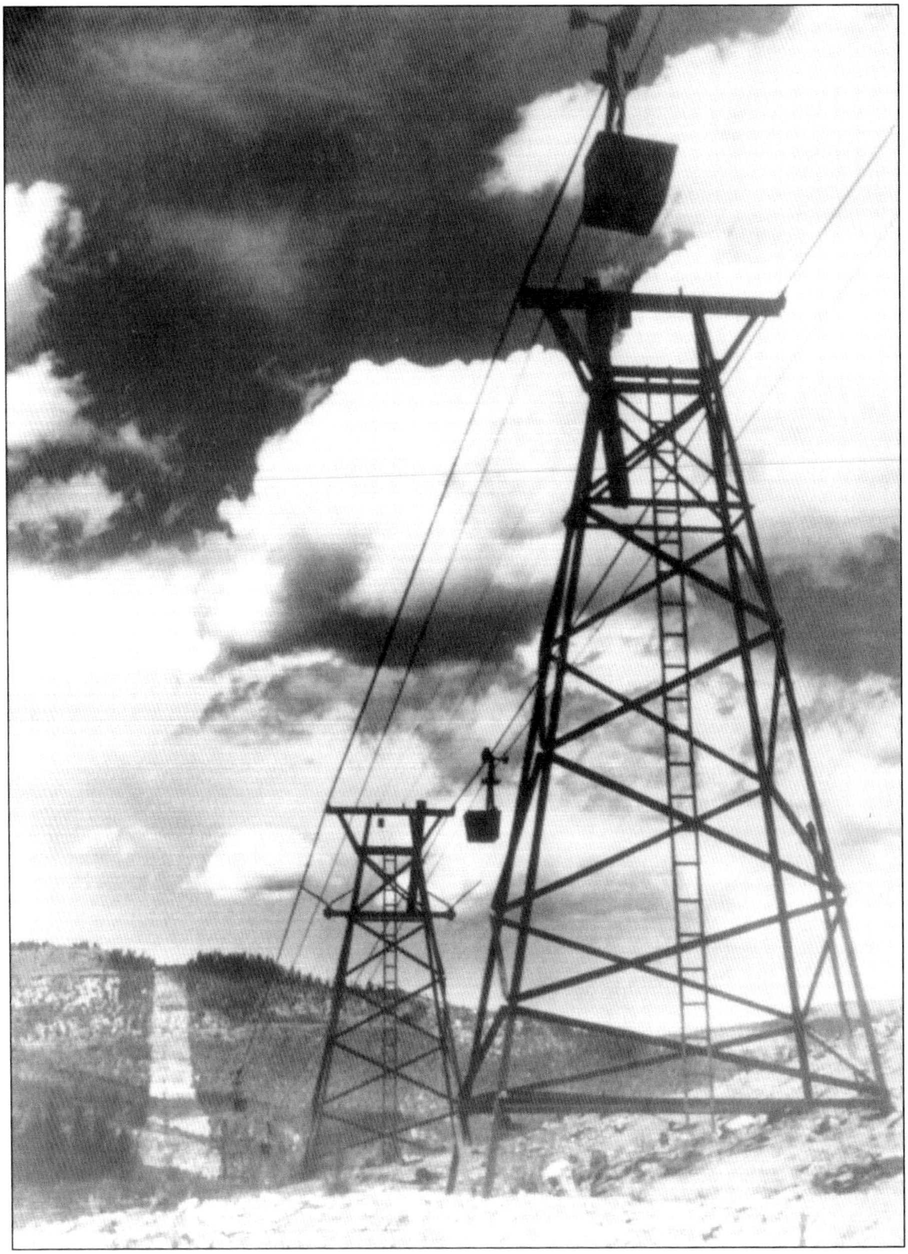

Getting ore from the mine, almost 8,000 feet up in the mountains, to the railroad station at Glorieta, nearly 20 miles away by road, was a problem. A suitable road or railroad up the Pecos Canyon would be a massive and expensive construction undertaking, and it was also opposed by several property owners who were concerned that their dude ranches would be compromised by the mine. The solution was an aerial tramway from the mine to the mill site (12 miles) and a rail spur from the mill to Glorieta (6 miles). To protect the tram from fire and windblown timber, a 200-foot right-of-way was prepared and cleared. The Riblet Tramway Construction Company of Spokane, Washington, won the contract with a bid of $313,000, with the tram to be completed and tested by January 1, 1927. At the time, it was said to be the longest such tramway in North America. (LM.)

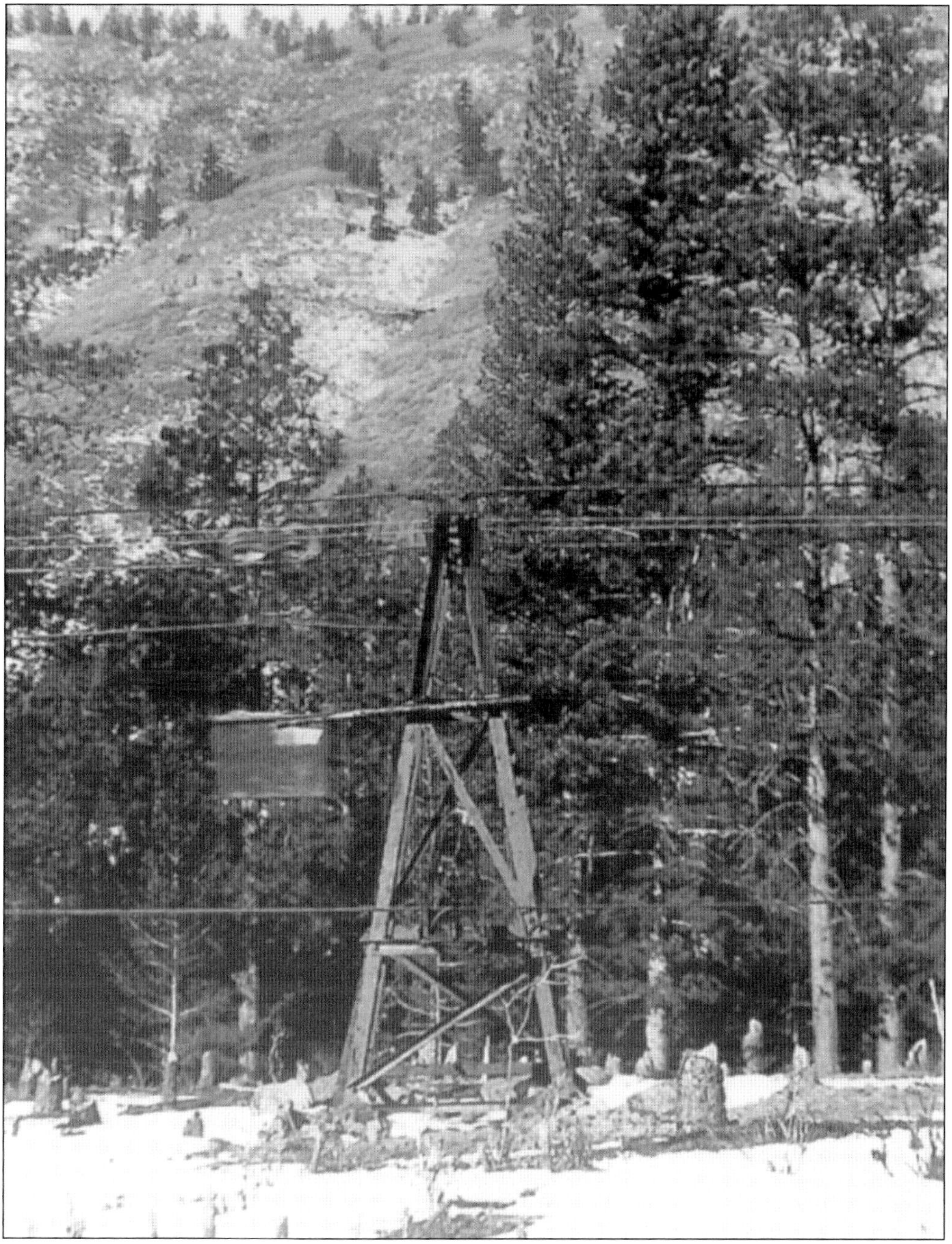

This photograph shows one of the lower towers. Individual buckets weighed 400 pounds and carried about 1,250 pounds of ore each. At full capacity, there were 400 buckets on the tram, each moving at a little over 5.5 miles per hour. In some places, the buckets would be a mere three feet off the ground, while some of the canyons were one mile wide and 1,000 feet deep. The system operated primarily by gravity, with power assists by a 100-horsepower motor at the mine and a 40-horsepower motor at the mill. During the life of the mine, any single bucket would have transported 5,734 tons of ore and made 9,174 round-trips. That is a distance of about 215,500 miles—22,500 miles short of a trip to the moon. (EI.)

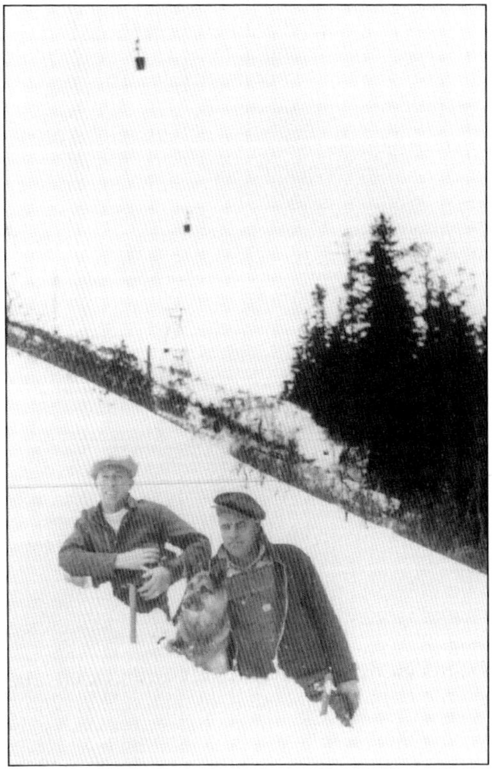

At left, Harold Walter and Ray Marsten check the tramline after a heavy snowfall. To ensure minimum downtime, a crew of two men rode the buckets every day to tighten bolts, oil moving parts, and inspect for wear and any problems. They carried a portable telephone to tap into a line strung along the towers. One would start at the mine, and one at the mill. When they met in the middle, they would hop off onto a tower and hop on another bucket for the return trip. If there was a problem, a repair crew would be sent out the next day. The repair crew below is operating the "iron mule," a small tractor powered by a Ford Model T engine. They are hauling a small, three-eighths-inch cable used to string larger cable for repairs and replacement (Both, LM.)

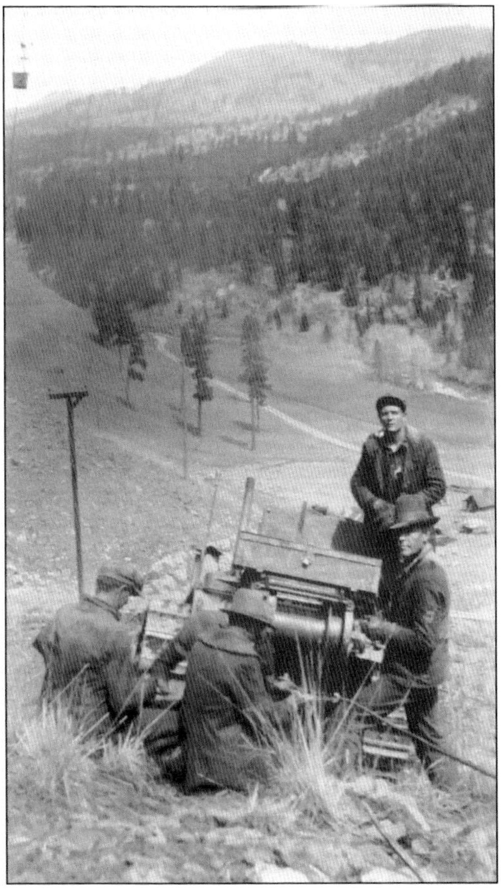

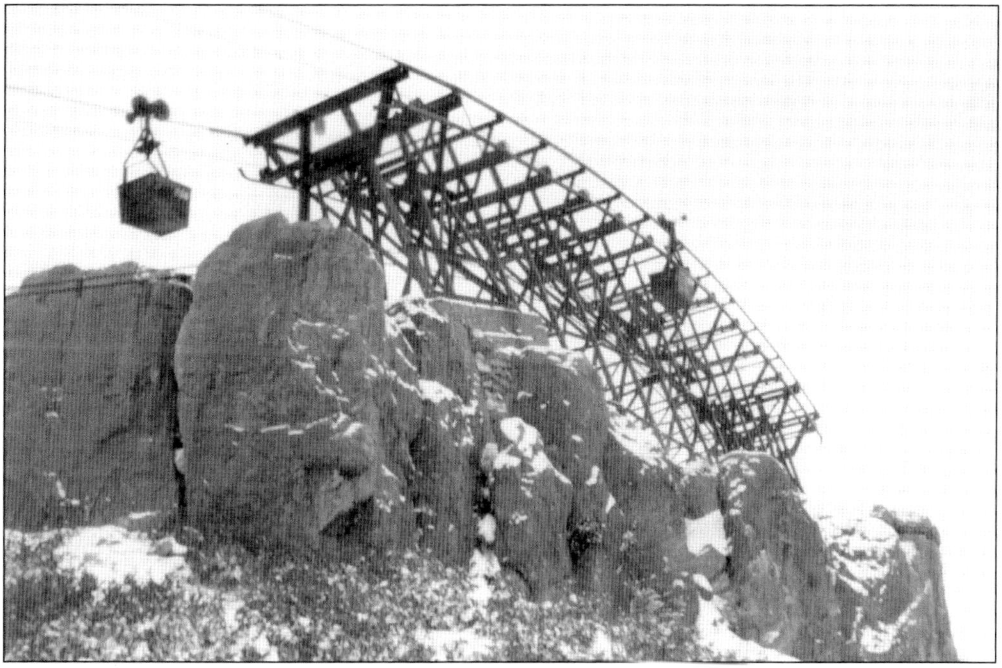

Much of the information about the tramway comes from a 1938 New Mexico School of Mines thesis, *The Aerial Tramway: As Used in the Transportation of Ore at the Pecos Mines*, by the mine's chief engineer, Eugene Carter Anderson (1892–1968.) After leaving Pecos, Anderson worked in potash mines near Carlsbad, New Mexico, as did a number of former Pecos Mine employees. The photograph above shows a tensioning station where the cable had to make an angle turn. One memorable accident occurred when young Norman Littrell grabbed onto a bucket. He failed to let go in time and, when he did, broke his arm in the fall. Word went out that the father of any boy caught riding the tram would be dismissed, and there were no more tram rides. The photograph below shows the mill described on the next two pages. (Both, LM.)

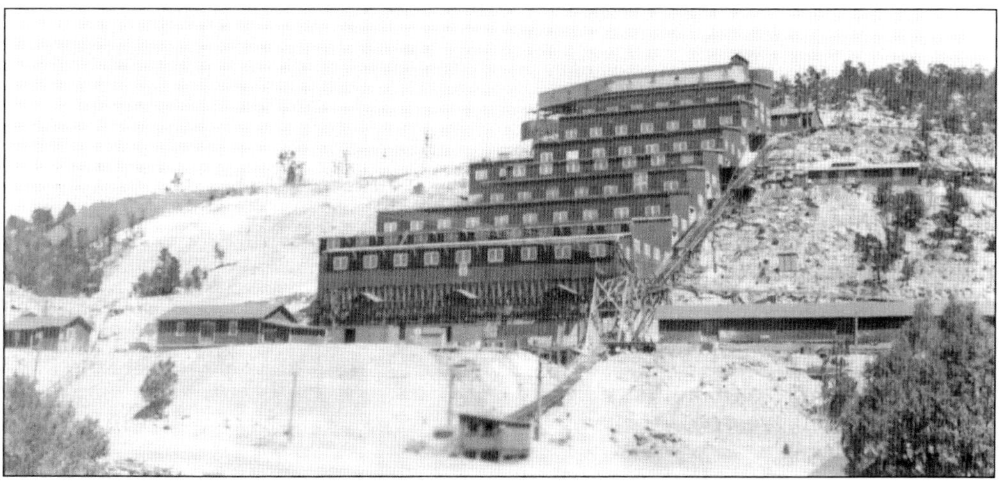

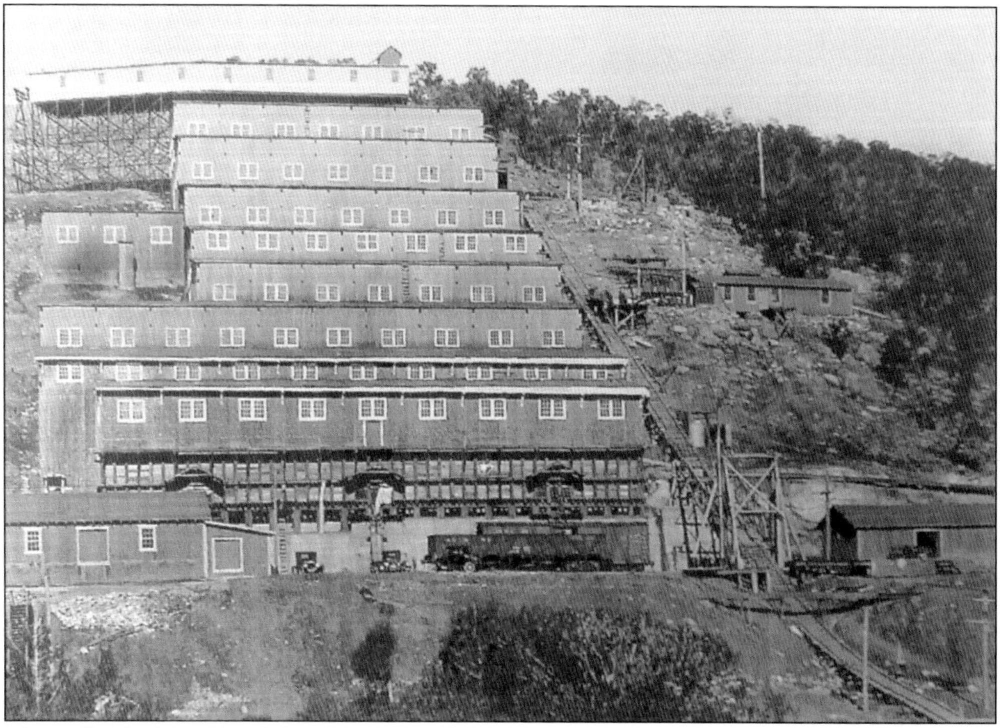

The mill, which prepared the ore so that metal could be extracted, was built in 1926 at a cost of $381,000. It was located just a few miles northwest of the village of Pecos in Alamitos Canyon. Power came from a 2,200-volt, coal-fired powerhouse just southeast of the mill, and water came through a 7,000-foot-long, eight-inch-diameter pipeline pumped from the Pecos River near the Valley Ranch. The mill treated the complex ore using a gravity-flow process of crushers, mixers with mica, and tanks with cyanide, cresylic acid, and xanthate to concentrate lead and lime, copper sulfate, pine oil, and xanthate to concentrate zinc. Up to 600 tons of ore per day were processed into lead and zinc concentrates. (Above, LM; below, NT.)

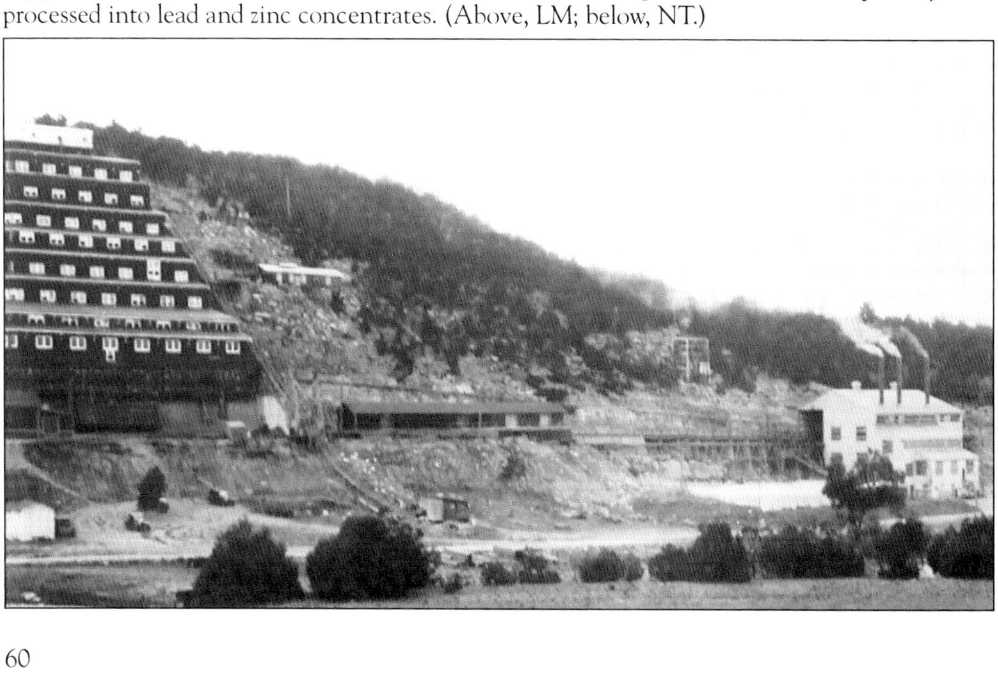

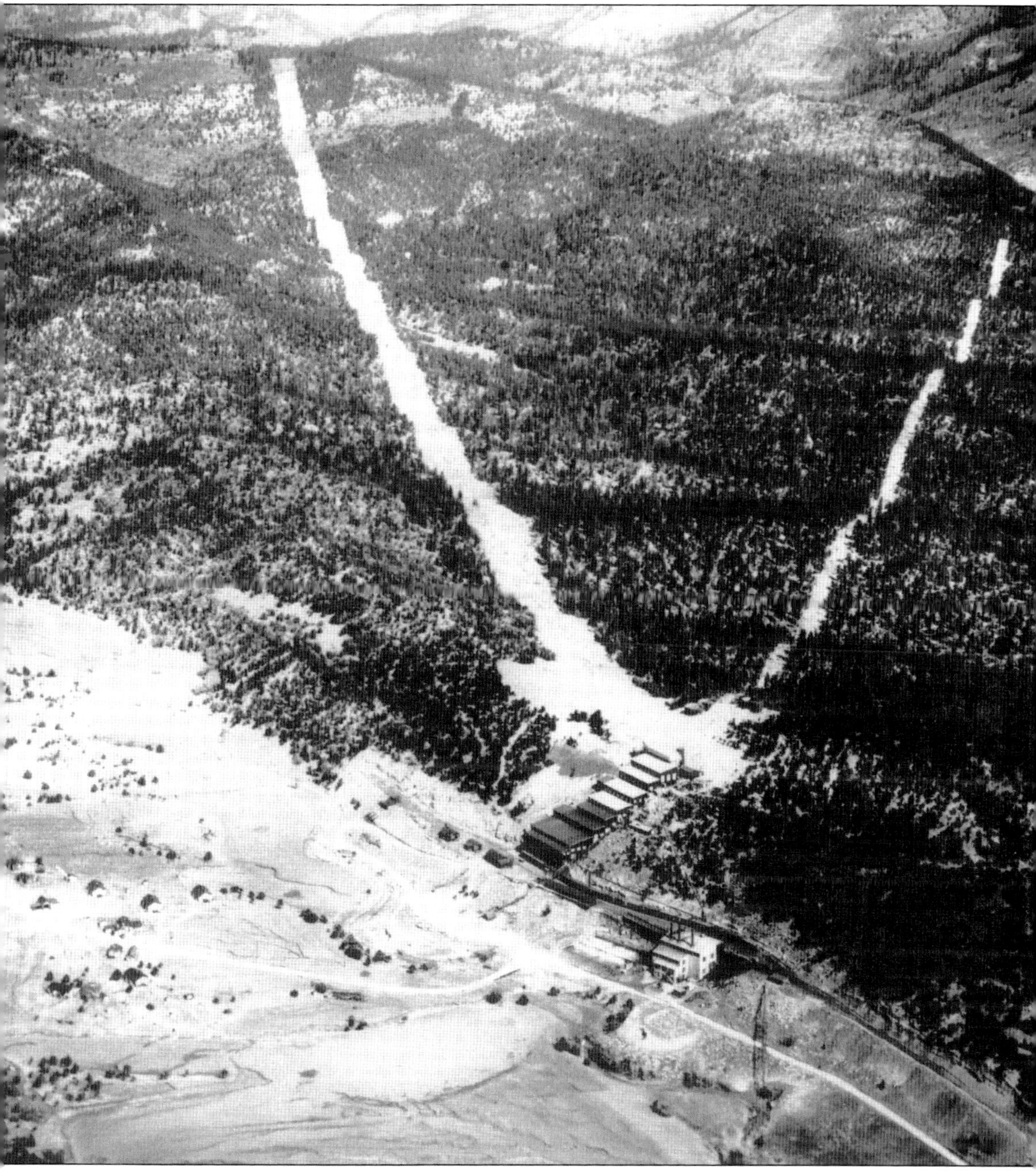

Coarse crushed ore from the mine came to the mill via the aerial tramway, the right-of-way of which is clearly visible in the photograph, and was deposited in a flat-bottomed wooden bin with a capacity of 1,800 tons. There were large water tanks on the hillside above the mill to provide water for ore processing as well as for fire protection. The ore concentrate from the mill was shipped on a six-mile rail spur to Glorieta for transport to smelters, where the metal was extracted. Zinc concentrate went to Oklahoma, and lead concentrate went to El Paso. Copper, silver, and gold were also removed at these two smelters. (LM.)

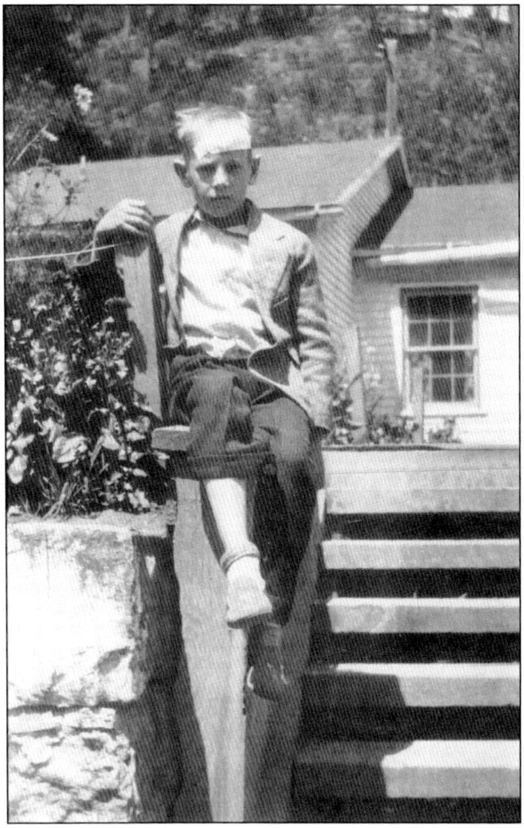

The mine, the mill, the tram, and the town are the framework for a story of people. And thanks to the writing of Leon McDuff in his book *Tererro*, a good portion of the human story is known. McDuff grew up in Tererro, moving there in 1925 at the age of five and not leaving until the town folded in 1939. The photograph below shows McDuff (left) and his constant companion Joe Matson Jr., son of the mine manager. They had many boyhood adventures and misadventures. In August 1930, while working as a golf caddy, McDuff was accidently struck in the head by a golf club thrown by a man frustrated at a bad shot. Dr. Warren George Smith pulled a silver quarter from his pocket, shaped it, and implanted it to fill the hole in McDuff's skull—note the bandage on his forehead. As of this writing, McDuff is 94 years old and always carries "two bits" with him. (Both, LM.)

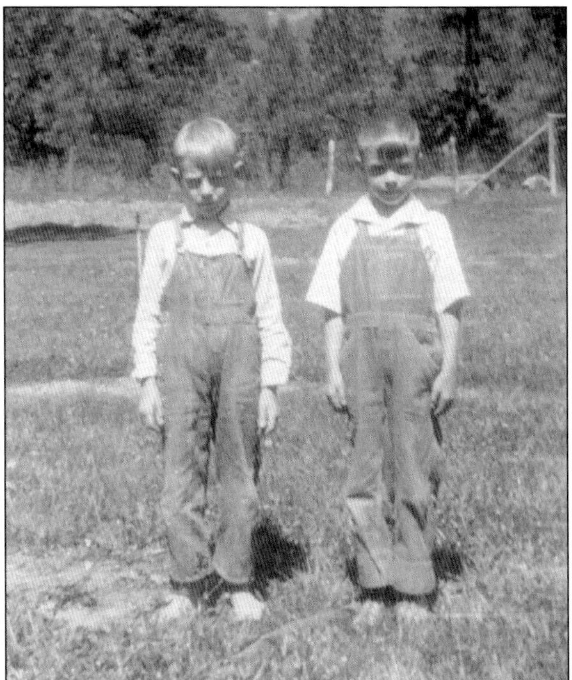

The photograph at right shows Leon McDuff in 1988 near a large pine tree in Tererro. The plaque on the tree is in memory of Joe Matson Jr. (1921–1987), whose ashes are scattered beneath the tree. While McDuff and Matson were some of the very first residents of Tererro, the man in the photograph below was one of the last residents, Happy Ley. He came to the area in 1929 as a ranch hand, working on most of the ranches in the area and eventually taking over the Tererro store. He married Delfina Hands, who was an employee of the Mountain View Dude Ranch. They raised their family in Tererro, and his son and his son's wife still operate the Tererro store and post office, the last remnants of the old mining town. (Right, LM; below, MH No. 1215.)

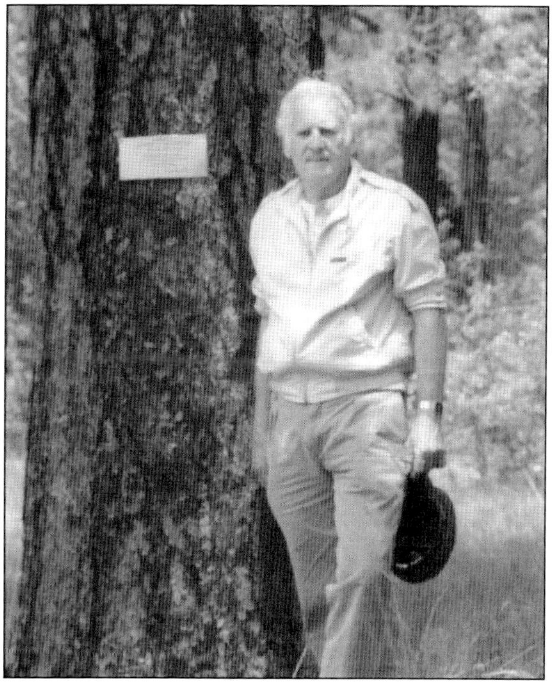

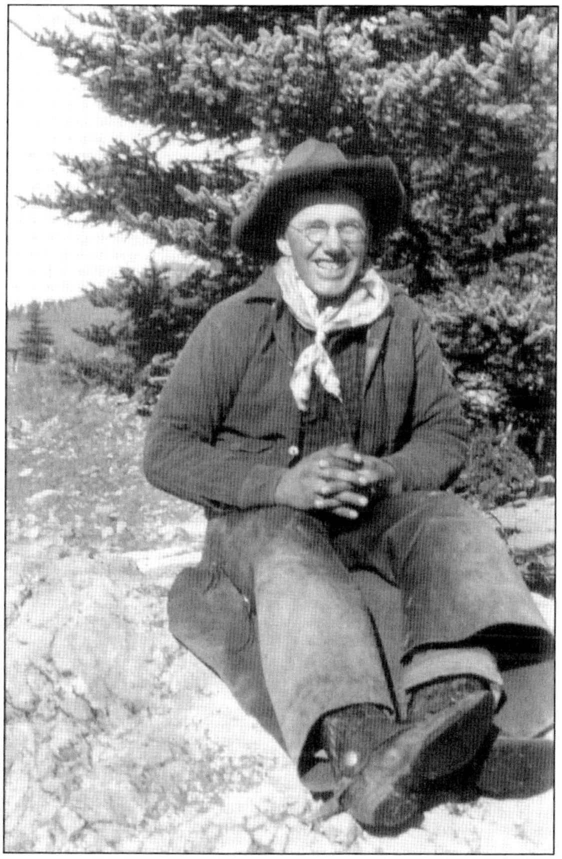

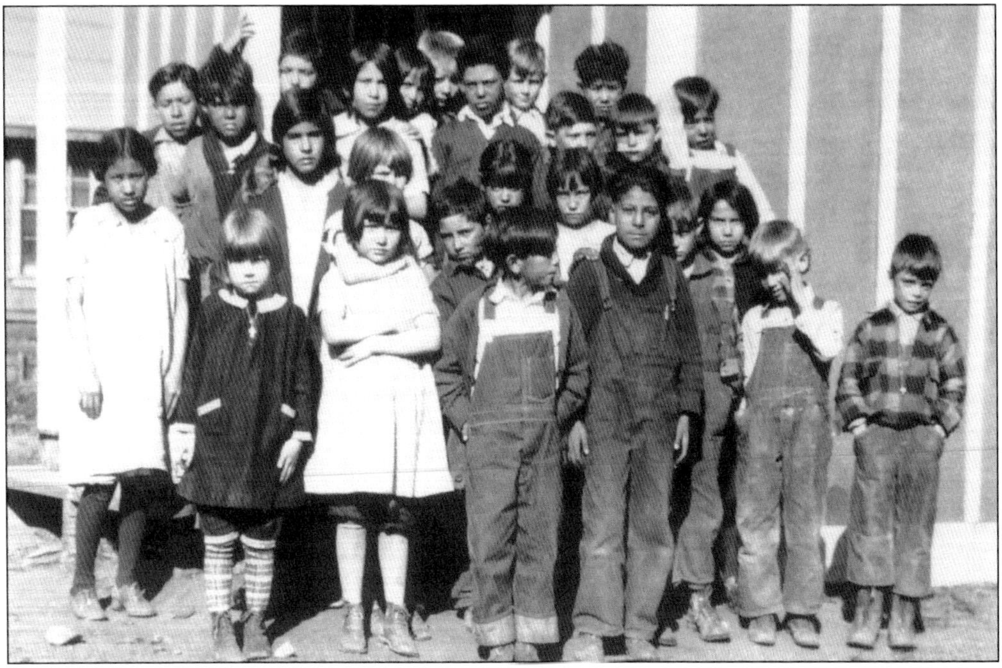

Seen here are the second, third, and fourth grades at the Tererro school in 1927. Leon McDuff and Joe Matson Jr. are on the far right in the first row. On the far left of the first row is Jane MacDonald. Billy and Mrs. MacDonald, Jane's mother, were said to be a brother and his widowed sister. However, when another daughter was born, it came out that they were in actuality husband and wife. The reason for the ruse was never revealed. (LM.)

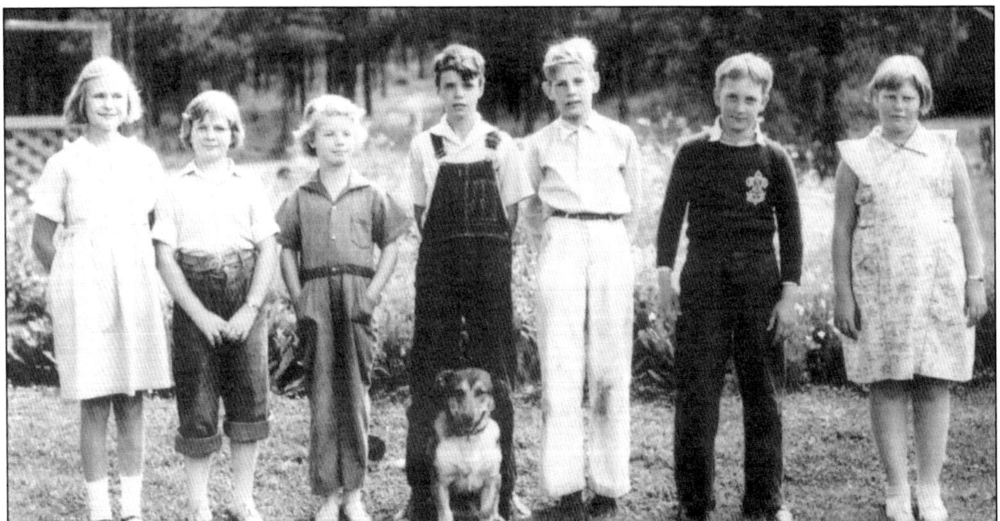

This photograph shows local kids at mine manager Joe Matson's daughter Alice's birthday party. From left to right are Betsy Anderson, the daughter of mine engineer Eugene Anderson; Lorraine Smith, daughter of Tererro physician Dr. Warren George Smith; Alice Matson; Joe Matson Jr.; Leon McDuff; Dick Smith, brother of Lorraine; and McDuff's sister LaVoyse McDuff. Dr. Smith was a 1908 graduate of Cornell University, had studied in Florence, Italy, and had been captured in Mexico by Pancho Villa's troops and forced to provide medical attention to them. (LM.)

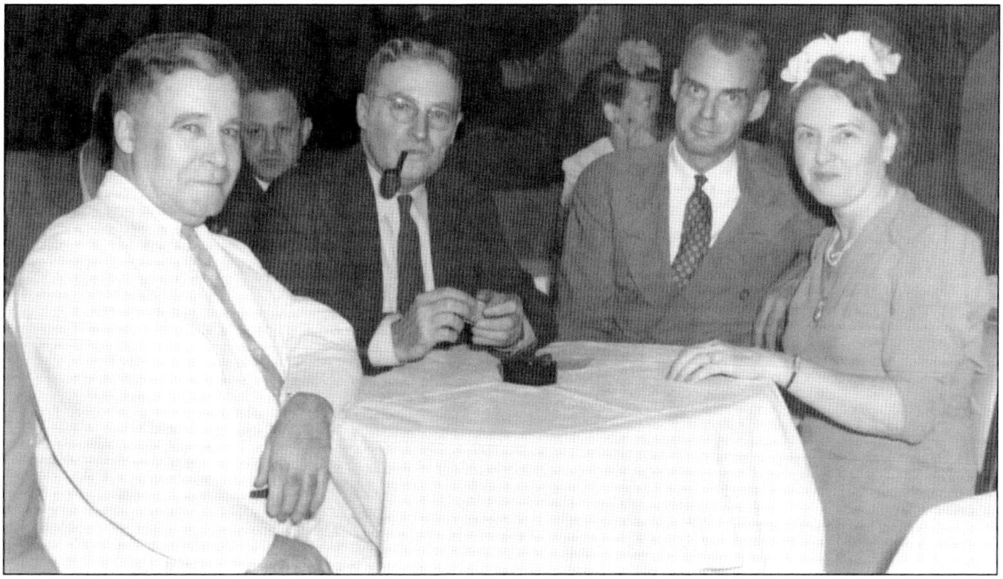

Seen here on a night out in the late 1930s are, from left to right, Herbert D. Bemis (1884–1969), superintendent of the Pecos mill; Joseph T. Matson, Pecos mine manager; and Mr. and Mrs. Charles Scott. Bemis was transferred to Pecos in 1926 from the Climax Molybdenum Mine in Colorado and stayed in Pecos as mill superintendent until the Pecos mine closed. Scott was the chief engineer of the Shafter Mine, a silver, lead, and gold mine in southwestern Texas. (LM.)

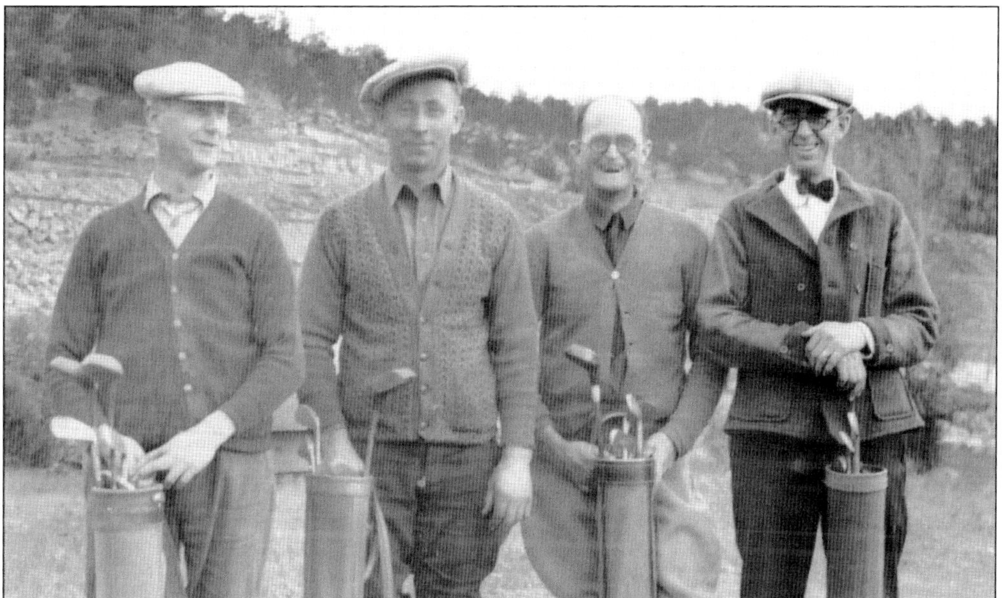

In the 1920s and 1930s, the typical workweek was six days, and some of the miners at Tererro even worked seven days a week. But a few also found time for recreation; there was a baseball diamond and a nine-hole golf course. Seen here on the links in the 1930s are, from left to right, Richard Wheelock Sr., Ole Lee, mine engineer Eugene Anderson, and an unidentified person. (LM.)

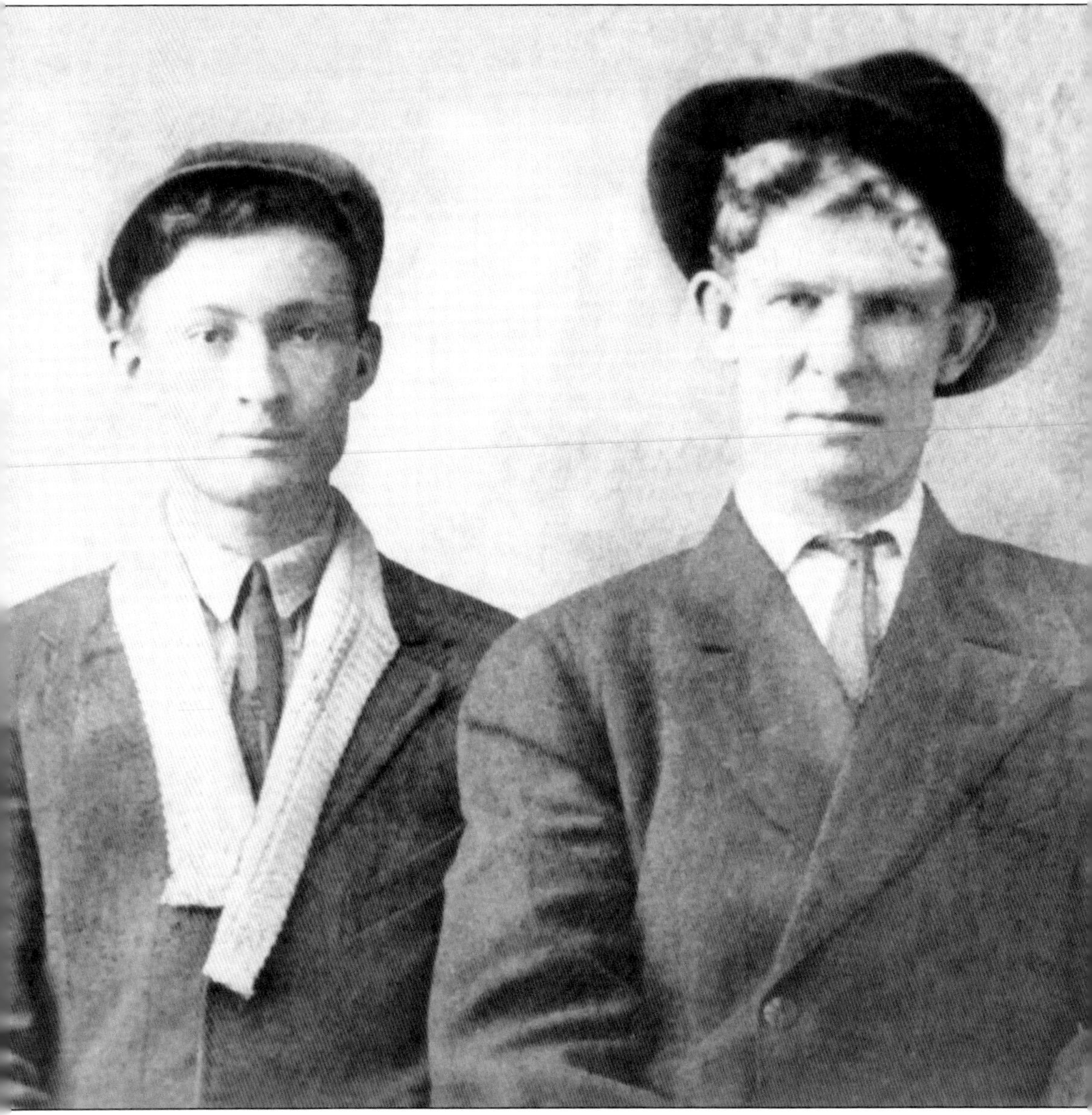

Seen here on the right is Nathan Addis "Jake" McGuire (1884–1954), a mine foreman on the night shift. He is credited with warning of dangerous conditions one night and not letting his men work that shift, thereby preventing them from all being killed by an explosion later that same night. During Prohibition, he also brewed beer in his basement, many bottles of which blew up one evening, much to his surprise—as well as that of a visiting preacher. His son Marvin "Buddy" McGuire (left) was known as the "Tererro Mafia" for running liquor and gambling operations, and perhaps other vices. Another son, Thomas McGuire, was the engineer for the train from Lamy to Santa Fe. (EI.)

Four

VILLAGE AND VALLEY

This chapter looks at the village of Pecos and its immediate surroundings, the geographic center of the area addressed in this book. The population and commercial center of the region has shifted through time from the Pecos Pueblo and Spanish Mission, to the Hispanic/Genízaro villages, in particular San Miguel del Vado (covered in the next chapter), and, ultimately, to the village of Pecos, where it has been from the early 20th century to the present.

Occupation of the Pecos region dwindled following the 18th-century decline at Pecos Pueblo, and the upper reaches were still quite remote well into the 19th century. Dalton Canyon, about nine miles up the Pecos Canyon from the village of Pecos, is said to be named for the Dalton family and to have served as a hideout for the famous gang of outlaws, although this is probably an apocryphal story.

The initial settlement of the village of Pecos is poorly known, but it most likely occurred by the 1820s. Within 10 years, it had become a thriving community centered around large haciendas and a central plaza.

Early structures were made with flat, dirt roofs, but by the 1880s, pitched metal corrugated roofs became common, and they were often placed directly over the original flat roofs. There would have been some prestige in having a pitched roof, because it precluded problems of snow removal and the inevitable rain of dust coming down from a flat, dirt roof. Pitched roofs were built of imported terneplate (sheet steel coated with an alloy of 80 percent lead and 20 percent tin).

The 1860 federal census reports that there were four gristmills and many farmers. Cattle and sheep raising, along with various field crops grown primarily for local consumption, were mainstays of the local economy until well into the 20th century. The post office was established in 1883.

Tourism promoted outdoor recreation, hence the creation of the Lisboa Springs Fish Hatchery, the oldest in the state. Awareness of the scenic beauty of the area led to guest ranches and summer homes, such as Fir Tree House, the only Frank Lloyd Wright house in New Mexico, a private residence not visible or open to public.

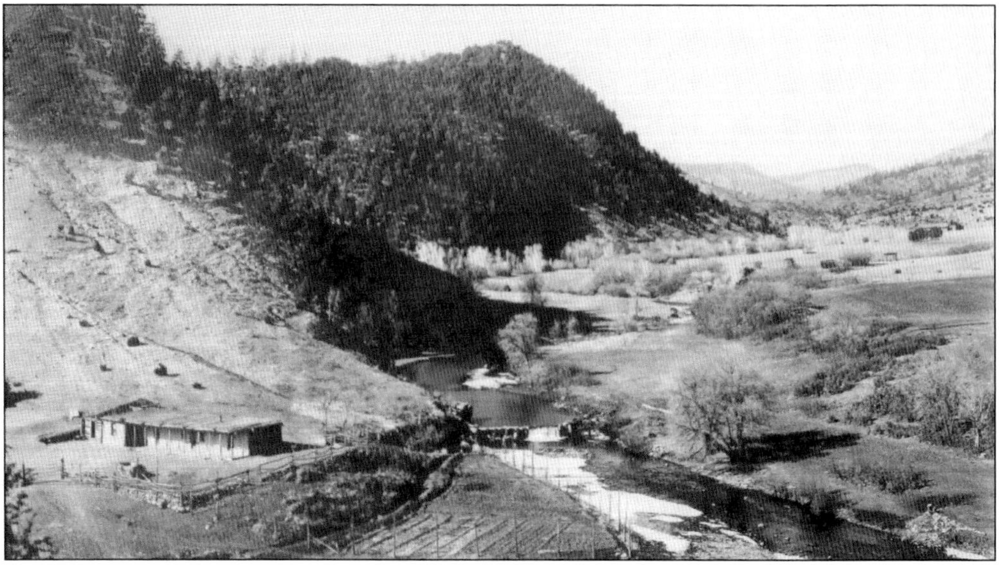

The upper Pecos Valley, a few miles above the village of Pecos, is seen here in the late 19th century. At the lower left near the Pecos River is a Hispanic ranch with a Pueblo-style flat roof. Also in the foreground is an irrigated field, primarily for local use. Grazing land and open fields cover much of the rest of the valley. (NT.)

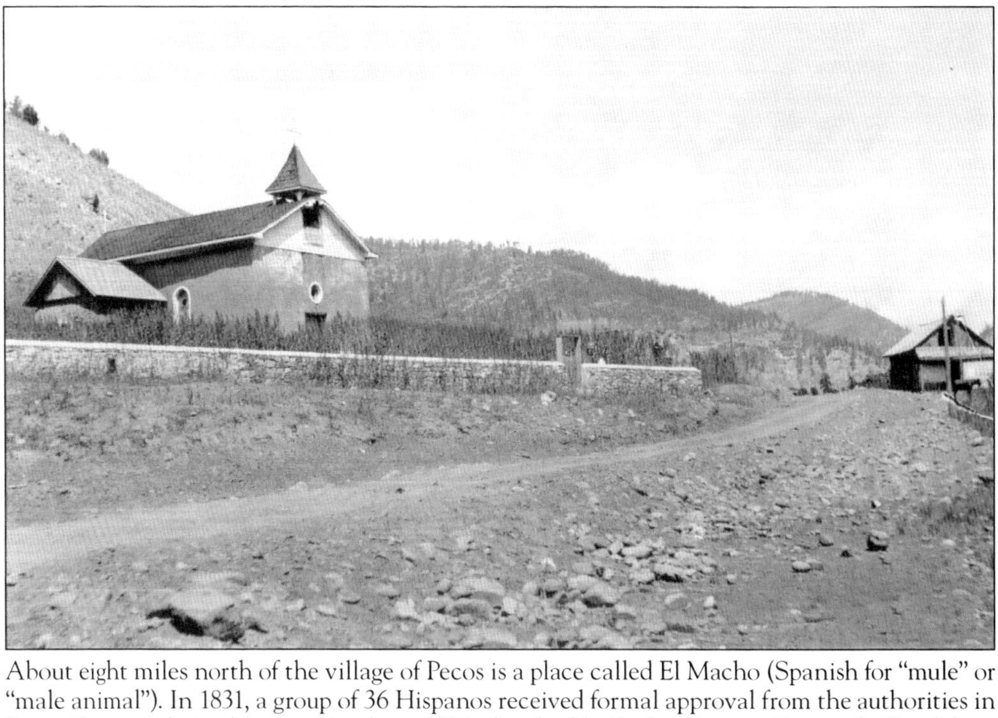

About eight miles north of the village of Pecos is a place called El Macho (Spanish for "mule" or "male animal"). In 1831, a group of 36 Hispanos received formal approval from the authorities in Santa Fe to settle in this area. By about 1834, they had built the Nuestra Señora de Guadalupe Church, pictured here, although they did not obtain official approval from the Archdiocese of Durango, Mexico, for the building of a church until three years later, in 1837. (MH No. 1055.)

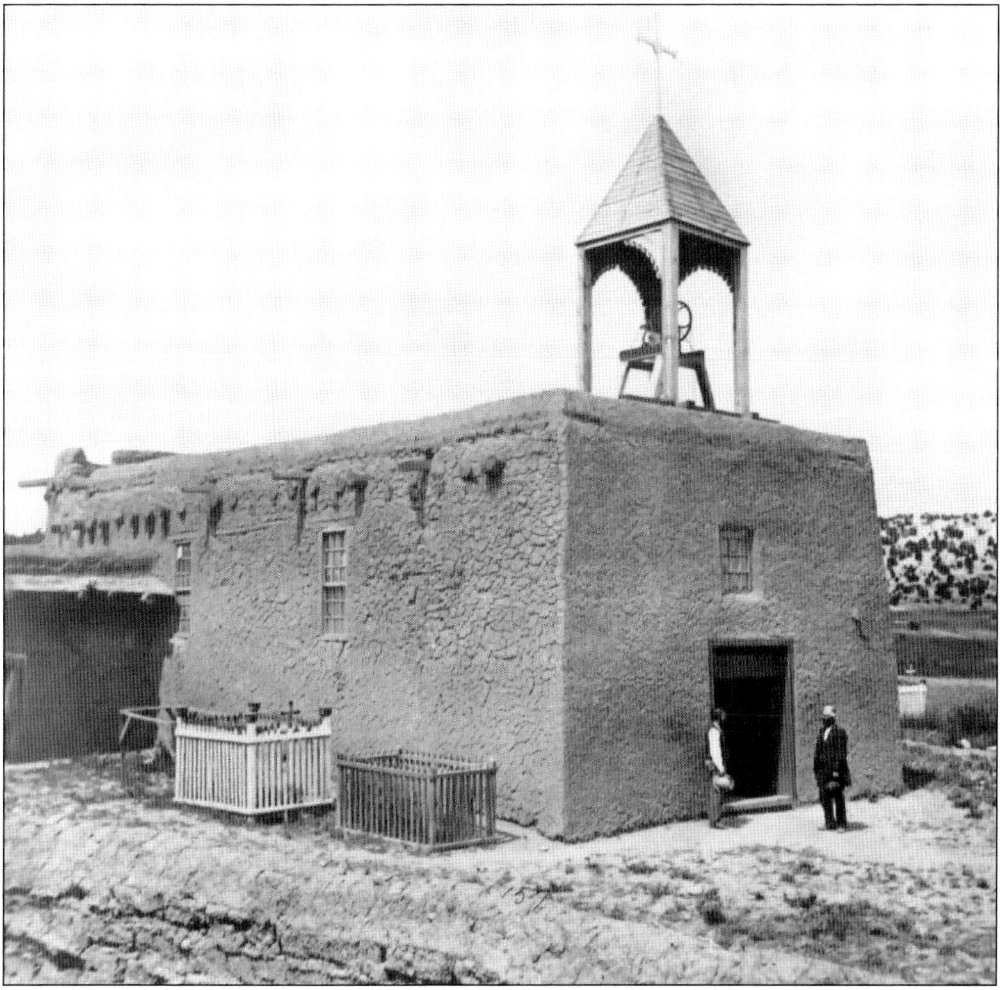

The photographs on this page are of the original church in the village of Pecos, Nuestra Señora de los Ángeles y San Antonio, in 1880. This church was on the same site as the later 1904 St. Anthony's Church (see page 75). As with the El Macho church, it was constructed in 1834, with formal approval granted in 1837. In 1900, it burned down. The photograph of the interior at right shows corbels, perhaps salvaged from the old Pecos Mission. This photograph also shows the original 18th-century painting of Our Lady of the Angels over the altar, entrusted to the Village of Pecos when Pecos Pueblo was abandoned in 1838. It survived the 1900 fire and proved to be the work of famous Mexico City religious painter Juan Correa. It now hangs 60 feet above the altar in St. Anthony's. (Above, NMSRCA; right, PNHP No. 1880.)

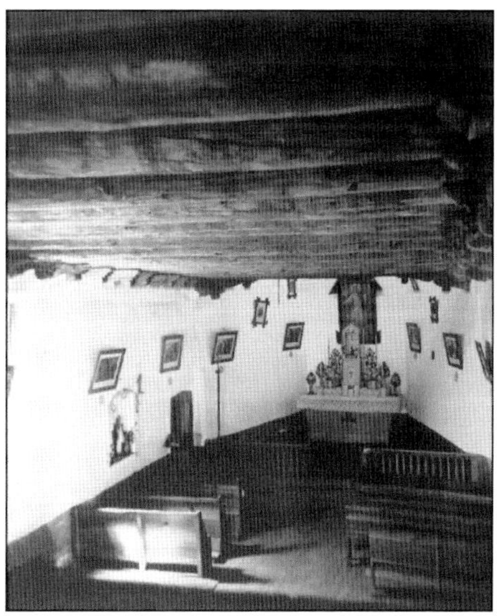

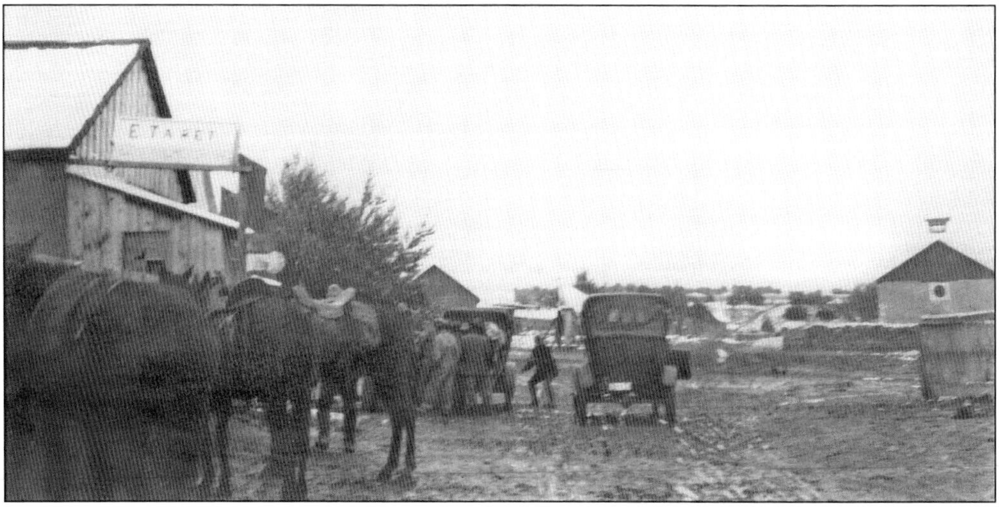

The photographs on this page show Thad Slaughter's (see page 43) return from a deer hunt up the Pecos Valley some time in the mid-1920s. A family story tells of the hunters having been surprised by an early snow storm, and after digging their cars out of the snow, barely making it back to Pecos Village. Having reached town, a group of locals inspects the hunter's success in front of the E. Tabet store, the N. Candelaria Cash Store, and a saloon; nothing more is known of these businesses. (Both, SS.)

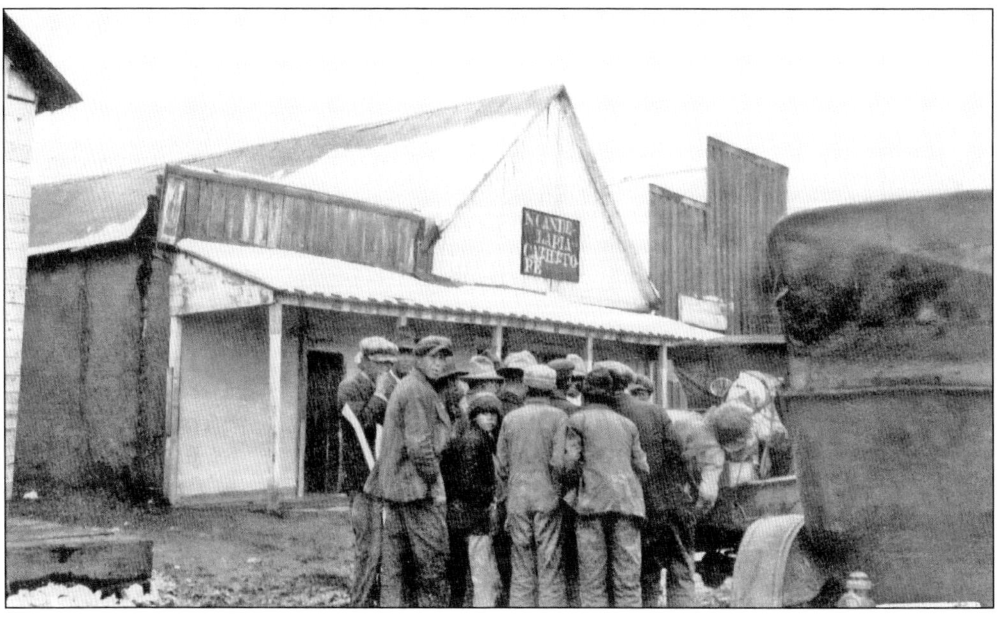

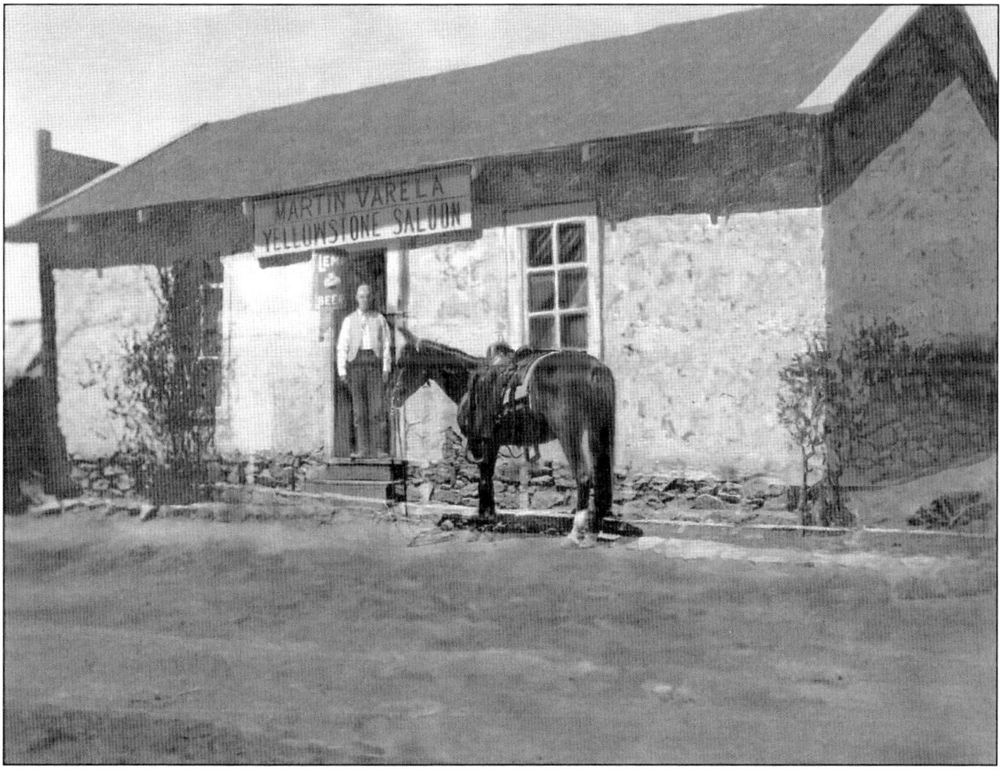

This drawing is based on a 1911 photograph of Martin Varela (1867–1929) at his Yellowstone Saloon in the village of Pecos. When the Varelas first came to Pecos is not known, although the family's New Mexico roots go back to 1598. Martin and his wife, Juanita, had six daughters, Miguela, Delfinia, Cleofes, Ramocita, Petronila, and Antonia, as well as one son, Lamberto. Lemp Beer, advertised on a giant beer can above the door, was made from 1864 to 1919 in St. Louis and was the first beer distributed by refrigerator car, in about 1890, from coast to coast. (Drawing by Joe Mildenberger; courtesy of NMSRCA.)

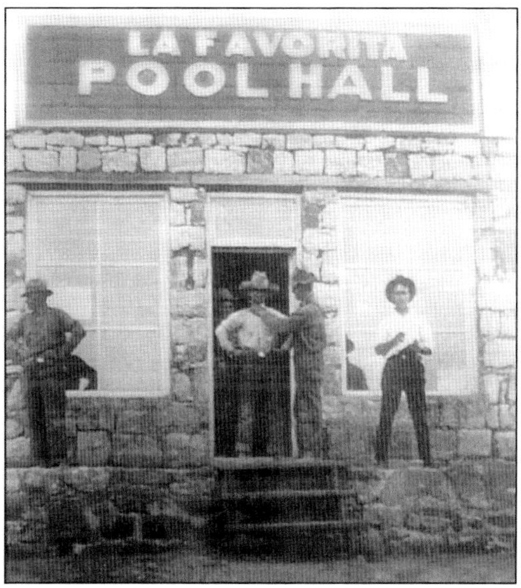

This photograph is of Teodulo Herrera's pool hall. Herrera came to Pecos in 1925 from Las Vegas, New Mexico, because of the Tererro Mine—not to work in the mine, but rather to sell to the miners. He soon established a number of retail businesses in the village of Pecos. The La Favorita Pool Hall is now the Lone Star Bar. (J&TH.)

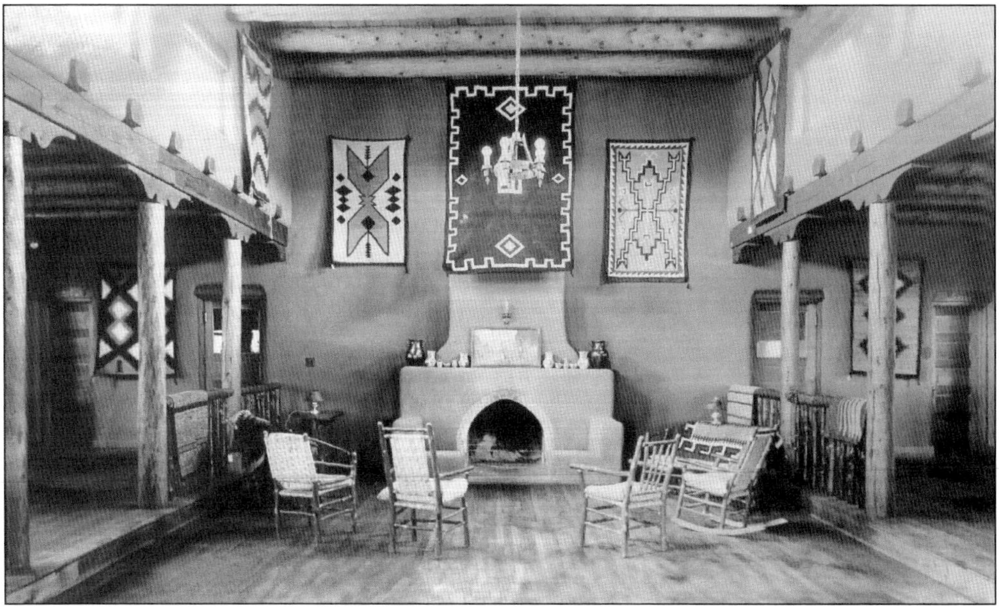

The Casanova Club, still in operation, was built about 1910 as the Western Mercantile. In the 1920s, it became Harrison's Casanova Club, a bar and restaurant on pre-1937 Route 66. Harrison grew apples and, during Prohibition, made cider. As a boy, Ed Irvin remembers stopping at the Casanova Club to enjoy a glass of cool cider; his father would have a glass from a different cask and was much more talkative thereafter. (NT.)

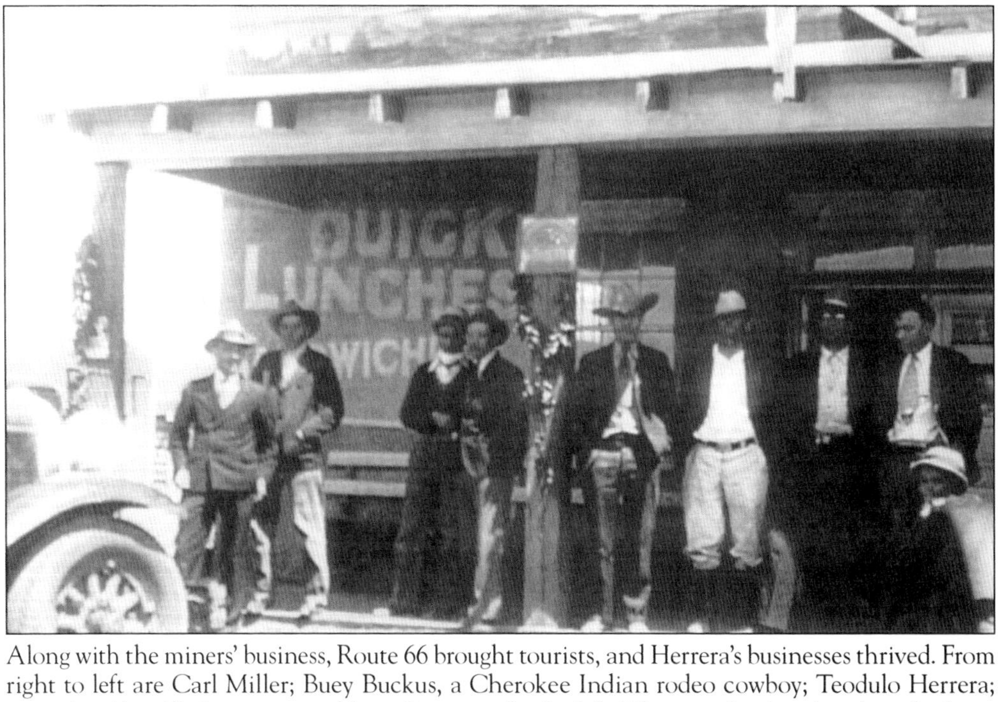

Along with the miners' business, Route 66 brought tourists, and Herrera's businesses thrived. From right to left are Carl Miller; Buey Buckus, a Cherokee Indian rodeo cowboy; Teodulo Herrera; several unidentified persons; and Juan Pena, on the far left. The mural painted on boards above the store entrance was probably done by Sostenes Delgado, who painted a number of murals on buildings in Pecos. (J&TH.)

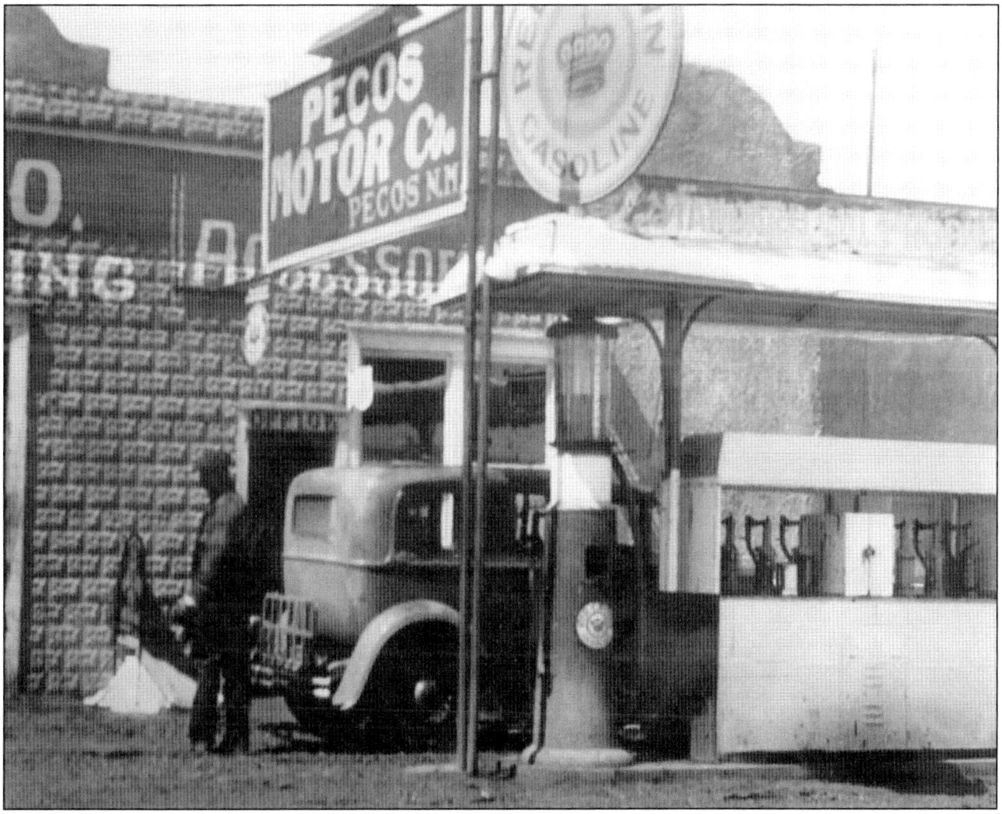

During the 1930s, "Pat" Patterson ran the Pecos Motor Company. It was one of a very few full-service automobile stops in the 120-mile section of Route 66 between Santa Rosa, New Mexico, and Santa Fe. This photograph shows a hand-crank gas pump about half full, along with a bank of six oil pumps, probably for different weights of lubricants. (J&TH.)

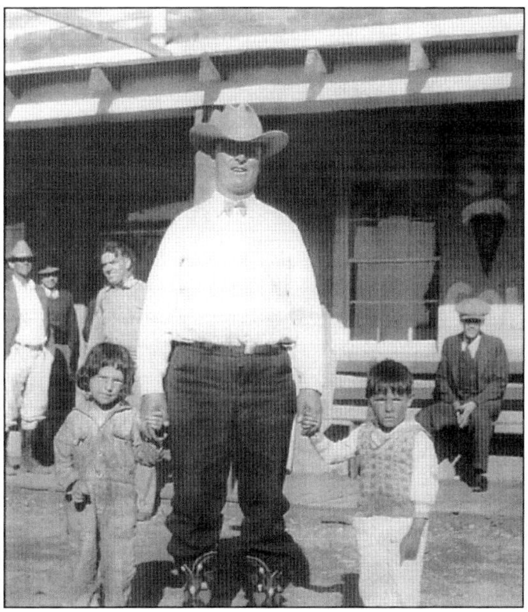

In this photograph, also from the mid-1930s, Teodulo Herrera stands in front of his store and restaurant holding the hands of two of his children. The little girl is Margie, and the boy is Teodulo "Tito" Herrera Jr. The man behind Margie is Carl Miller, and the man with the light hat and his pants tucked into his boots is Buey Buckus. (J&TH.)

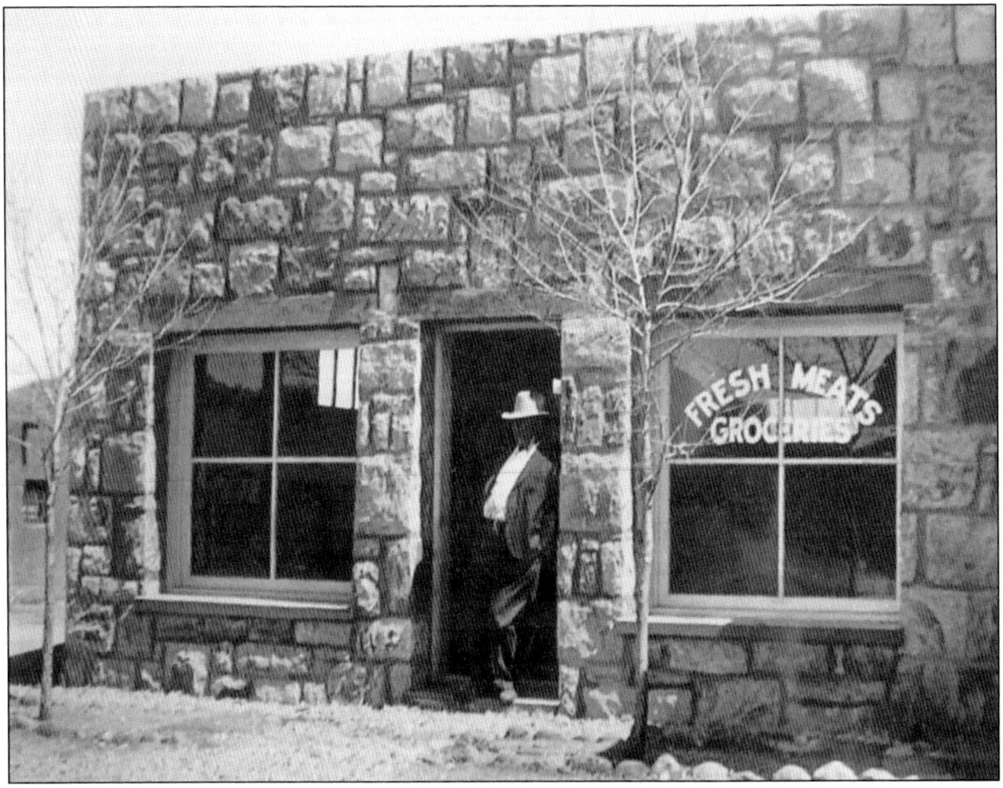

The little Herrera grocery store was a longtime business of Herrera's. He is seen above standing in the front door of his establishment; below, he is inside the store having a smoke. The two young men are Aldofo Perera (left) and "Freckles," as his son Tito Jr. was known. There are many familiar brands, many of them with the same logos they have today, if one looks carefully. Even Clabber Girl Baking Powder, gluten-free and certified Kosher, is unchanged today. Pecos can be very cold in the winter, hence the woodstove. (Both, J&TH.)

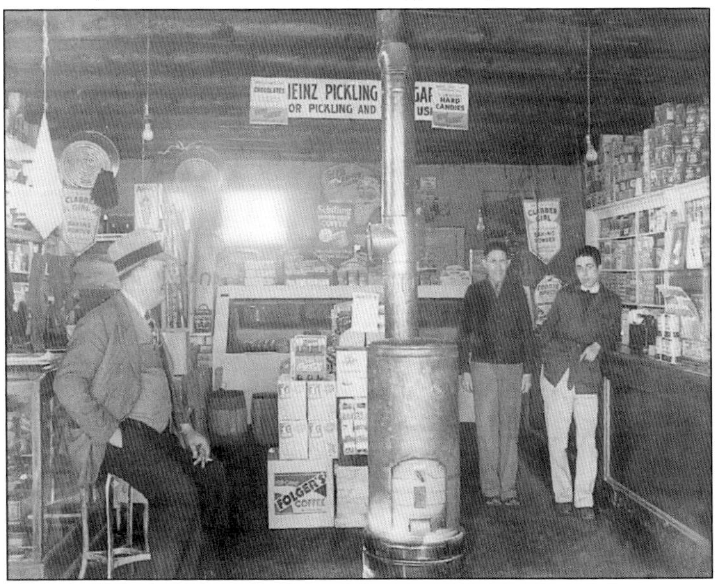

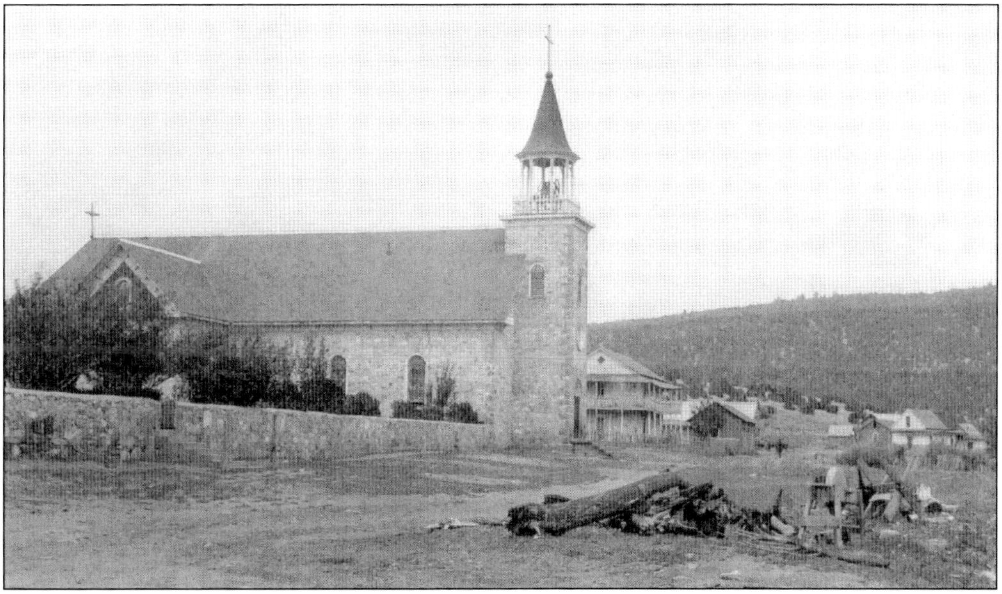

The current St. Anthony's Church in the village of Pecos (La Iglesia de San Antonio del Rio Pecos/San Antonio de Padua) was constructed in 1904–1906, following the fire that destroyed the original village church in 1900 (see page 69). This was during the time of New Mexico's famous French bishop Jean-Baptiste Lamy, and thus it was built of stone in the style of a French Gothic provincial church. In August, during the Feast of St. Porciúncula, there is a procession from St. Anthony's to the ruins of Nuestra Señora de los Ángeles Church. The photograph below is a bucolic scene of the river crossing near the village of Pecos in about 1910. (Above, NMSRCA; below, PNHP No. 1224-2.)

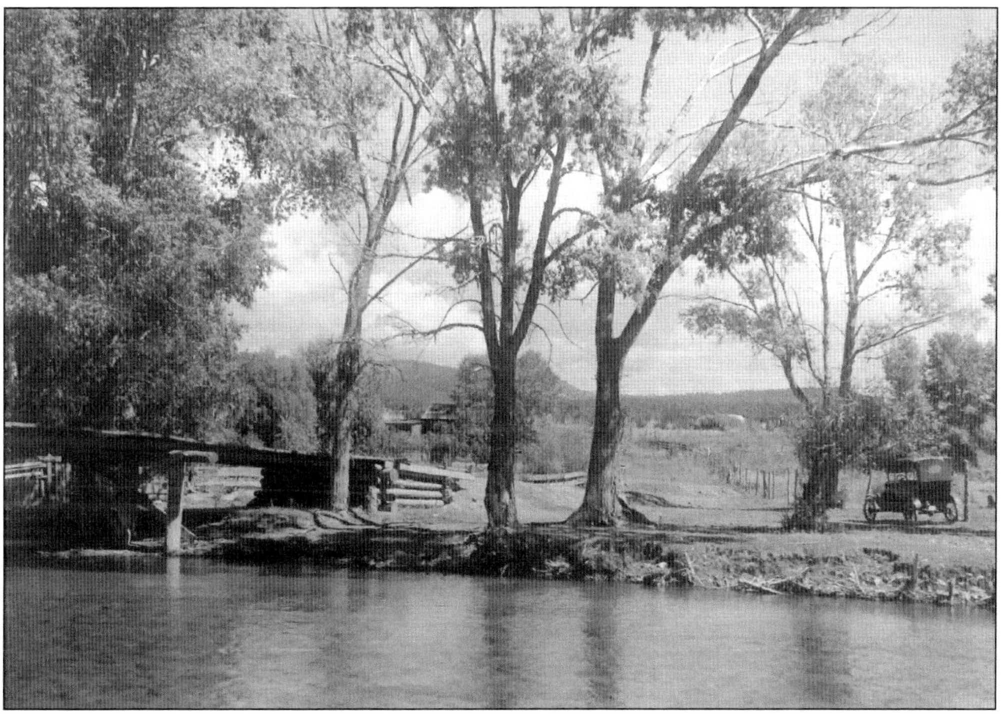

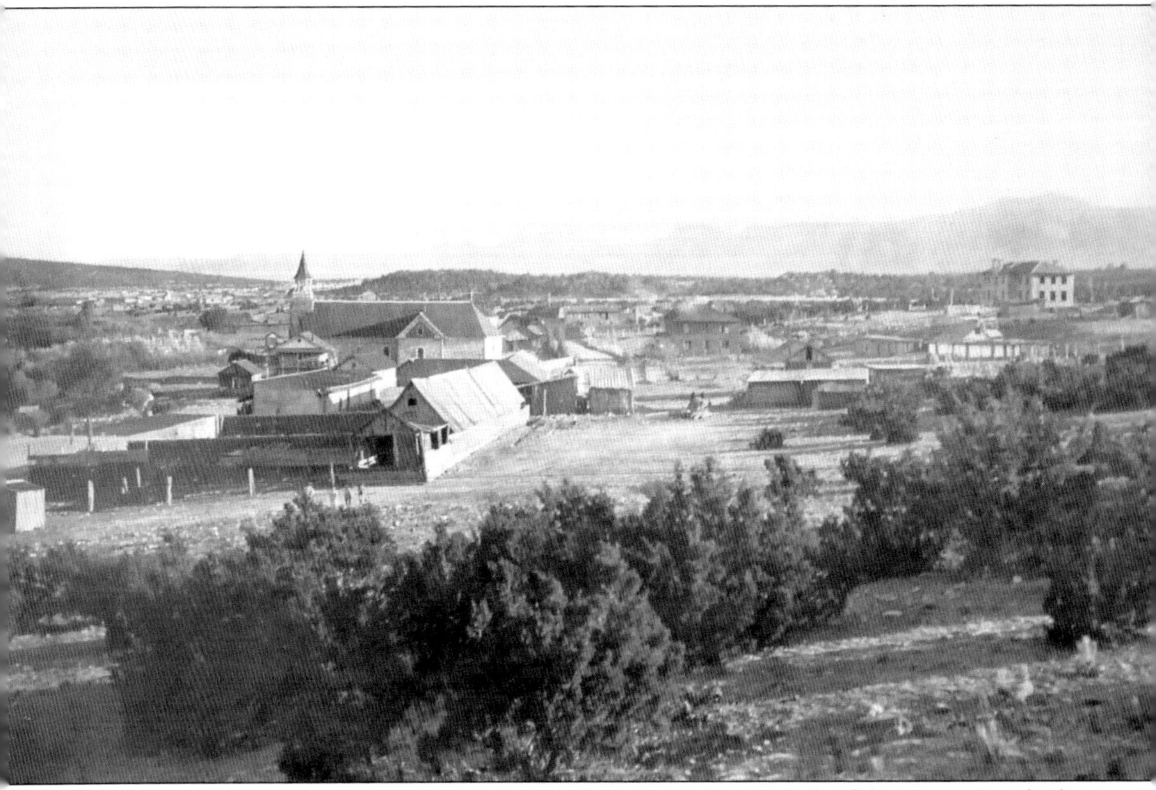

This 1931 view of the village of Pecos was taken from a hill just north of the community looking south. At the time, the population was just over 1,000 people; today, it is about 1,500. St. Anthony's Church dominates the photograph. The view would have been little changed in decades past, except for the larger buildings and high, pitched roofs. In the background is Glorieta Mesa. (PNHP No. 1215.)

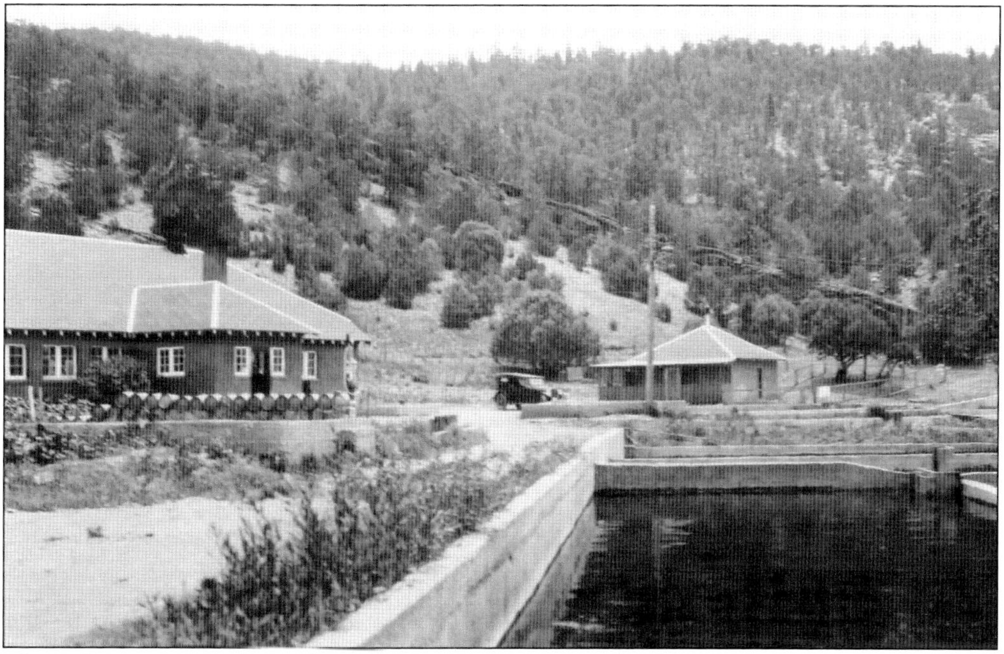

The Lisboa Springs Fish Hatchery is located two miles north of the village of Pecos. Established in 1921, it is the oldest hatchery in the state, and it is seen above shortly after it was placed into operation. Lisboa exclusively breeds trout, placing hundreds of thousands of fish each year primarily into the Pecos watershed. The original buildings and ponds are still being used and are open to the public. The photograph below shows May Walter, a teacher at the Tererro school from 1934 to 1939, fly-fishing for trout on the Pecos River near Tererro in the 1930s. (Above, NT; below, LM.)

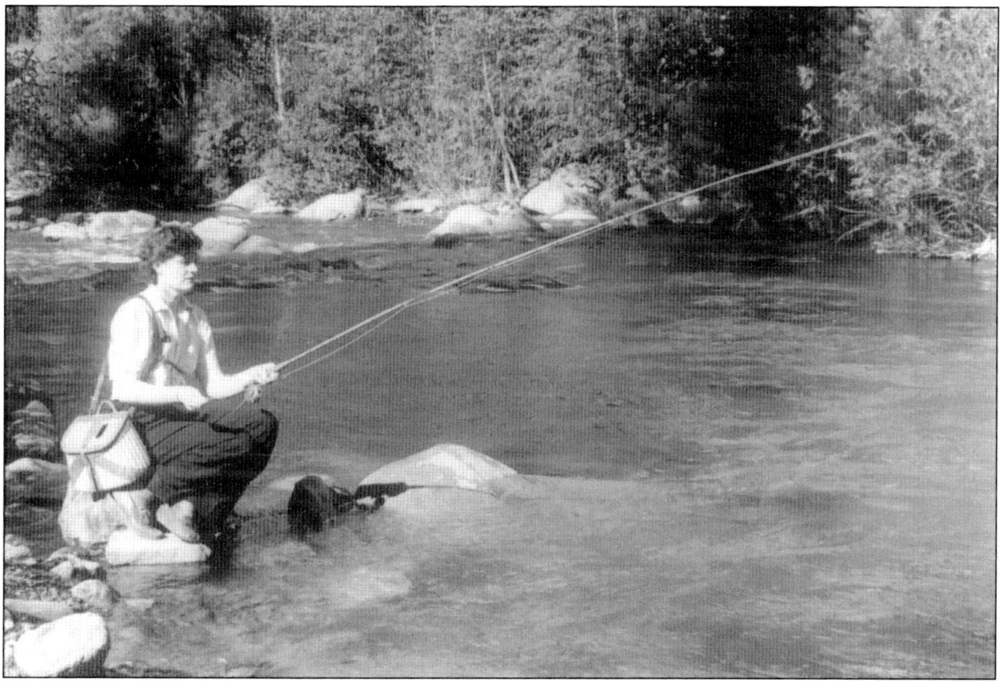

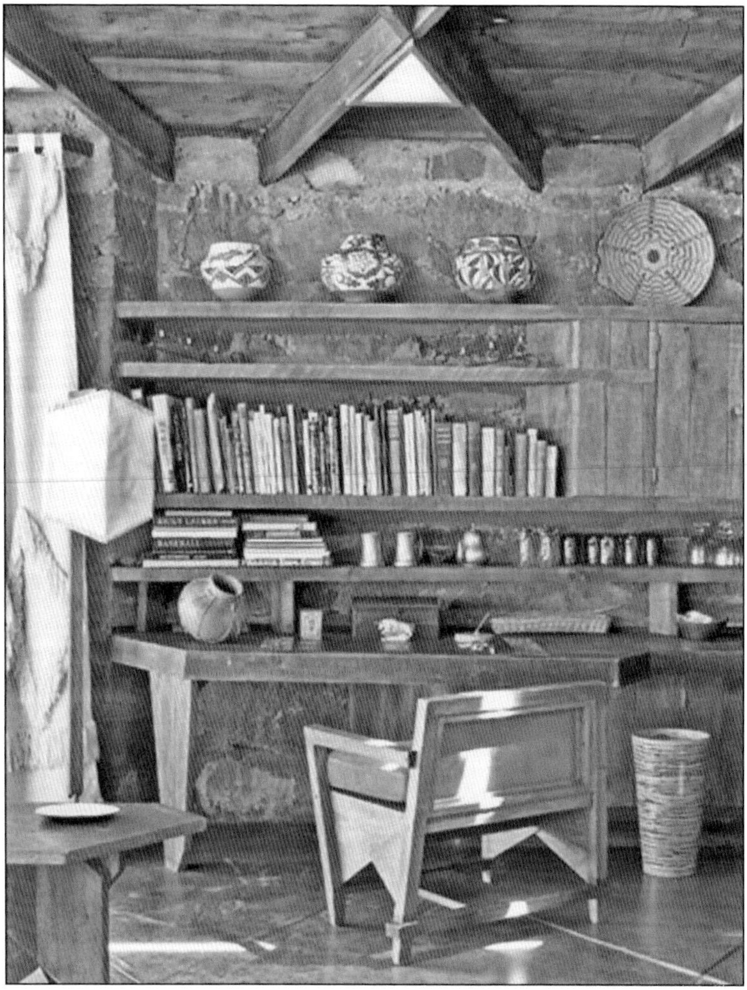

A few miles north of the village of Pecos is the inappropriately named Fir Tree House (there are no fir trees in Pecos; only pines). This is the only complete Frank Lloyd Wright house in New Mexico. It was built in 1948 on the banks of the Pecos River and has been subsequently added onto in a manner sympathetic to the original house. The angular wooden house has a massive stone fireplace, as well as built-in furniture. The house is a private residence owned by descendants of the first owner and is not open to the public or visible from the adjacent road. (Both, CSWR.)

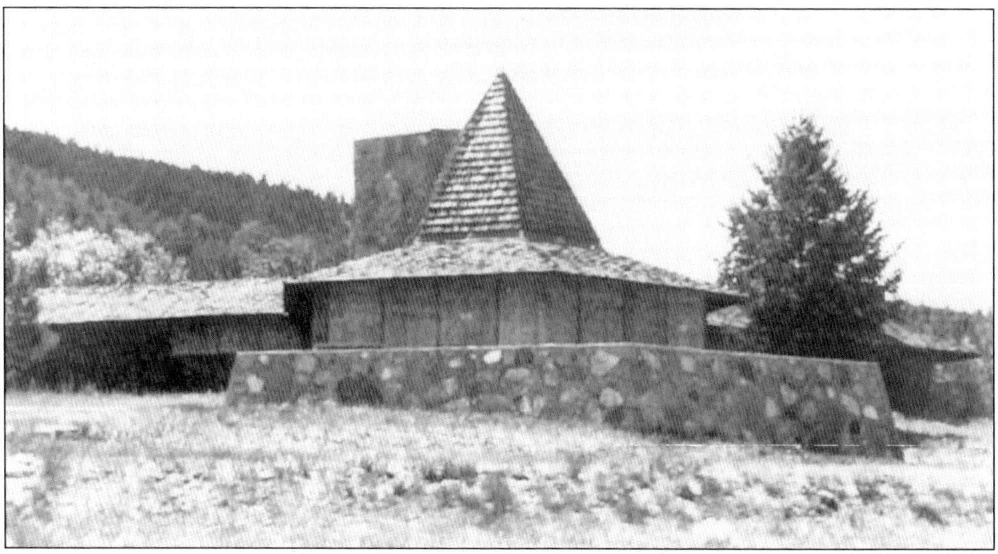

Five

Genízaros and Raiders

Less than 15 miles southeast of Pecos Pueblo, adjacent to the Pecos River, is a series of villages originally established as defensive settlements in an exposed frontier area subject to raids by Comanche and Kiowa Indians from the plains to the east, as well as Apaches and Navajos from the north and west. They were occupied by Hispanic colonists, some Pecos Pueblo Indians, a few converted Comanche Indians, and, primarily, Genízaros.

Genízaros were and are principally of Native American heritage, from both Mexican and New Mexican tribes. Initially, they were slaves, servants, and indentured workers, but, because of their close association with the Spanish, they lost their tribal affiliations. They comprised a substantial component of the region's entire population by the early 1800s. *Genízaro* is a Spanish word derived from the English word "janissary," which is an adaptation of the Ottoman Turkish word *yeniçeri*, for the foreign boy slaves that were trained as the sultan's elite guard.

In 1794, colonization was authorized by the Spanish government in Santa Fe for San Miguel del Vado ("St. Michael at the Ford," because of its proximity to a crossing of the Pecos River; later a Santa Fe Trail crossing). Today, it is forgotten, but in the 19th century, it was one of the most important towns in northern New Mexico. Satellite communities at San Jose, Villanueva, and El Cerrito, among others, were soon established nearby, and settlement slowly extended to agriculturally suitable locales all along the Pecos River.

The villages started as communities surrounded on all sides by houses with windowless outer walls. Access was restricted through heavy gates. These villages all exhibit the four distinct types of architectural development in New Mexico: flat-roofed, Pueblo-style dwellings with exposed roof beams (vigas); Spanish Colonial haciendas, churches, and commercial buildings; what is known as the "territorial style," with simple Greek pediments above doors and windows, along with brick-capped cornices; and 20th-century features, especially high, pitched metal roofs.

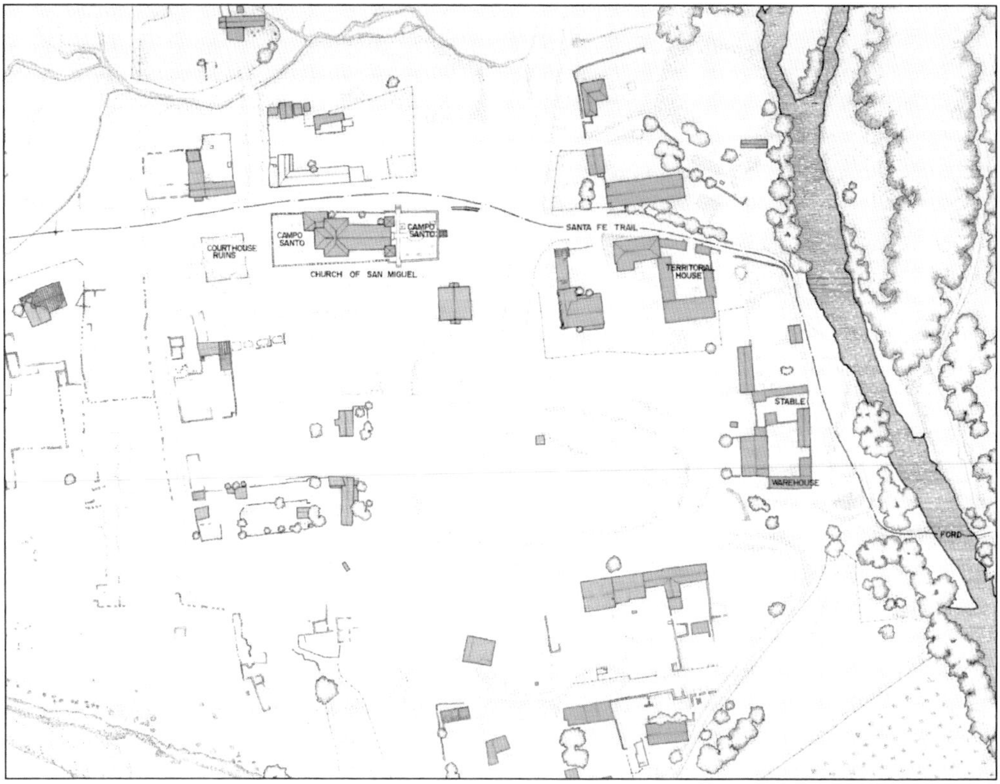

San Miguel del Vado ("St. Michael at the Ford") was officially established in 1794 by Gov. Fernando Chacon, who appointed Lorenzo Marquez to lead 51 settlers, 13 of who were Genízaros, to a ford on the Pecos River where there was an earlier Genízaro settlement. San Miguel was the port-of-entry for travelers and goods coming into Mexico from the United States. In the mid-19th century, it was the sixth-largest town in New Mexico, and it was the county seat of San Miguel County until 1864. By 1821, raiding had become so bad that a detachment of 21 soldiers was stationed here. Seen above is the plan of the village in 1933, and the photograph below shows the interior courtyard of a residence. (Above, HABS; below, NMSRCA.)

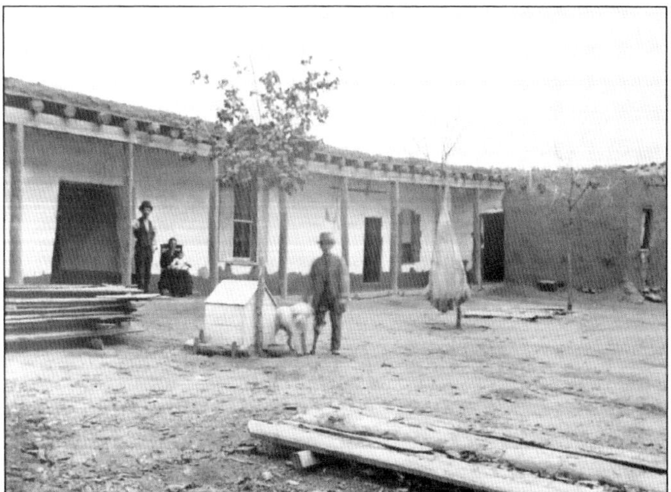

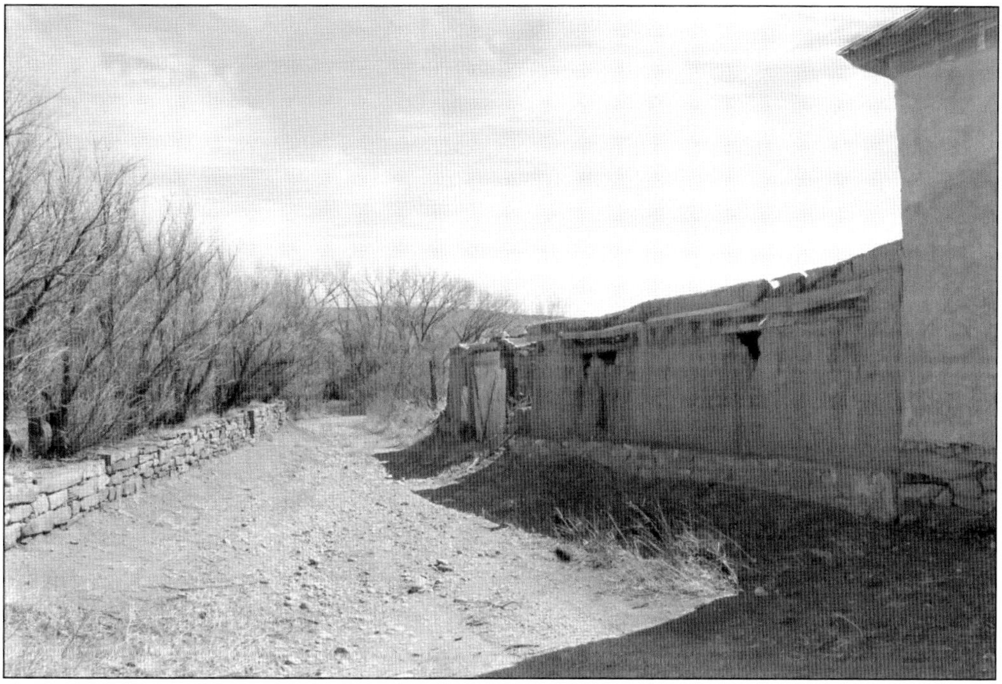

The Territorial House is a complex of buildings around a central courtyard with wagon access directly to the Santa Fe Trail, seen above in the 1970s. It was a saloon and dance hall and, later, a general store. There were servants' quarters, animal stalls, hay storage, and a blacksmith shop. In the 1840s, a customs duty of $500 per wagon had to be paid upon entering New Mexico, so wagons were often "double-loaded" outside of town to minimize the duty. (Above, AC; below, HABS.)

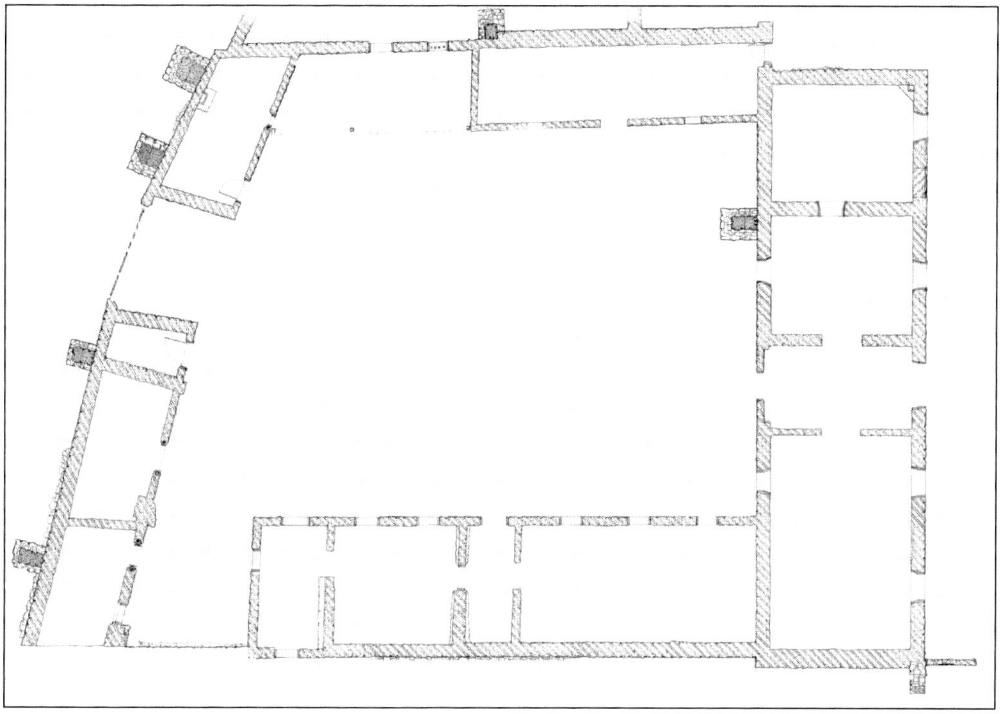

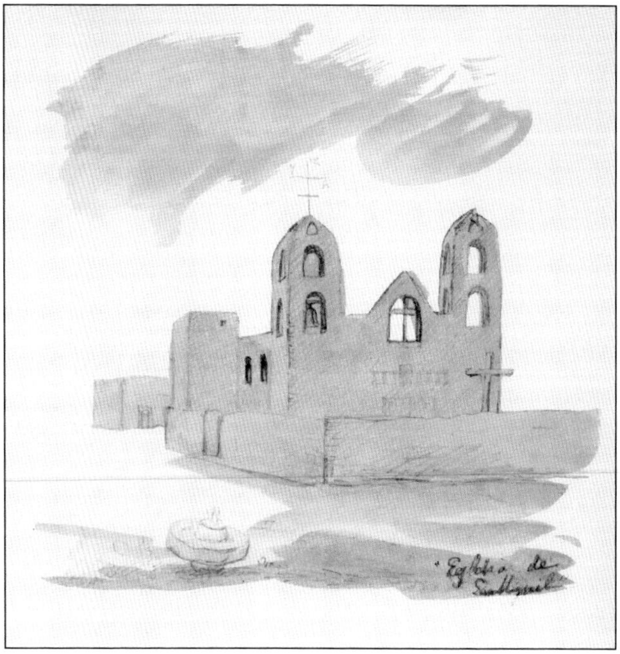

The images on this page and the facing page show the evolution of the San Miguel Church. Genízaros of the new settlement petitioned the bishop of Durango, Mexico, for a chapel in 1804, which was under construction in 1805. However, some wood from the church dates to the 1790s, so there may have been an earlier church. Other beam dates indicate a major remodel in about 1816. Church offices relocated from Pecos to San Miguel in 1829. The illustration at left shows the church as sketched on September 25, 1846, by Lt. James William Abert, a topographical engineer with General Kearny's army during the Mexican border campaign (see page 13). (AC.)

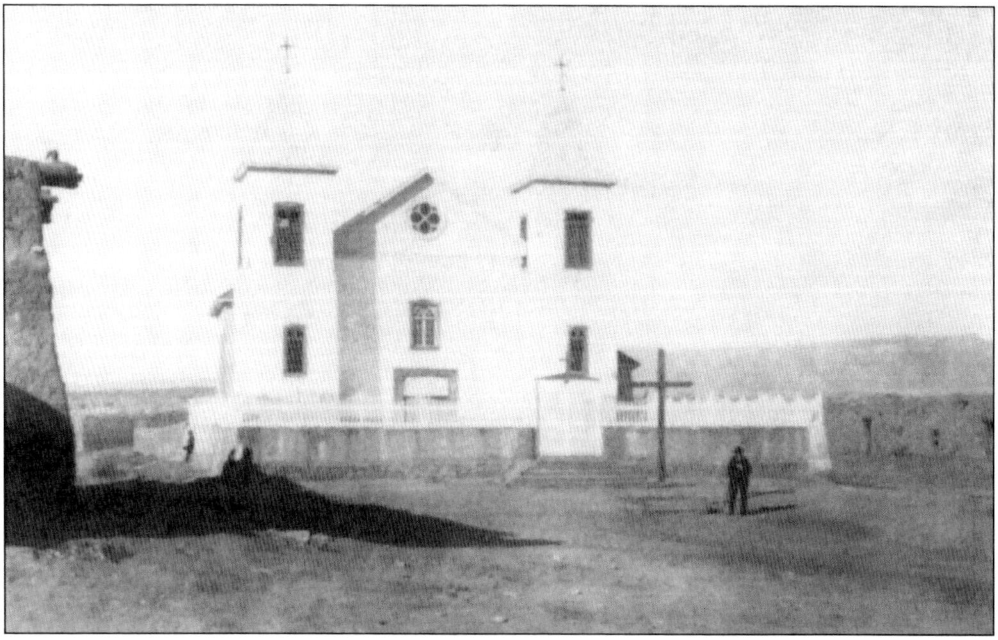

This photograph shows the San Miguel Church in 1882. The bell towers were rebuilt in 1866. (NT.)

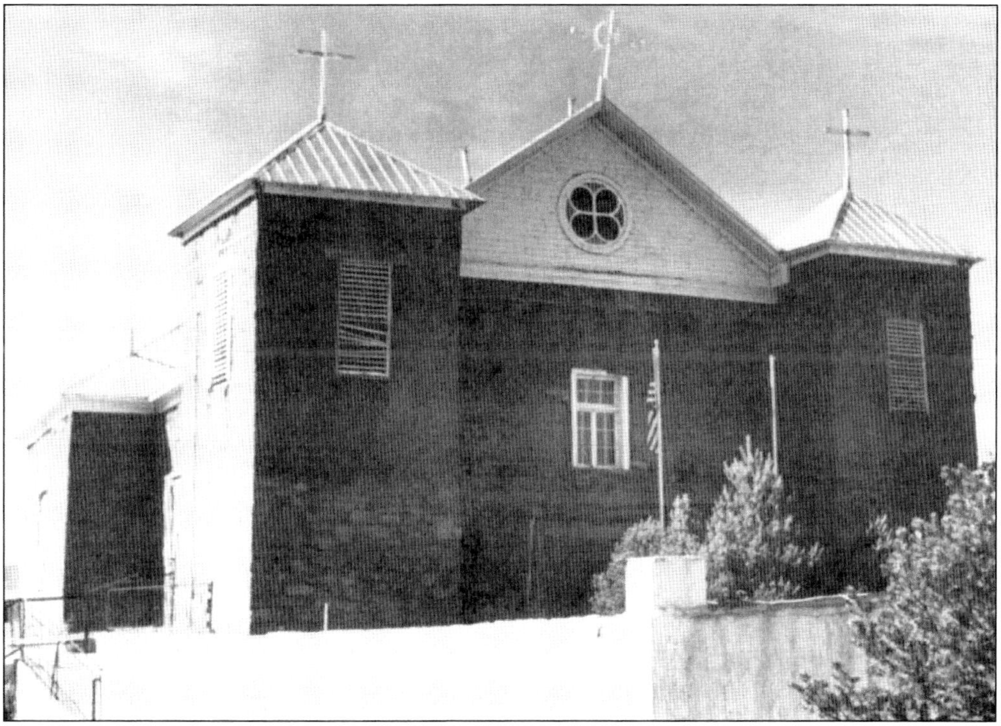

The photograph above shows the San Miguel Church in the early 1970s. The windows have been changed and the tops of the towers lowered from their appearance in the 1880s. There is no exterior plaster at this time, and the stone walls of this fortress-like church are clearly exposed. The photograph below shows the interior of the church in the 1960s. The original roof vigas are under the pitched roof but are now hidden by insulation and planking. A large statue of unknown age of St. Michael with wings and sword is visible by the side of the main altar. (Both, PNHP.)

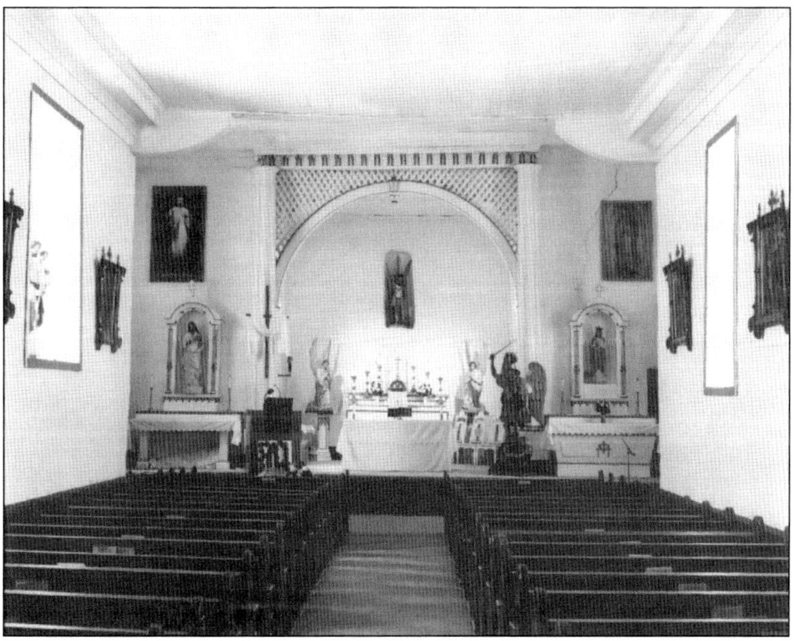

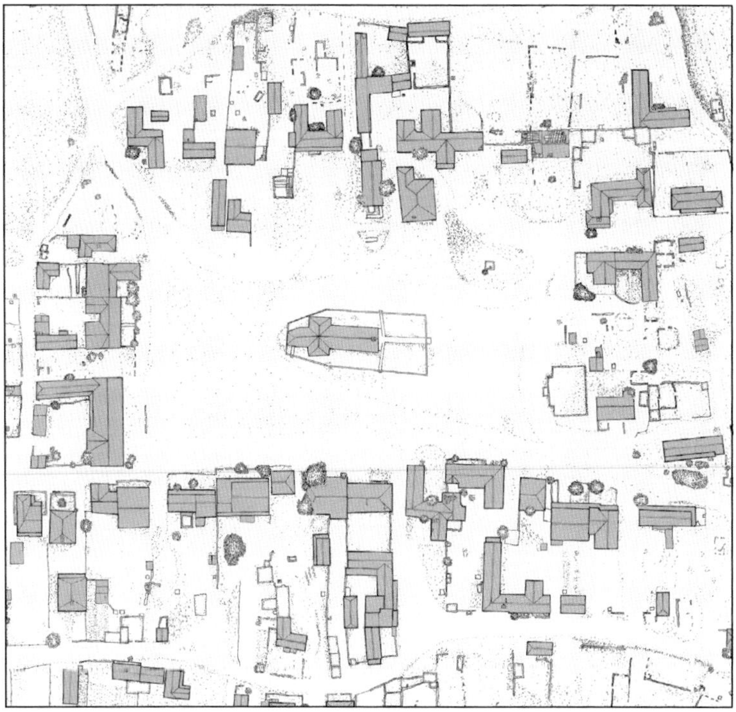

Both images on this page are of the village of San Jose del Vado, located where Interstate 25 crosses the Pecos River today, about two miles north of San Miguel. In 1822, San Jose became a stop on the Santa Fe Trail. The 1933 plan at left clearly shows the fortified nature of the village, with connected houses enclosing the plaza and the 1826 church in the middle. It is one of the best-preserved such village layouts remaining in New Mexico. (HABS.)

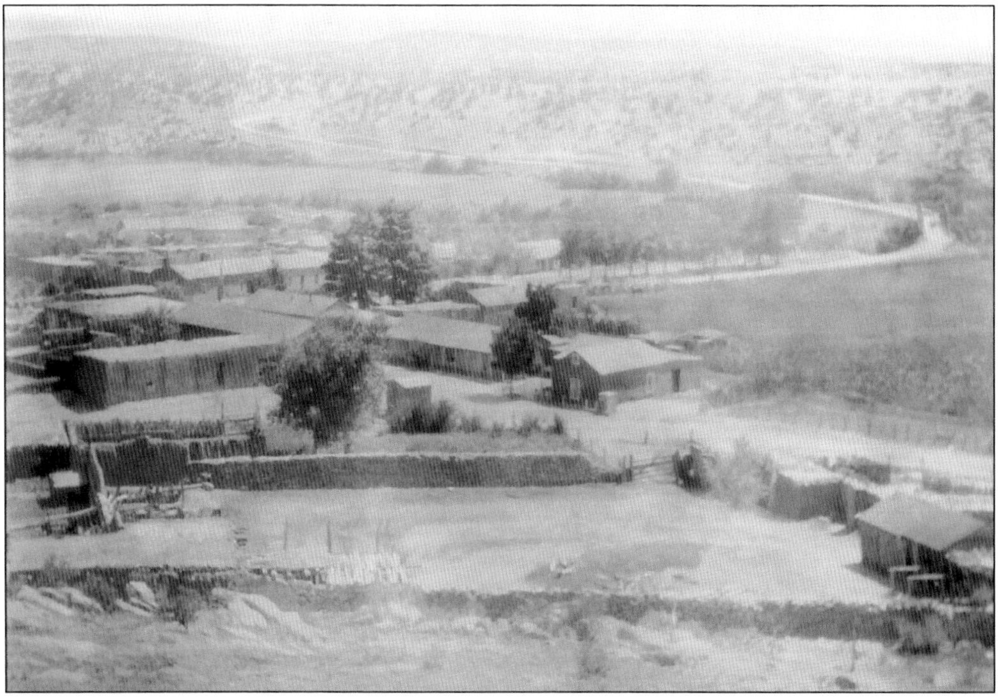

As with San Miguel, San Jose was officially established on the San Miguel del Vado/Bado grant in 1794 at the site of a Genízaro settlement. Daily passenger stagecoach service between Independence, Missouri, and Santa Fe forded the river here from 1846 to 1862. (NT.)

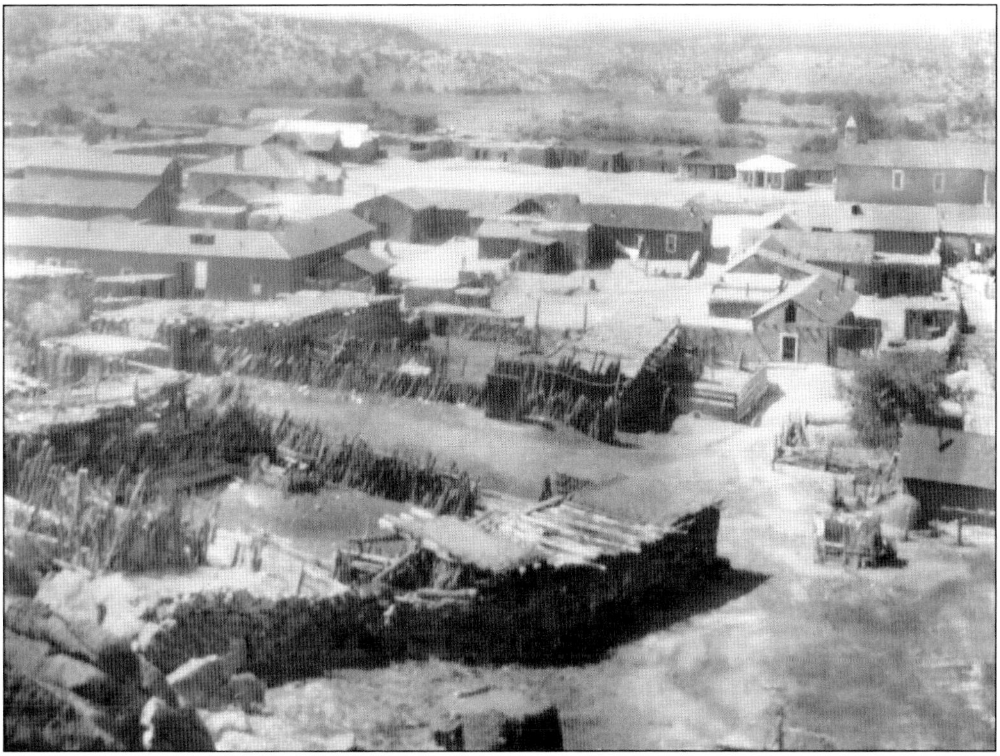

The stage station was probably located across from the plaza opposite the church. Both the photograph above and the one on the opposite page were taken some time in the late 19th century. In 1858, a US post office was established in San Jose, and it has operated there intermittently ever since. The 1879 construction of the railroad, which bypassed San Jose, eliminated the need for the stagecoach and most of the traffic on the Santa Fe Trail. Today, San Jose is frozen in the 19th century. The photograph below shows "territorial style" molding surrounding a traditional New Mexico corner fireplace. (Above, NT; below, CSWR.)

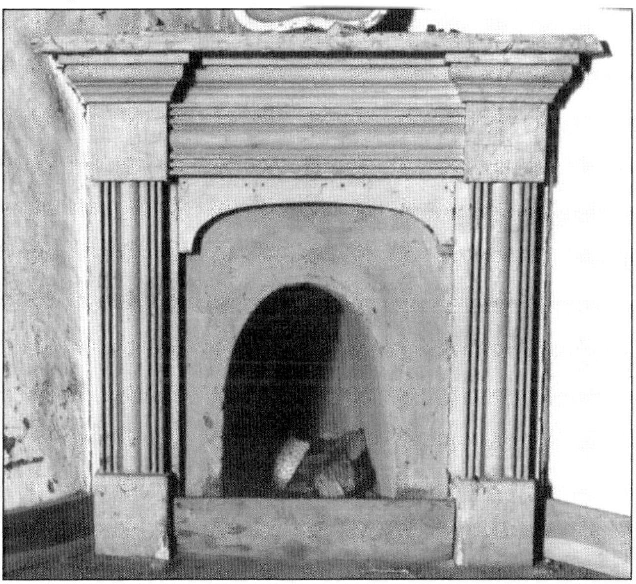

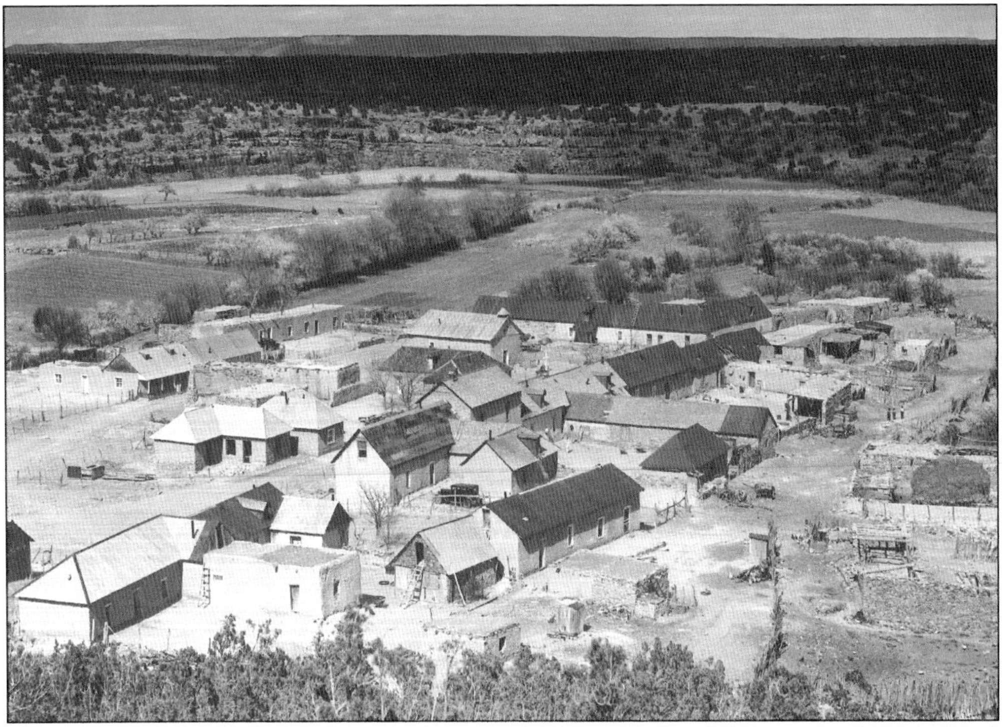

In April 1941, photographer Irving Rusinow, under the auspices of the Bureau of Agricultural Economics, took a series of 94 photographs of El Cerrito. The images on these two pages are from this series. The photograph above, from the bluff overlooking the village, clearly shows the enclosed central plaza with the church in the middle. The settlement was founded by settlers from San Miguel in about 1810. The photograph below shows the village church, Nuestra Señora de los Desamparados, built in 1888. (Above, USNA No. 521147; below, No. 521216.)

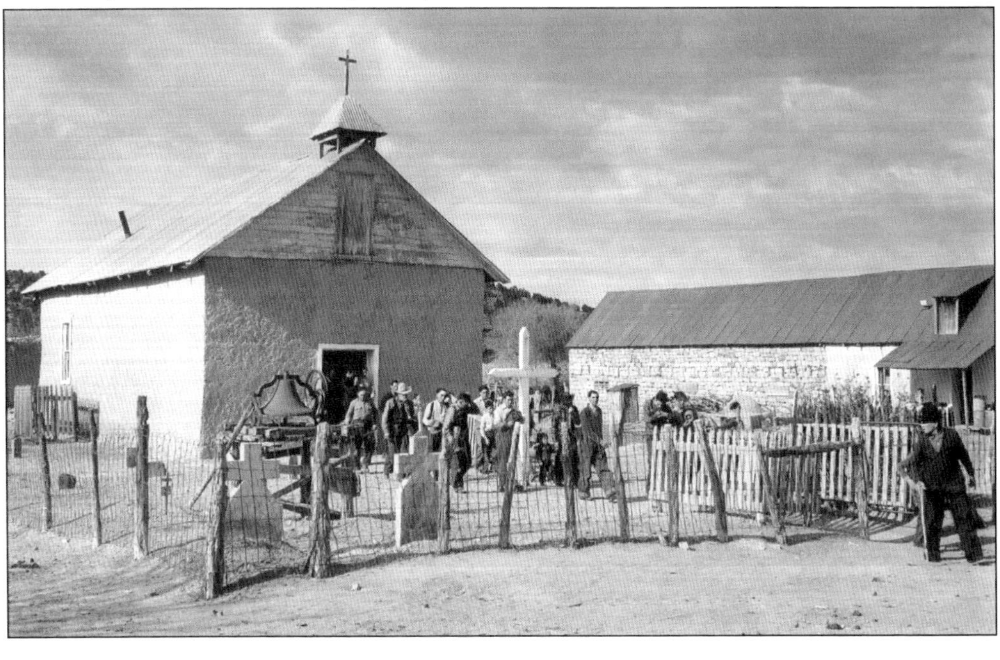

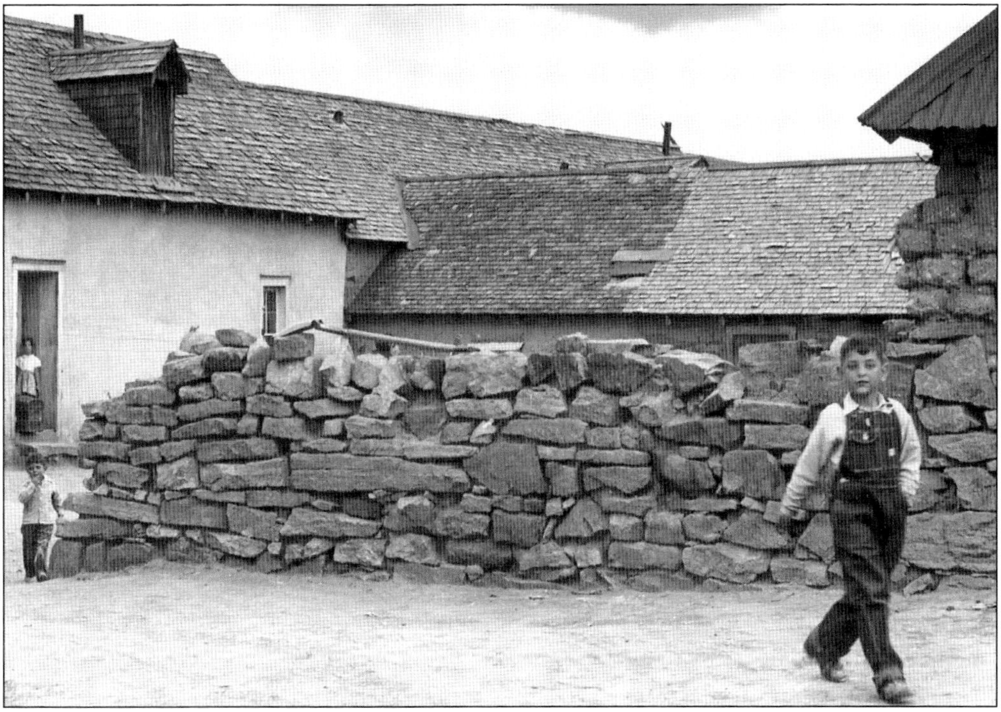

The photograph above is of one corner of a connected house compound, typical of the villages discussed in this chapter. These houses would originally have had the flat roofs associated with Native American Pueblo architecture, several of which can be viewed in the village overview on the opposite page. The photograph below is an interior shot of one of the oldest houses and shows a man descended from some of the earliest residents of El Cerrito. Note the large number of religious pictures, as well as the photograph of a relative with snapshots of other relatives and perhaps friends stuck under the edge of the frame. (Above, USNA No. 521149; below, No. 521124.)

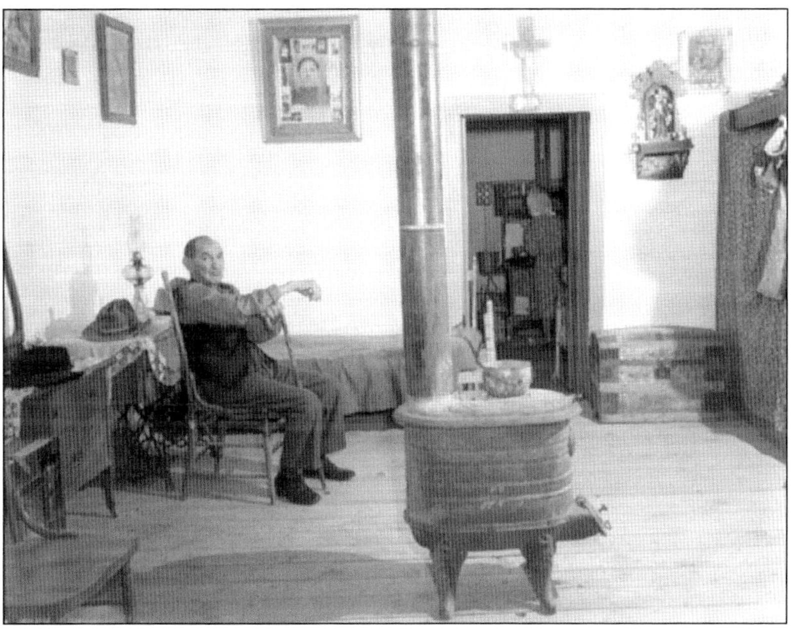

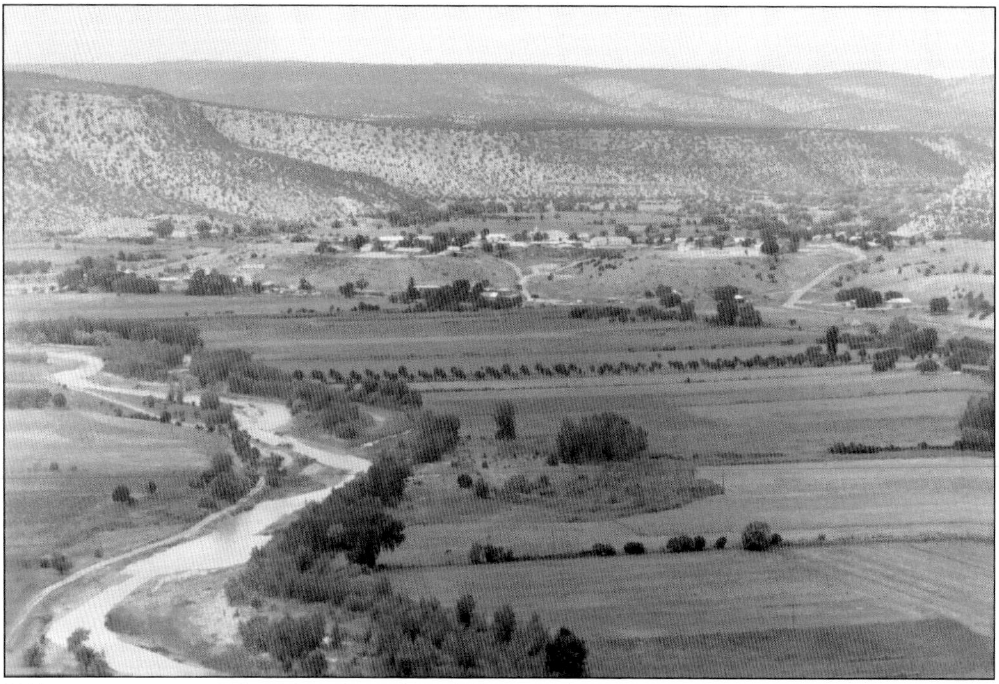

Villanueva, meaning "New Town," was founded in 1808 by Baron Marianos and Jose Filipe Madrid. Originally, it was called La Questa, or "the Hill." There may once have been a watchtower, or *torreon*; however, there was never a perimeter wall. These two photographs show Villanueva overlooking the Pecos River. This town, and others along the Pecos, were home to Ciboleros, buffalo hunters. In October, they would ride east to West Texas with long lances and either trap buffalo in ditches or ride alongside them and spear them. Josiah Gregg, in *The Commerce of the Prairies* (1844), describes these hunts. This is also where, in 1841, Gov. Manuel Armijo captured the Texas–Santa Fe Expedition after they claimed the area for Texas. (Both, CSWR.)

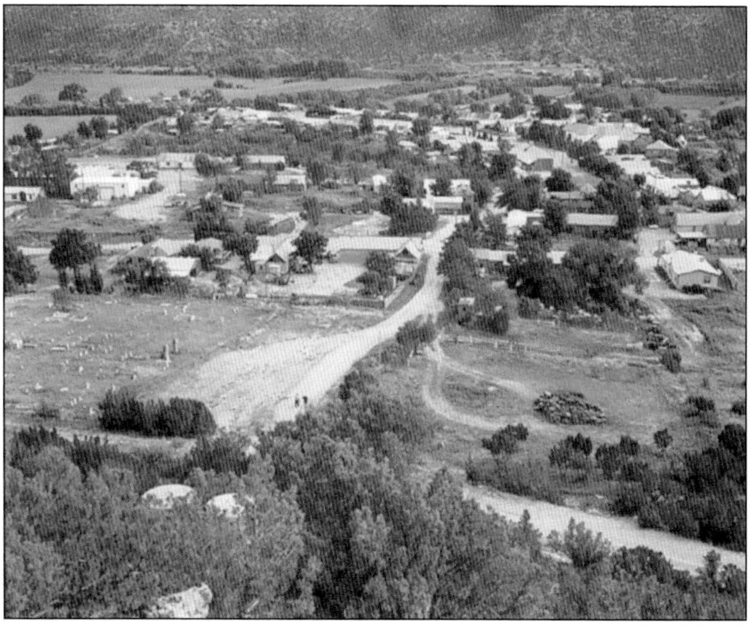

The church at Villanueva, Nuestra Señora de Guadalupe, was originally constructed in 1816, although it was not officially licensed until 1831, probably because of tension between the church and the Mexican government at that time. The photograph at right shows the church with the stone facing that was added to the adobe structure some time in the mid-20th century. The interior shows original carved corbels, with a statue of Our Lady of Guadalupe hanging over the main altar. In 1890, the name of the community was changed to Villanueva. Electricity was not installed until 1949. (Right, CSWR; below, NT.)

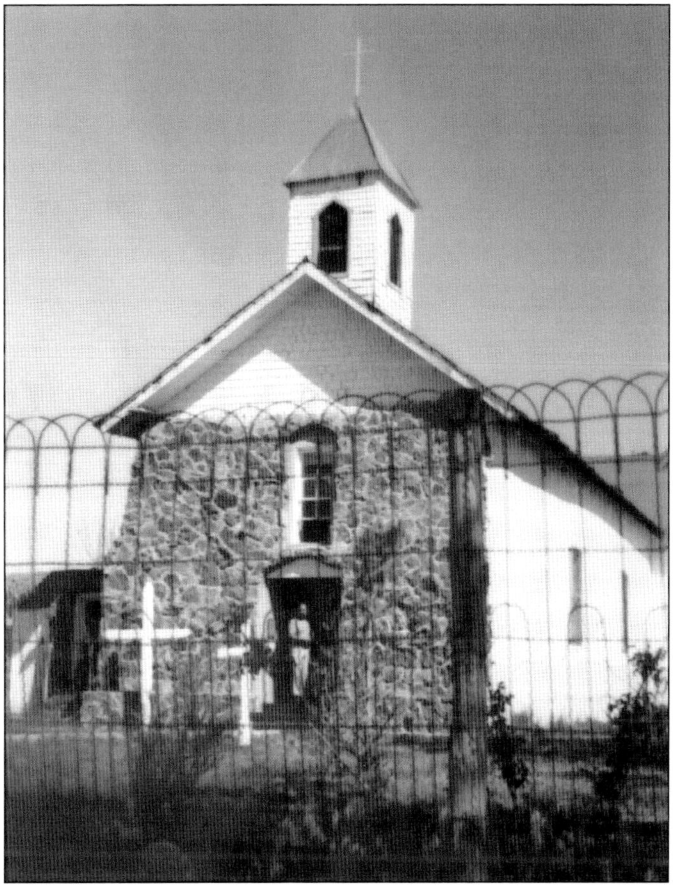

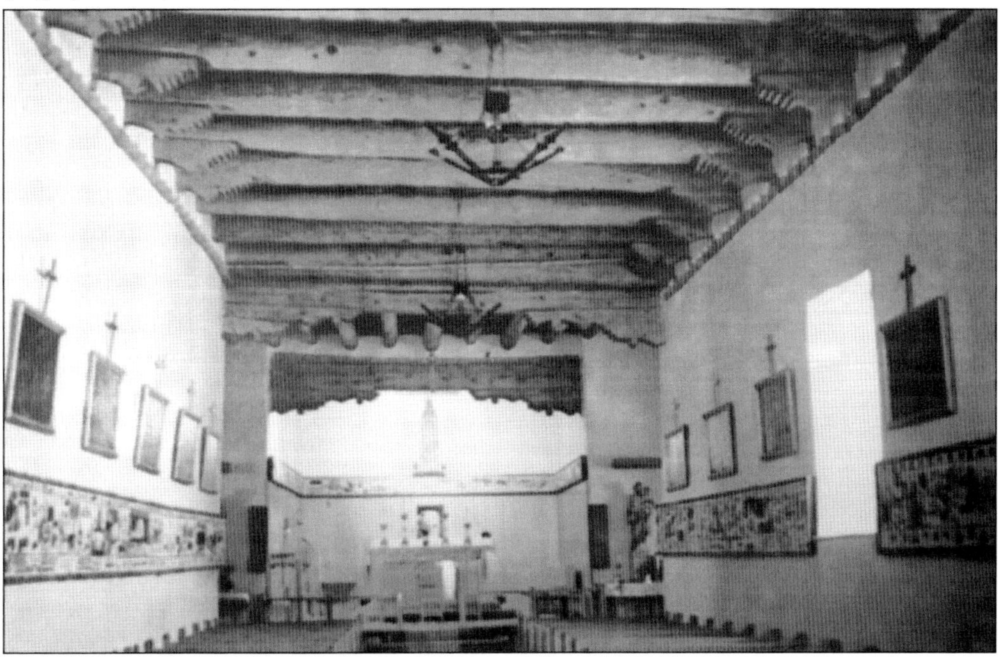

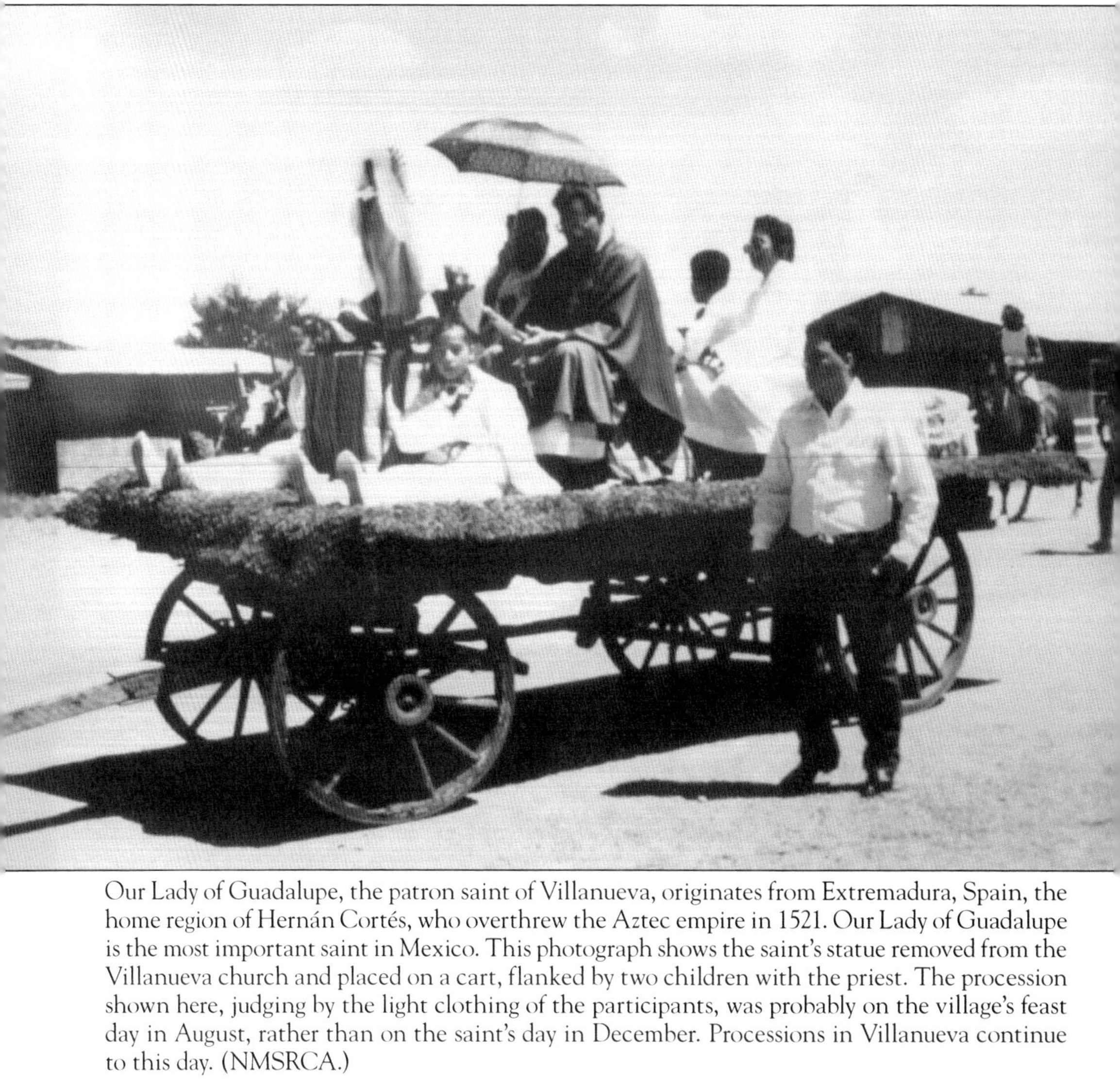

Our Lady of Guadalupe, the patron saint of Villanueva, originates from Extremadura, Spain, the home region of Hernán Cortés, who overthrew the Aztec empire in 1521. Our Lady of Guadalupe is the most important saint in Mexico. This photograph shows the saint's statue removed from the Villanueva church and placed on a cart, flanked by two children with the priest. The procession shown here, judging by the light clothing of the participants, was probably on the village's feast day in August, rather than on the saint's day in December. Processions in Villanueva continue to this day. (NMSRCA.)

Six

Ranches and Dudes

Much of the Pecos watershed area, from Spanish settlement until well into the 20th century, was used as summer, and, in some cases, permanent, range for cattle and sheep. As livestock density increased, native grass cover was diminished and environmental degradation occurred. Grazing was managed by the US Forest Service; however, by the 1960s, grazing permits were limited. In 1996, possession or transport of domestic goats or sheep was terminated on public lands in the Pecos region. Today, sheep grazing has been eliminated from the region, as has much of the cattle grazing.

Well into the 20th century, local cattle were driven to railroad stations at Rowe, Glorieta, and Lamy and then shipped to Kansas or California.

Starting in the late 19th century, ranchers found that tourists were more profitable than cattle. The dude ranch craze saw considerable activity along the Pecos River, especially given its close proximity to mountain wilderness.

Los Pinos is the only active older ranch remaining today. Mountain View Ranch was the largest on the upper Pecos; Irvin's on the Pecos had indoor plumbing; and Valley Ranch was an Indian Detour stop. The Valley Ranch had rodeos on Sunday afternoons to entertain the guests, where local cowboys got the chance to "show their stuff;" in exchange, they sometimes received tips from spectators. Valley Ranch was the "fanciest" of the Pecos-area guest and dude ranches.

Because few images were found of cattle and sheep operations, this chapter focuses on dude and guest ranches, the latter of which had more amenities and were not as rustic.

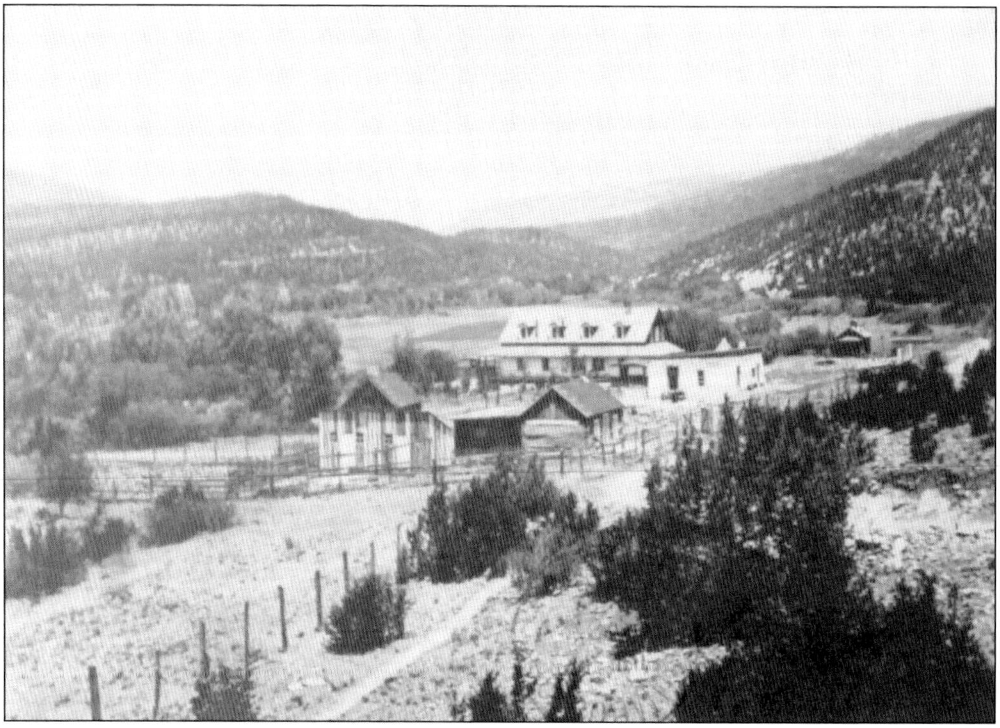

Valley Ranch was one of the earliest guest establishments in the Pecos Valley. It started as a cattle ranch in the 1880s and operated as a full-service guest ranch from 1908 to 1947. It is now a Benedictine monastery and retreat. Along with other guest ranches, it also catered to health seekers, often tuberculosis patients attracted by the region's pure, dry climate. The photograph below, from a Valley Ranch brochure, shows guests preparing for a day excursion. (Above, NT; below, AC.)

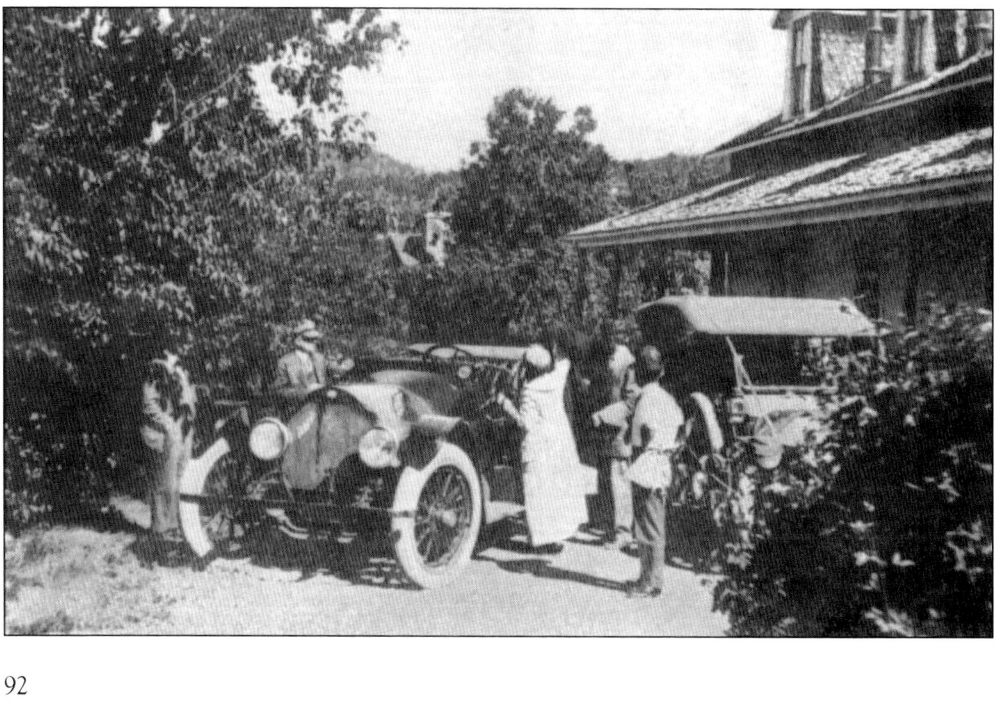

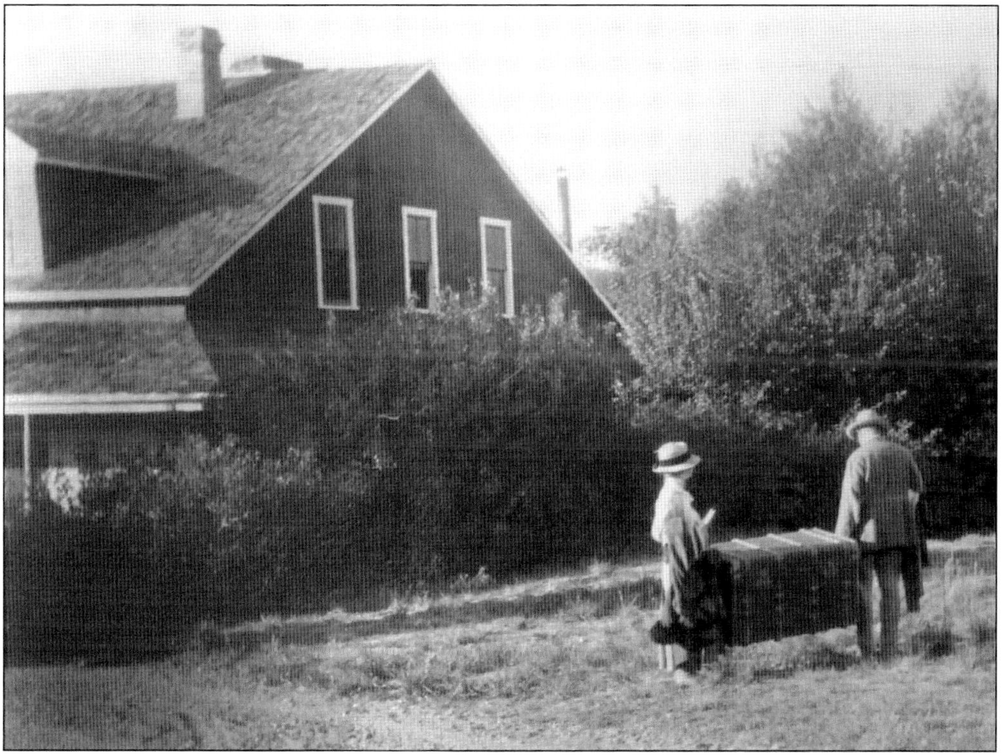

At first, guests at Valley Ranch stayed in the main two-story ranch house, a few smaller buildings, and wood-floored tents. The photograph above shows Rachel and Warren Lothrop lugging their trunk to their accommodations behind the tennis court. There were no porters in 1915. The photograph below, from about 1920, shows the old ranch house in relation to the new Santa Fe–style Apache Inn. When the Tererro Mine and mill were built in 1925, an agreement was made for the mine's use of Valley Ranch water from the Pecos River in exchange for free electricity to the ranch. (Above, PNHP No. 1448-6; below, NT.)

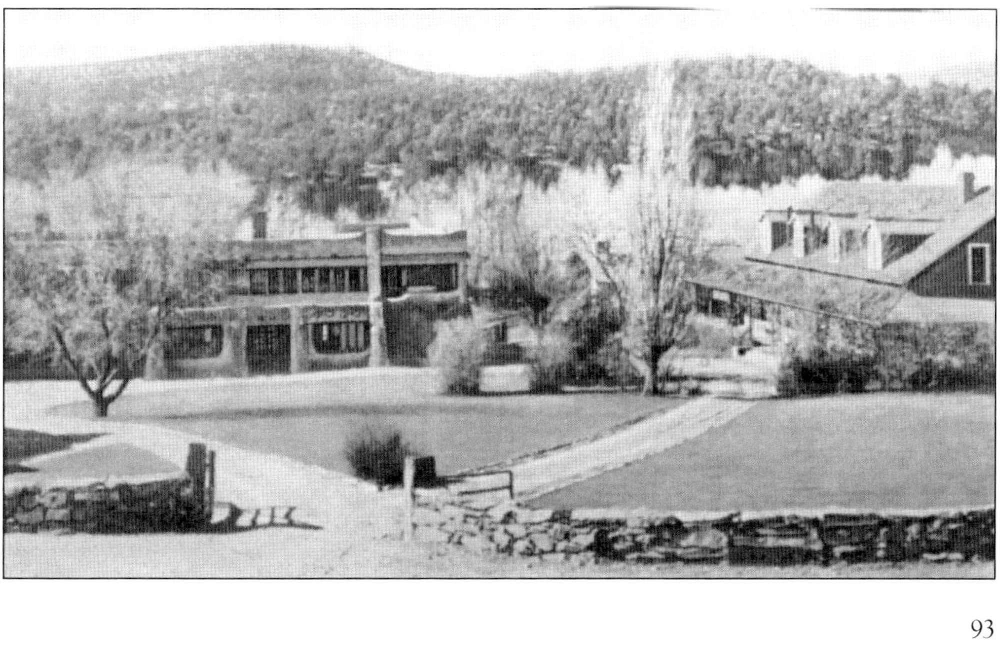

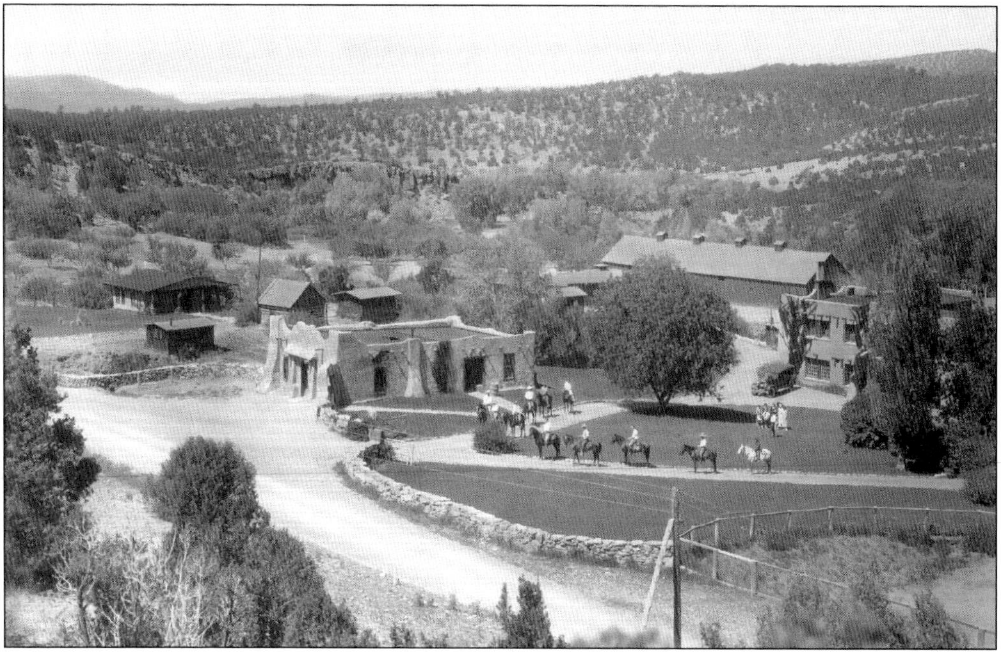

From the mid-1920s through the 1930s, Valley Ranch was a regular lunch stop on the AT&SF/Fred Harvey Indian Detour tours, following a stop at the Pecos Mission Church ruins and before it proceeded on through Glorieta Pass and ended at the La Fonda Hotel in Santa Fe. The topically named Valley Ranch Apache Inn was one of a very few commercial restaurant operations used by the Indian Detour that was not operated by Fred Harvey, but it was subject to strict Fred Harvey inspections. The dining room was on the second level, allowing for cool summer breezes to waft through the building. This building and the main building at Bishop's Lodge, near Santa Fe, were constructed from identical plans, with the same fixtures and landscaping. For more information, see Arcadia Publishing's Images of America: *Santa Fe's Historic Hotels.* (Above, DD; below, NT.)

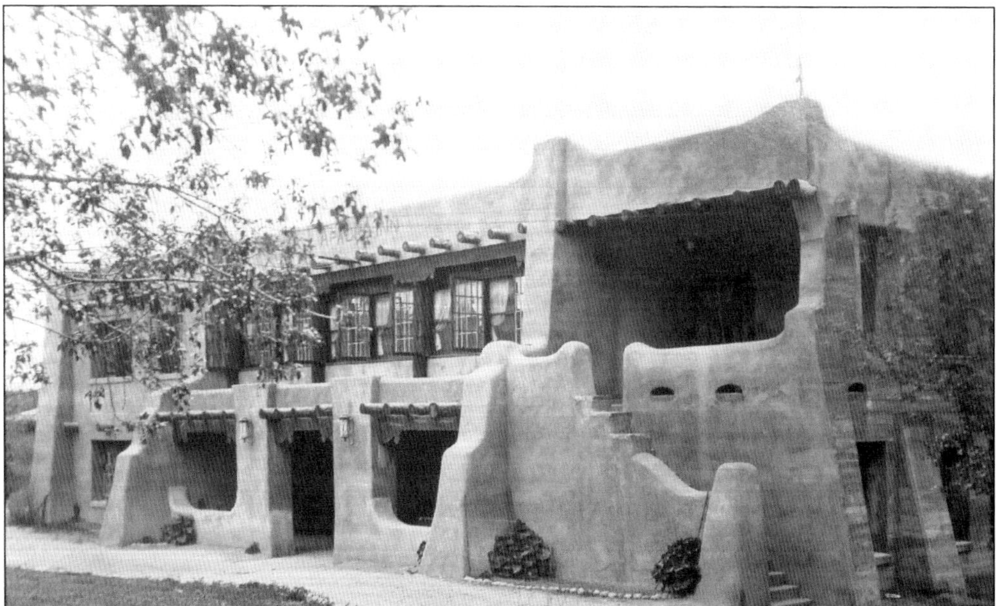

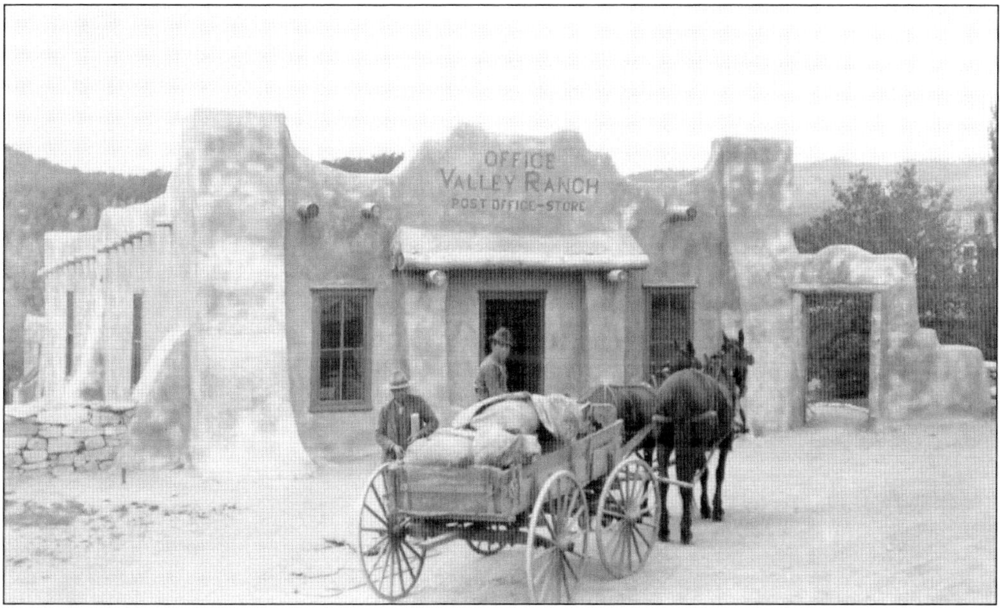

Valley Ranch had its own post office from 1908 to 1950. It was primarily for the convenience of guests, but it also served portions of the upper Pecos Valley until the Tererro post office was established in 1927. The photograph above shows the Valley Ranch post office and store after it had been given a Santa Fe–style makeover some time in the early 1920s. The photograph below shows the guest ranch at the height of its popularity in the late 1920s, when it was complete with a golf course. Note the tents, which were especially popular with health-seekers. The south side of the post office and store is facing the road. (Both, NT.)

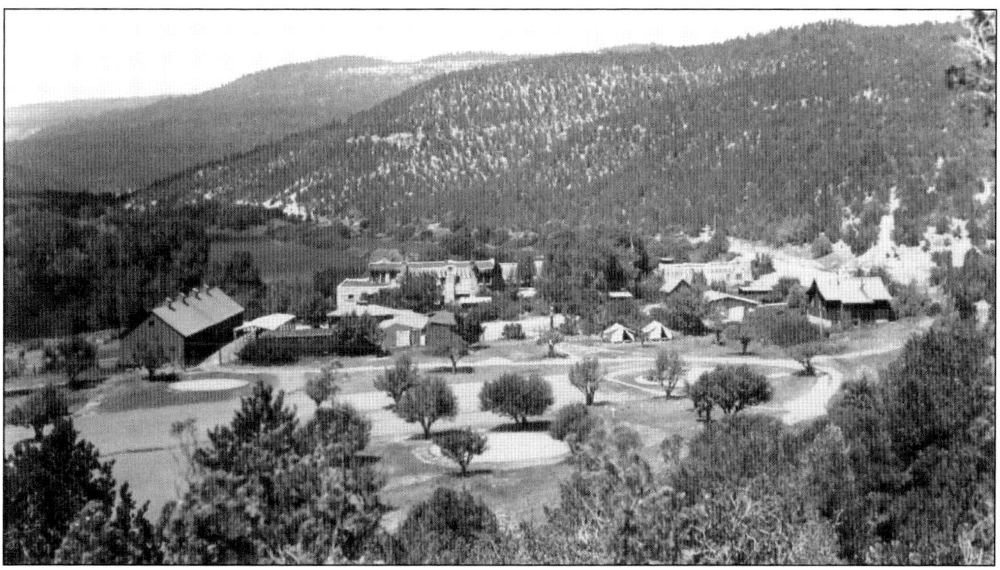

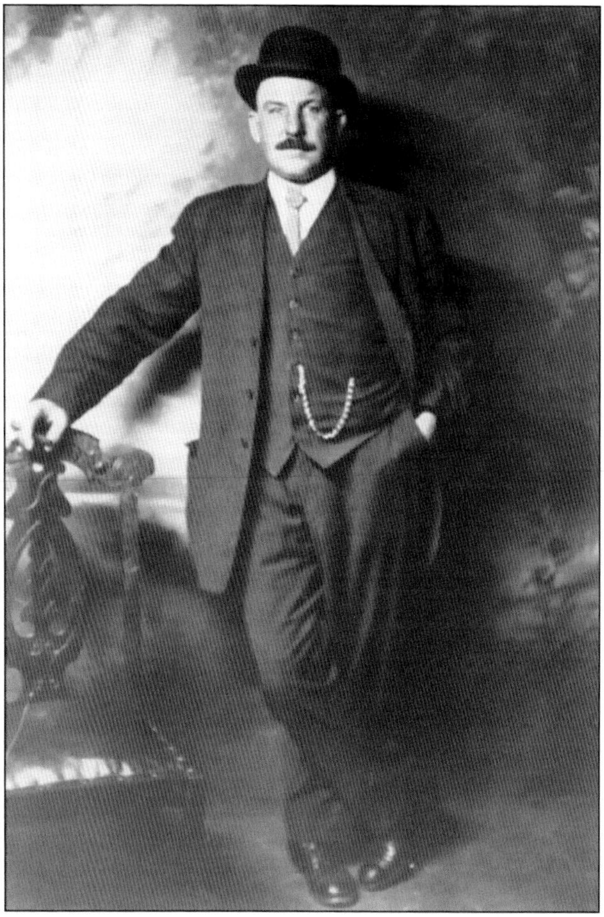

Edward "Ed" Irvin (1870–1948) and his wife, Rachel Elizabeth Closson Irvin (1878–1947), visited Santa Fe from Pennsylvania. After seeing Pecos, they decided that was the perfect place for a dude ranch. They purchased property about 10 miles north of the village of Pecos and operated Irvin's on the Pecos from 1908 until 1935. The image at left is a studio photograph of Ed about the time he came to New Mexico. The 1915 photograph below shows family and friends at the recently opened dude ranch. Elizabeth Irvin is in the white dress next to Forest Ranger Johnson, the Irvins' son Tom is sitting on the ground, and Ed Irvin is standing looking to his right. (Both, EI.)

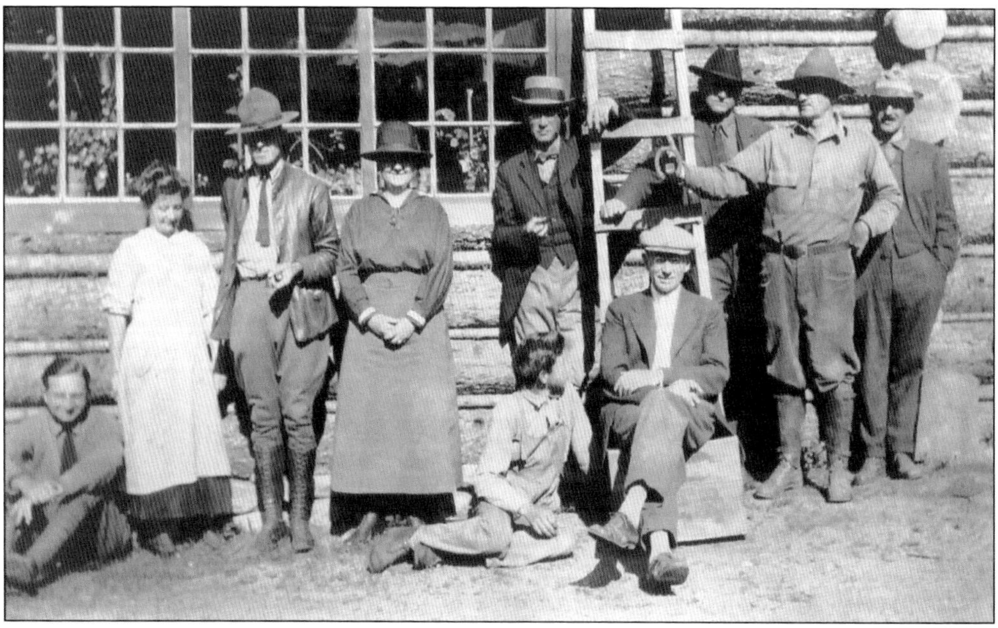

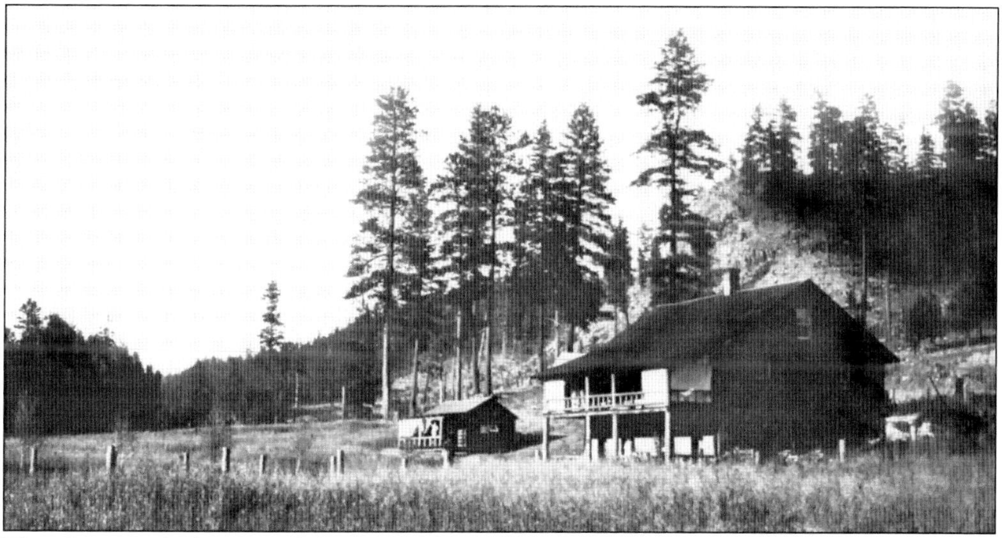

The photograph above is of the Irvin ranch house in 1910. One of the guest cabins is to the left. Irvin's on the Pecos was as much a guest ranch as a dude ranch, having indoor plumbing, a dining room, electric lights, a separate recreation room, and a swimming pool. The Irvins also raised their own poultry and vegetables. From 1921 on, the Lisboa Fish Hatchery kept the Pecos River, along with various other mountain streams and lakes, well stocked with trout. At that time, there were four types of trout in the river: rainbow, brown, eastern brook, and the native cutthroat. The photograph below shows the 1930s Irvin family home on Willow Creek, a couple of miles north of the dude ranch. (Both, EI.)

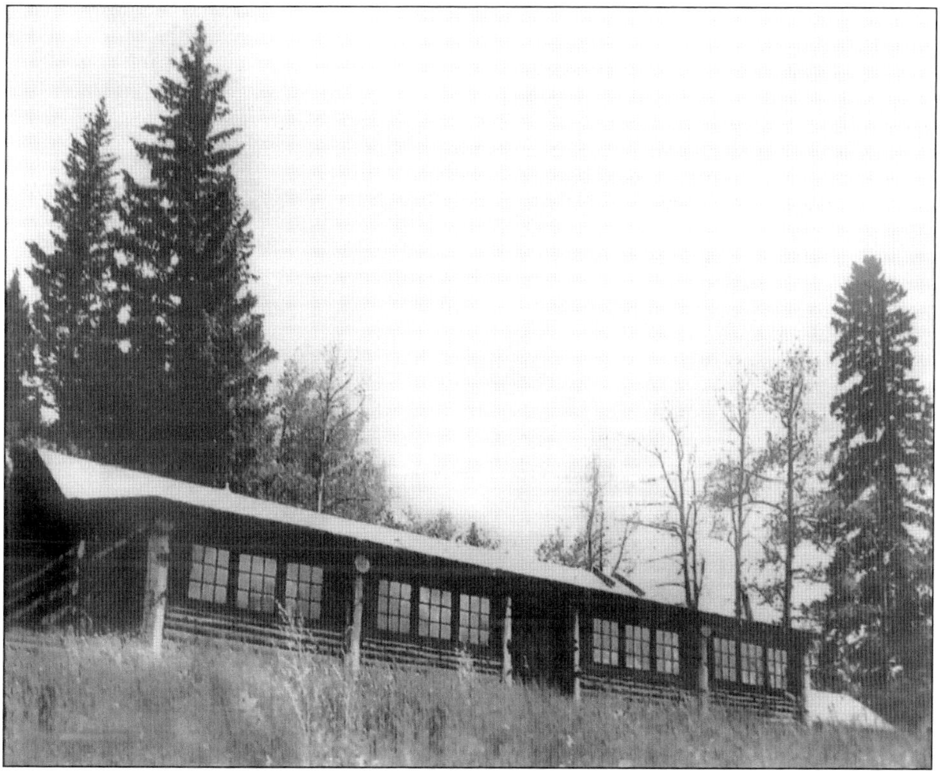

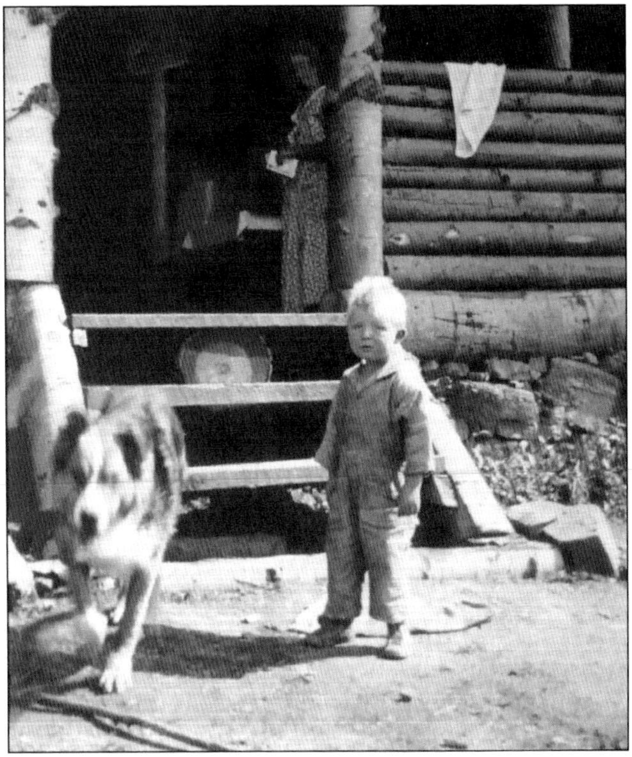

Ed Irvin's grandson, also named Ed, grew up at the ranch with his dog Moses and still lives in the immediate area today. Irvin's on the Pecos was a year-round operation, advertising ice-skating, snowshoeing, and skiing from January through March, along with plenty of wood, electric lights, and indoor lavatories. However, keeping the roads open was no small task. The photograph below shows "Little Ed" and his father, Tom, on the ranch's Caterpillar 28, manufactured between 1931 and 1935. These were the first of the yellow Caterpillar tractors. Note the earlier, originally horse-drawn, road grader they are pulling behind them. (Both, EI.)

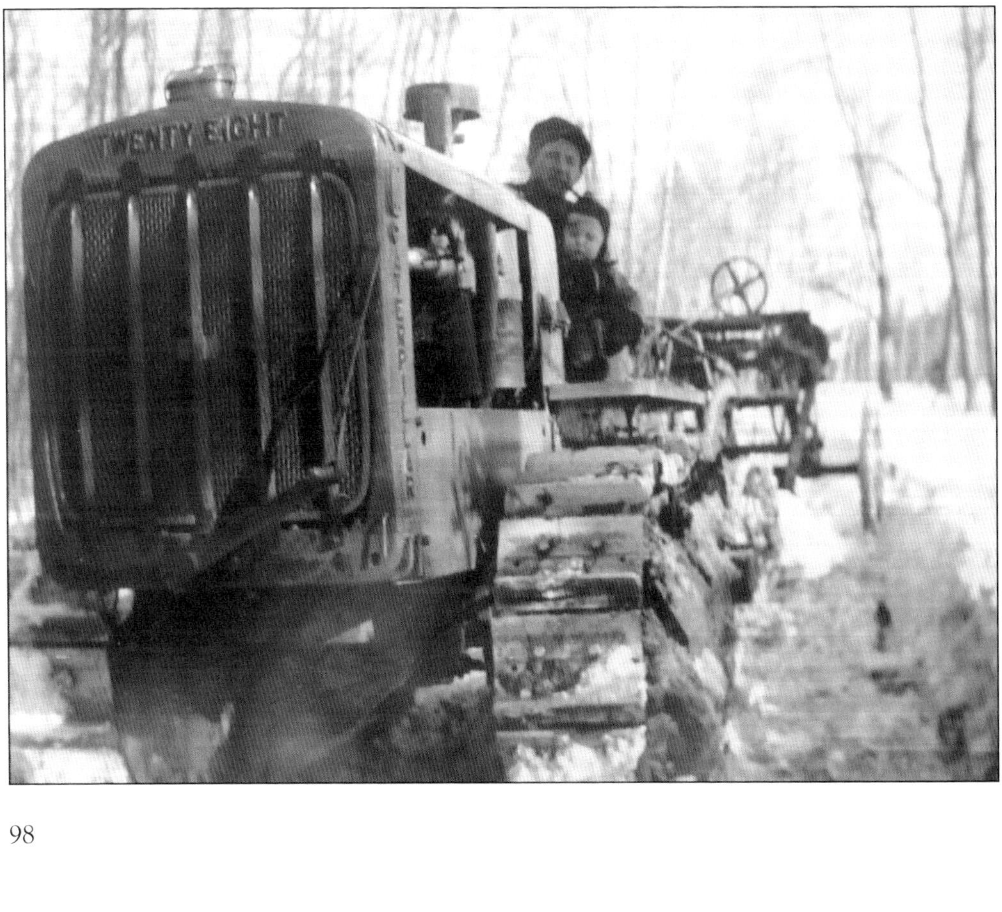

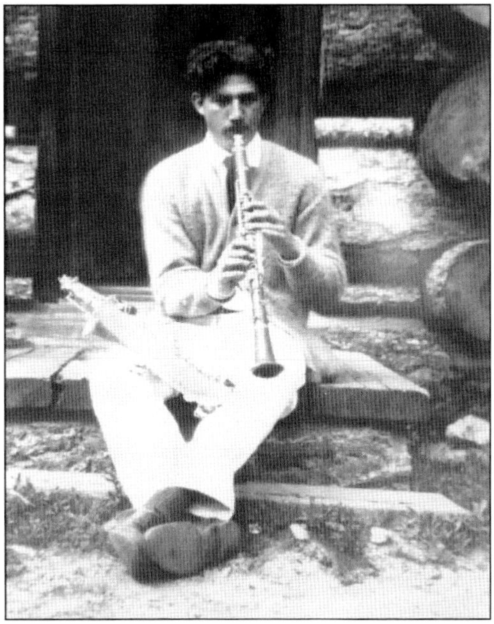

Tom Irvin became a civil engineer. He was also a musician, playing saxophone, clarinet, and trombone in the ranch's Blue Goose Orchestra, which was comprised of family and friends, with guests occasionally sitting in. They played every Friday and Saturday night. Below, Tom is standing next to what looks like a 1922 Studebaker Big Six, although the triangular radiator badge is odd. It was said to be the fastest car in the canyon. (Both, EI.)

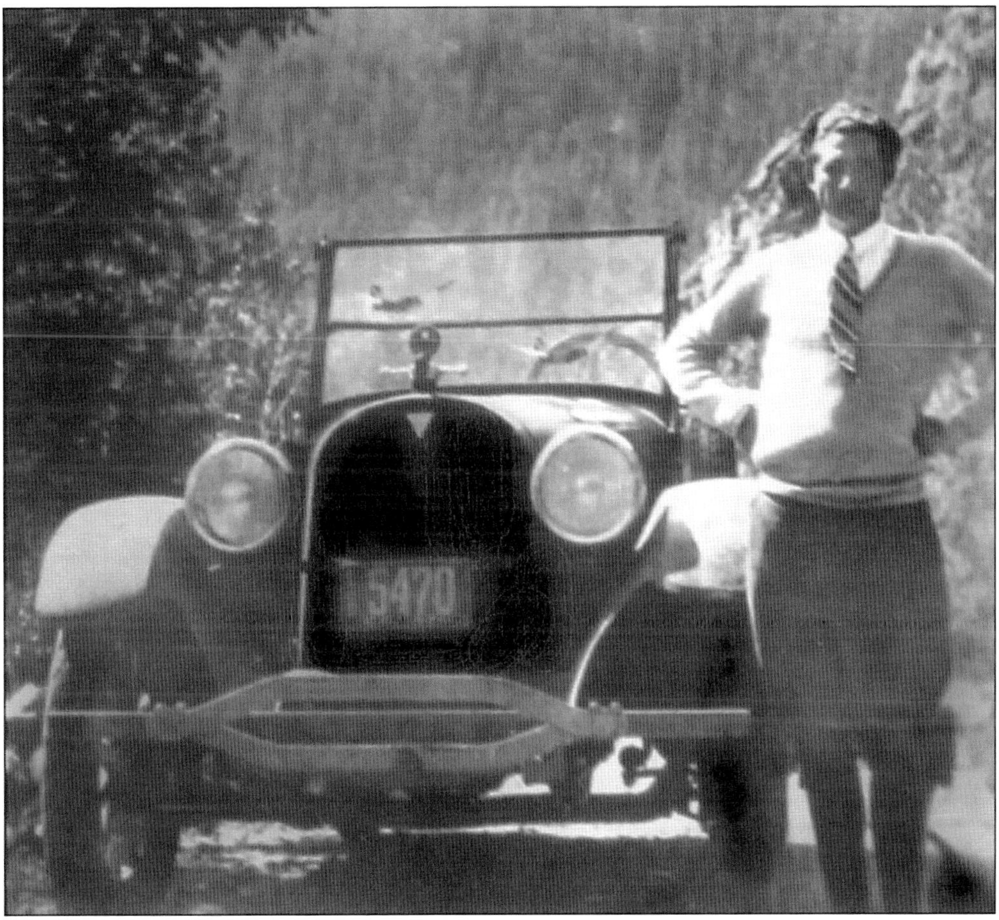

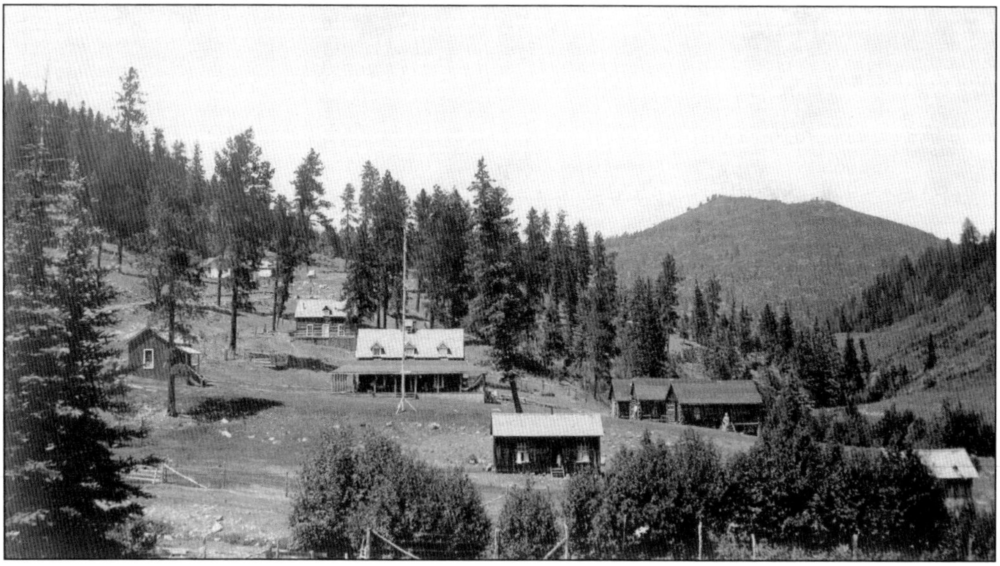

Nearly 20 miles north of the village of Pecos, at the end of the road, at the confluence of Winsor Creek and the Pecos River, is Cowles, named for the Cowles brothers, who prospected the area in the 19th century. In 1915, Henry U. Mudge, who had had a cabin there since 1896, purchased the Mountain View Ranch from George Ritzheimer and opened it as a dude ranch. After Mudge died in 1920, it was purchased in 1930 by the original ranch manager, George "Skipper" Viles, from the Mudge estate. Skipper and his wife, Matie, operated Mountain View until 1945. It was expanded and improved greatly over the years and was one of the most popular of the mountain dude and guest ranches of the era. The ranch is seen above before 1922, and the main lodge is seen below before 1926. (Above, MH No. 001; below, No. 087.)

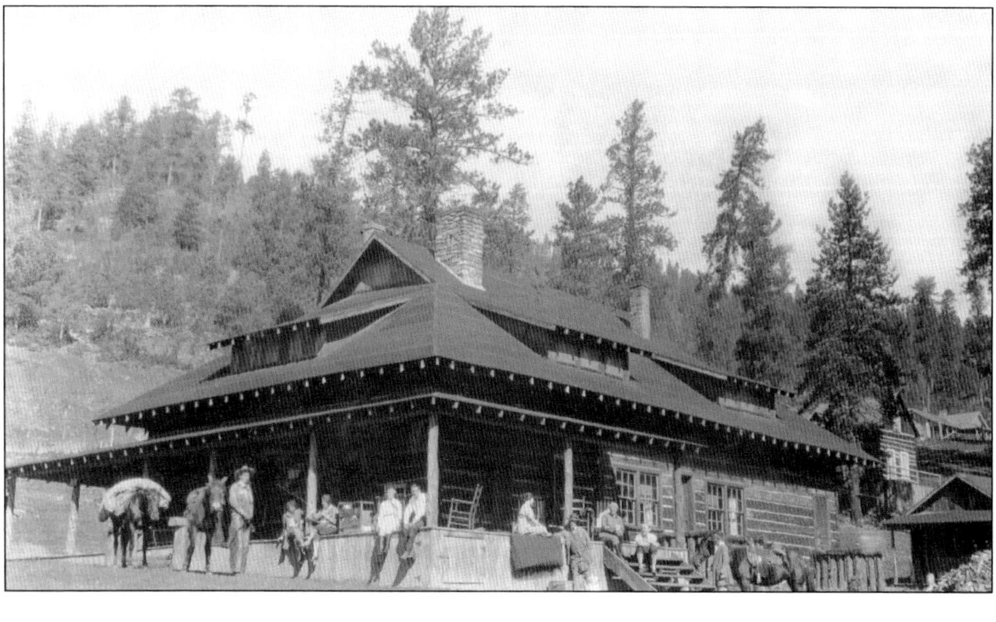

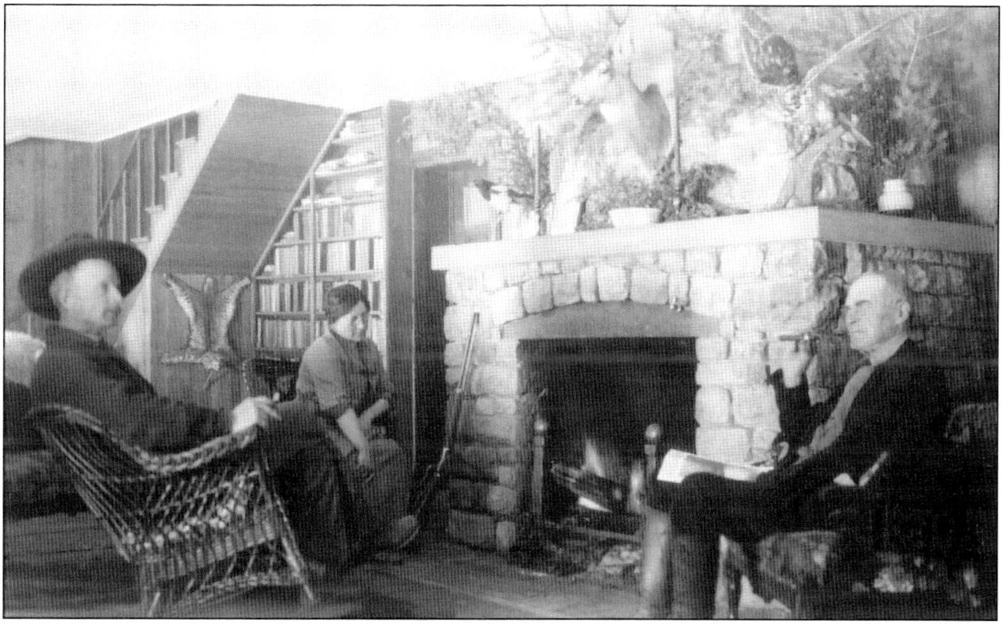

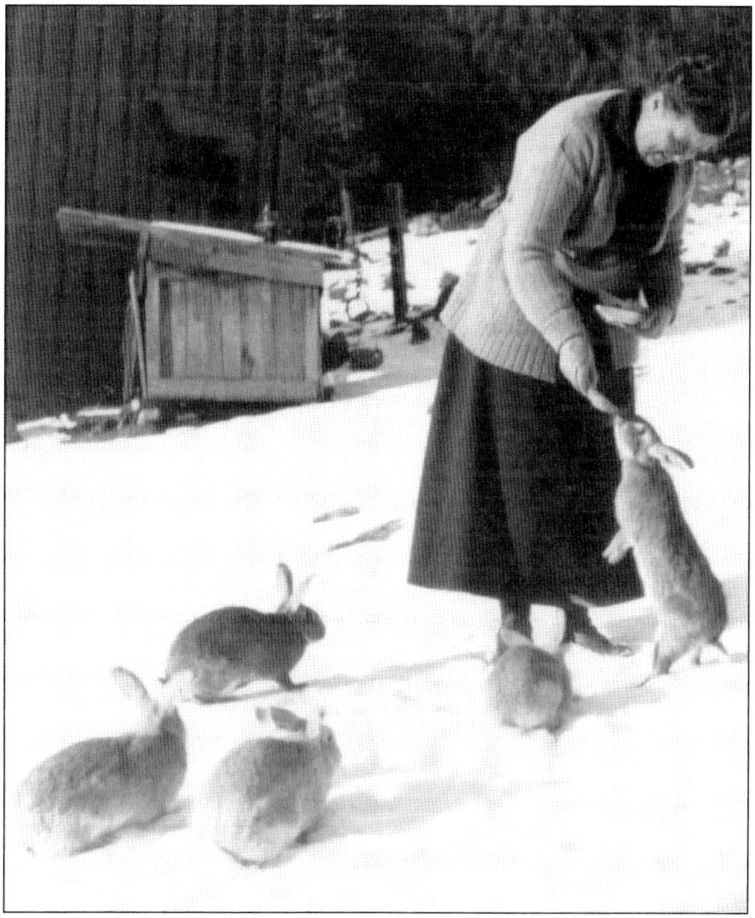

Seen above is the living room of the main lodge at Mountain View Ranch in 1924. Skipper and Matie Viles are sitting with Mr. Robertson, with the cigar, who ran the general store. The fireplace was rebuilt on a grander scale in 1922 by a Mr. Gardetti, when the main lodge was remodeled. Skipper was an accomplished hunter; in 1923, he killed the last grizzly bear in the Pecos region. On a less violent note, the photograph at right shows Matie, who loved animals, especially cats. Here, she is feeding pet rabbits in the snow in 1922. (Above, MH No. 1228; right, No. 819.)

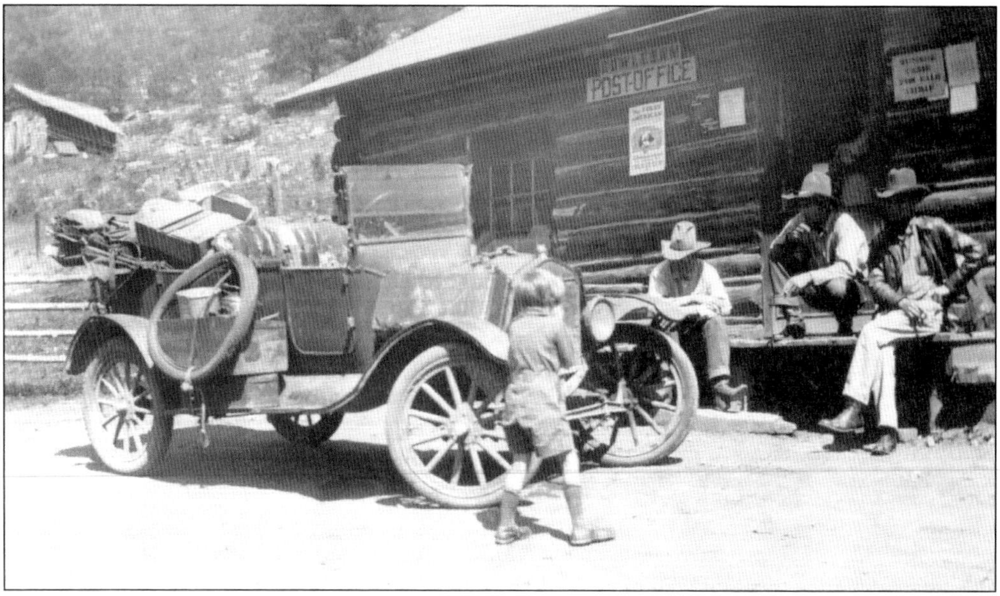

In 1905, Oliver Alexander, a mining engineer living at Willow Creek, near what was to become Tererro, established a post office at Cowles. There is no town of Cowles; this post office, in operation until 1965, served only a handful of summer cabins, Mountain View Ranch, Los Pinos Cabins, and Winsor's Cabins. The photograph below is of the interior of the post office and general store. There are postcards on the counter, and many of the product logos are familiar. In the early days, the only telephone at Mountain View was also in the store, so it served as the ranch office. Both of these photographs are from the early 1920s. (Above, MH No. 1854; below, No. 622.)

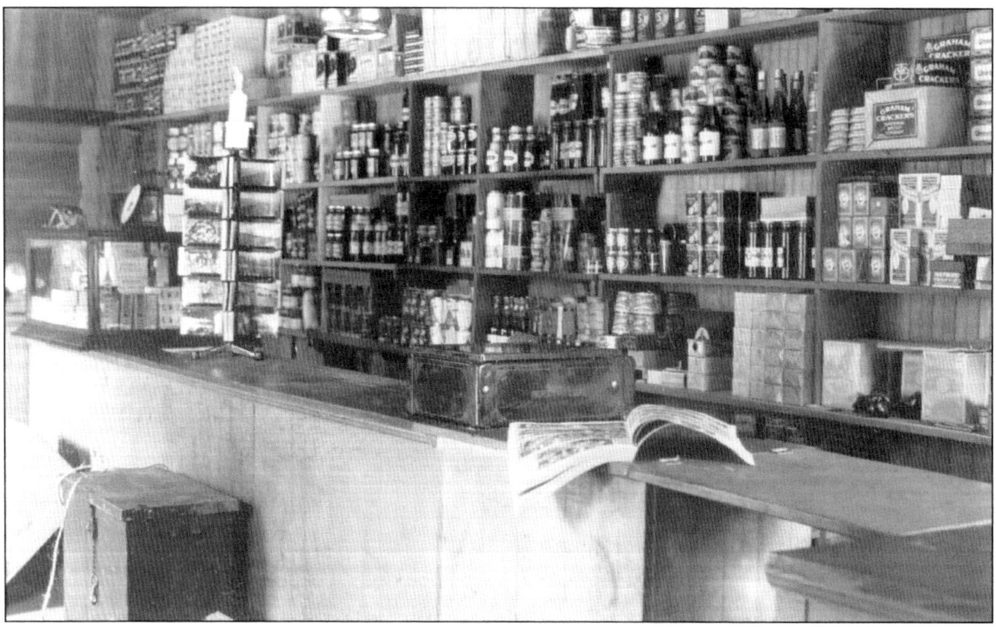

New Mexico, with its multicultural population struggling to get along in a beautiful but sparse environment, has long attracted "free spirits" and those who live "alternative" lifestyles. The two young women at right are on the grounds of Mountain View Ranch, with the ranch's iconic leaning pine tree in the background. (MH No. 409.)

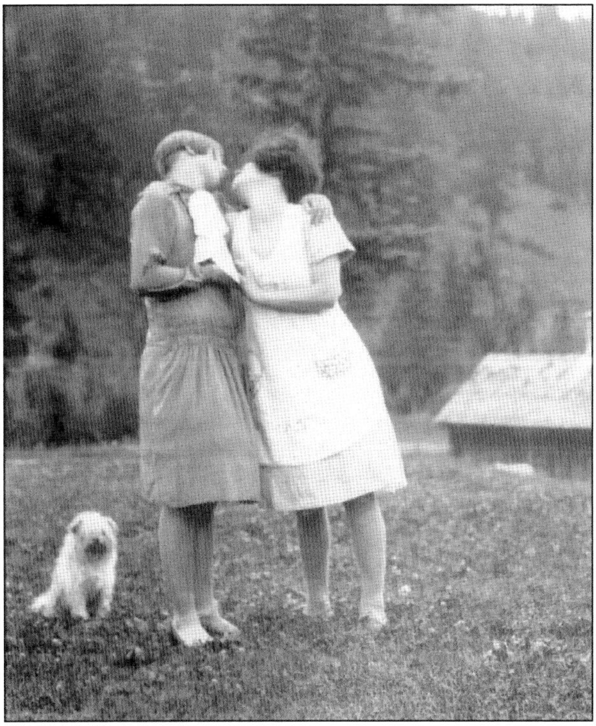

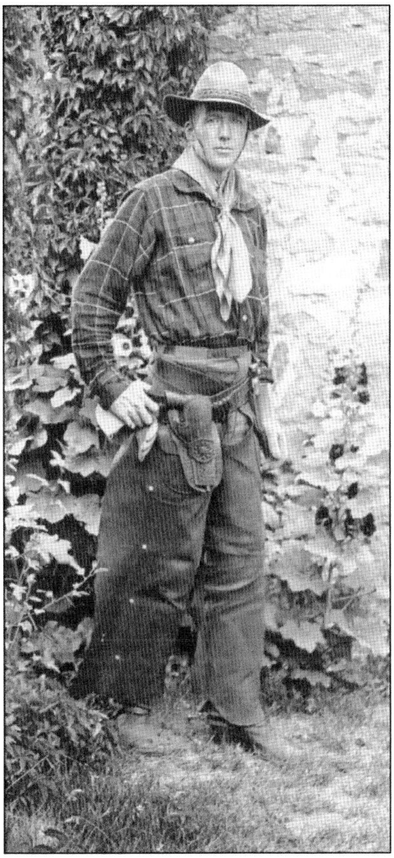

The photograph at left is thought to be of famous silent movie cowboy Thomas Hezikiah "Tom" Mix (1880–1940). Mix had spent time in Las Vegas, New Mexico, in 1915 and filmed a number of motion pictures there. He became enamored with northern New Mexico and stayed at Mountain View Ranch. (MH No. 424.)

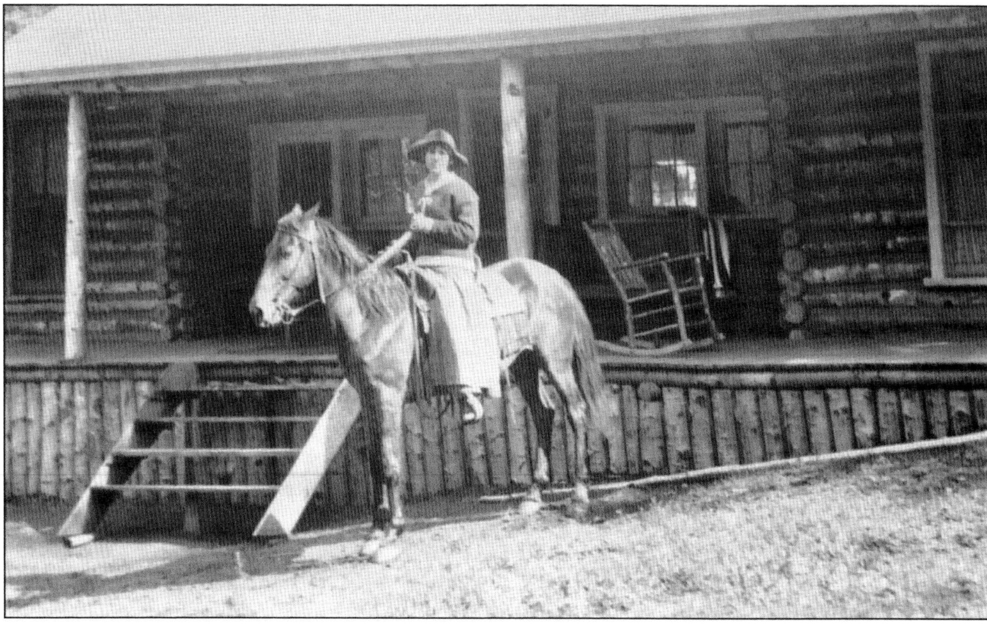

Los Pinos Resort (now Los Pinos Guest Ranch and Cabins), in Cowles, has been in continuous operation from the early 1920s to the present day. The main ranch building, seen below, was originally built in 1912 as a summer home for the Amado Chaves family. Chaves was active in New Mexico politics and served as superintendent of public instruction, mayor of Santa Fe, and as a territorial council senator. The photograph above, taken in 1914, is of his daughter Katherine Chaves on her horse Lady. Katherine married Bernard Winthrop Page in the 1920s and was dean of residents at Finch College in New York. She moved back to New Mexico in 1940 and managed the Los Pinos Resort until her death in 1961. (Both, KSP.)

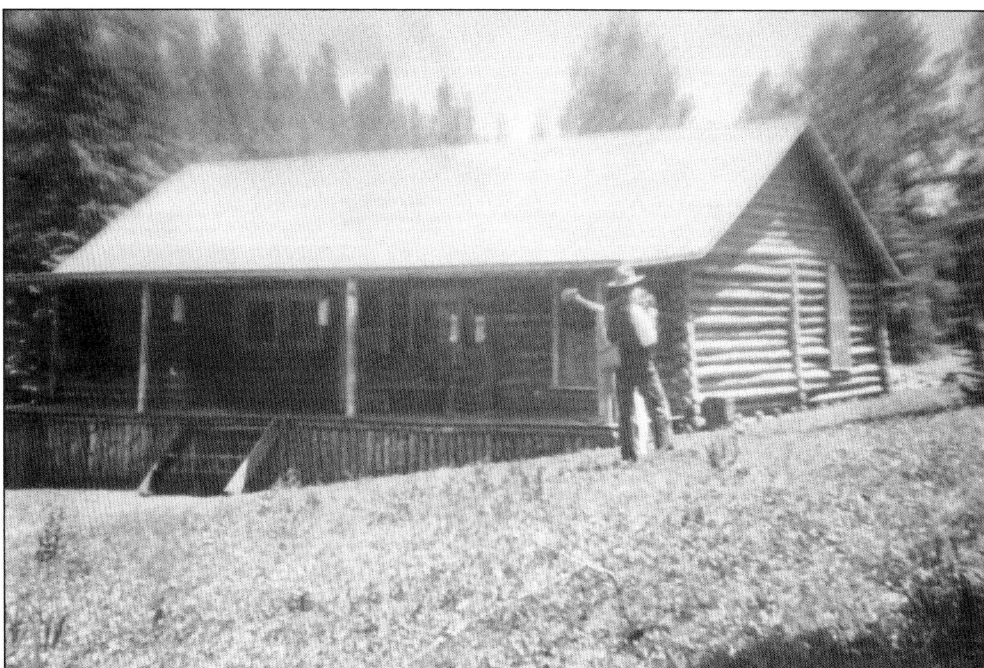

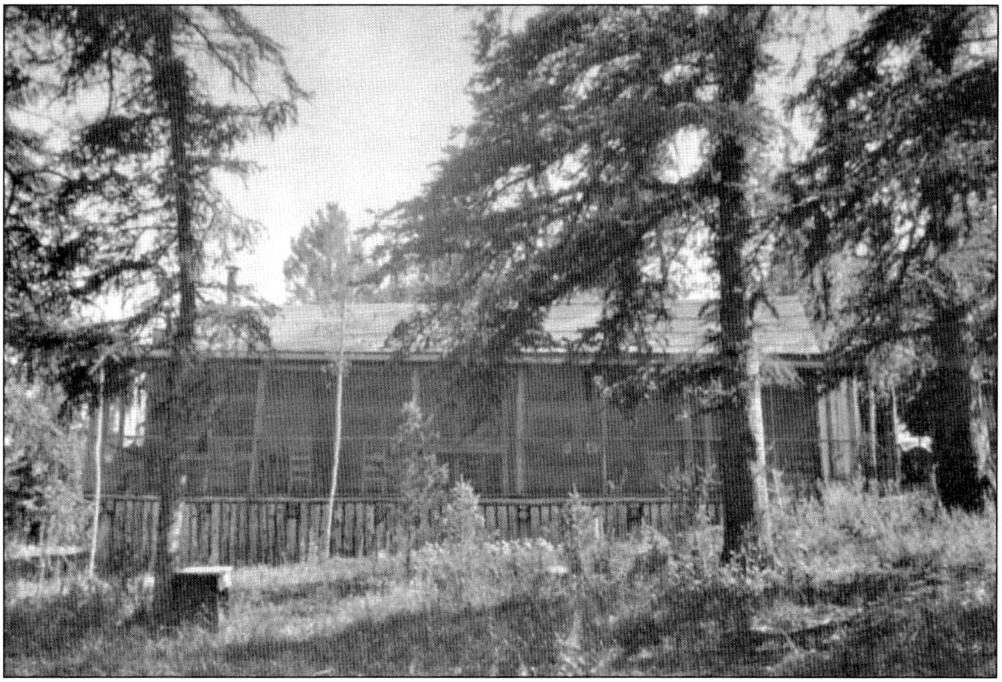

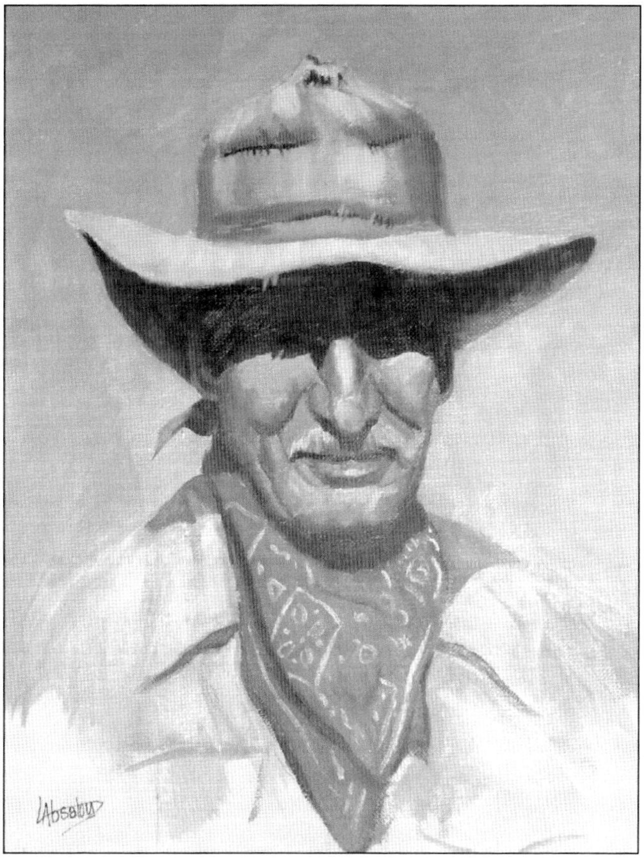

Los Pinos was expanded to a total of four individual aspen-log cabins. The photograph above shows one of the earlier cabins, built in the 1920s. The Los Pinos Resort has always stressed its remoteness and mountain charm, "where the road ends and the trails begin," while providing quality fare and comfortable accommodations. In the early 1960s, it was purchased by William A. McSweeney (1909–1996) and his wife, Alice Josephine McSweeney (1916–2009), and it remains in the McSweeney family today. The painting at right is of William. (Above, KSP; right, AM.)

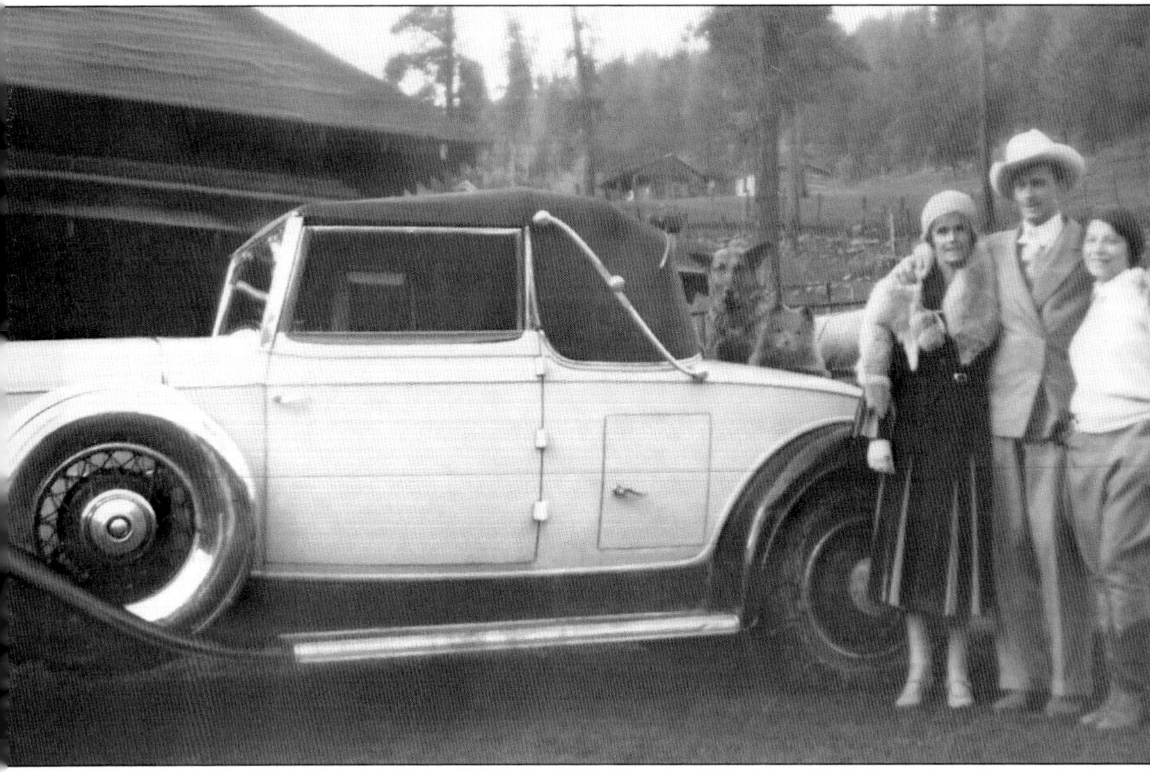

The final photograph for this chapter, taken in 1928, is of silent movie cowboy Tom Mix at Mountain View Ranch. The car is a 1927 Series 314 Cadillac Roadster. The two women with Mix and the two dogs in the rumble seat are unidentified. Note the fox-head stole worn by one of the women and the chains on the car's rear tires, no doubt to help with the often muddy road up to Cowles. (MH No. 1690.)

Seven

Forked Lightning and Hollywood

Forked Lightning Ranch at one time included what is now Pecos National Historical Park. It is named for a small, 880-year-old prehistoric pueblo ruin on the ranch property that was excavated by archaeologist A.V. Kidder in the 1920s.

The story of Forked Lightning begins with Polish immigrant Martin Kozlowski's stagecoach stop, tavern, and trading post alongside the Santa Fe Trail in the 1860s. Initially, Kozlowski used lumber taken from the ruins of the 18th-century Pecos Mission Church to construct buildings and corrals on his property. Much later, in 1925, it became the first headquarters for Forked Lightning Ranch, established by flamboyant rodeo promoter Tex Austin.

Austin was actually Clarence Van Nostrand, from Missouri, who found his calling as a Texas cattleman. In 1917, he became a successful rodeo promoter, taking rodeo indoors for the first time, including to Madison Square Garden in 1922 and Wembley Stadium in 1924, where over 113,000 Londoners saw a rodeo for the first time.

In 1925, he purchased the Kozlowski Pecos property and hired 30-year-old architect John Gaw Meem, soon to become famous as the articulator of the Santa Fe style, to design a ranch house for him. For more information, please see Arcadia Publishing's Images of America: *Albuquerque Deco and Pueblo* and Images of America: *Santa Fe's Historic Hotels*.

Following financial difficulties in the mid-1930s, Austin was forced to sell the ranch. In 1941, it was again sold, to Texas cattle and oil man E.E. "Buddy" Fogelson, who married actress Greer Garson in 1949. The ranch house soon became a center for Hollywood entertaining while also operating as a working ranch.

Today, the house and adjacent grounds are maintained as part of Pecos National Historical Park.

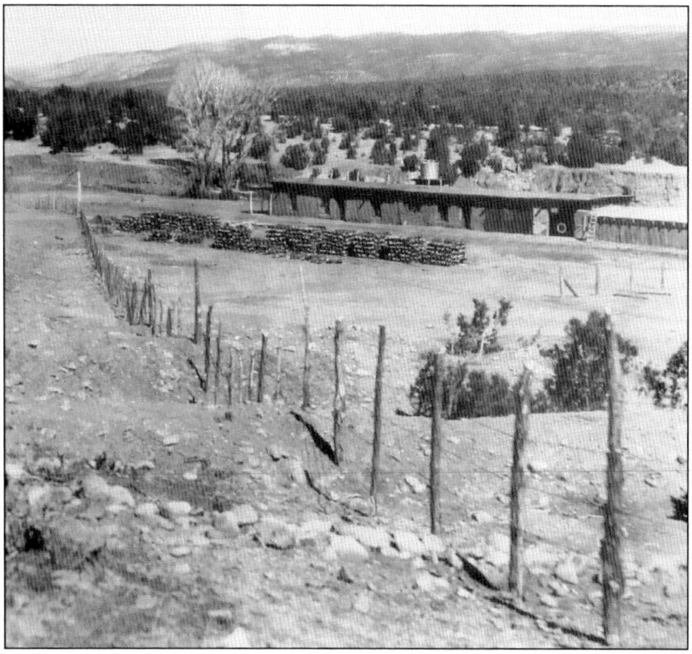

Martin Kozlowski first came to Pecos in 1846 as a member of the Missouri volunteers during the Mexican border campaign. He and his wife, Elena, had settled in the Pecos area by 1859 and established, based on a highly dubious title, a stop on the Santa Fe Trail. One of Kozlowski's sons is said to have been killed by lightning while removing beams from the old Pecos Church. In 1911, another son, Tomás, rebuilt parts of the store. The photograph at left shows the Kozlowski ranch in the late 19th century. (PNHP No. 4122.)

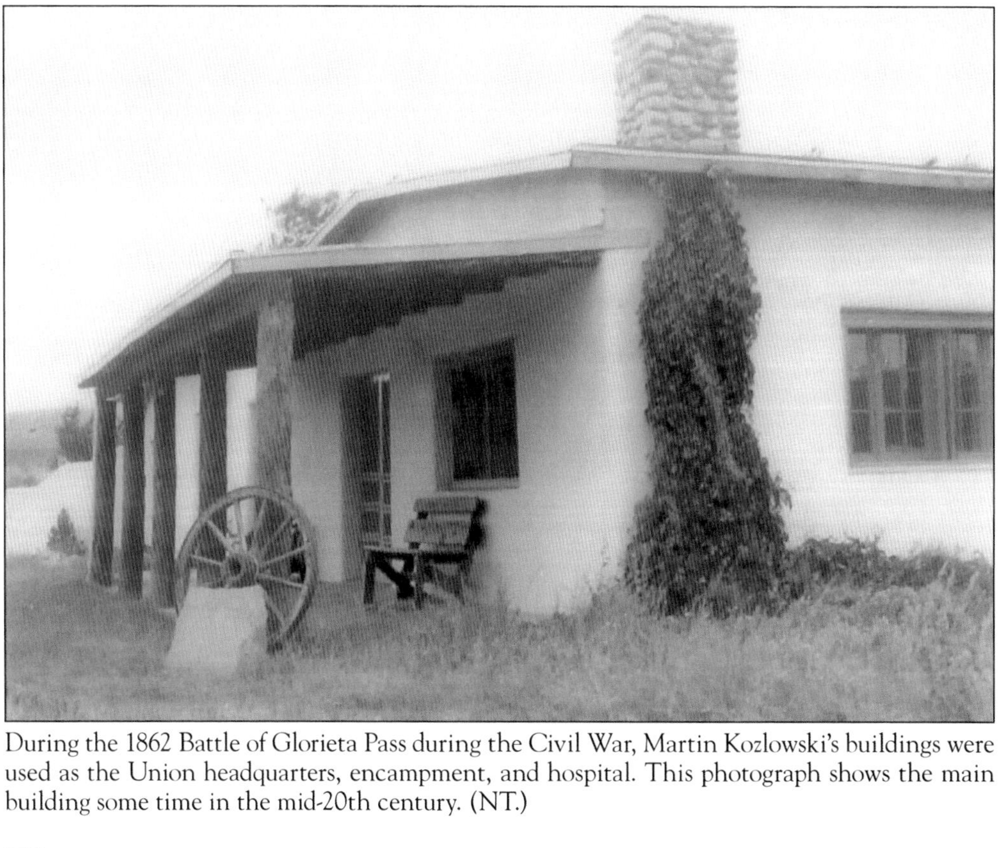

During the 1862 Battle of Glorieta Pass during the Civil War, Martin Kozlowski's buildings were used as the Union headquarters, encampment, and hospital. This photograph shows the main building some time in the mid-20th century. (NT.)

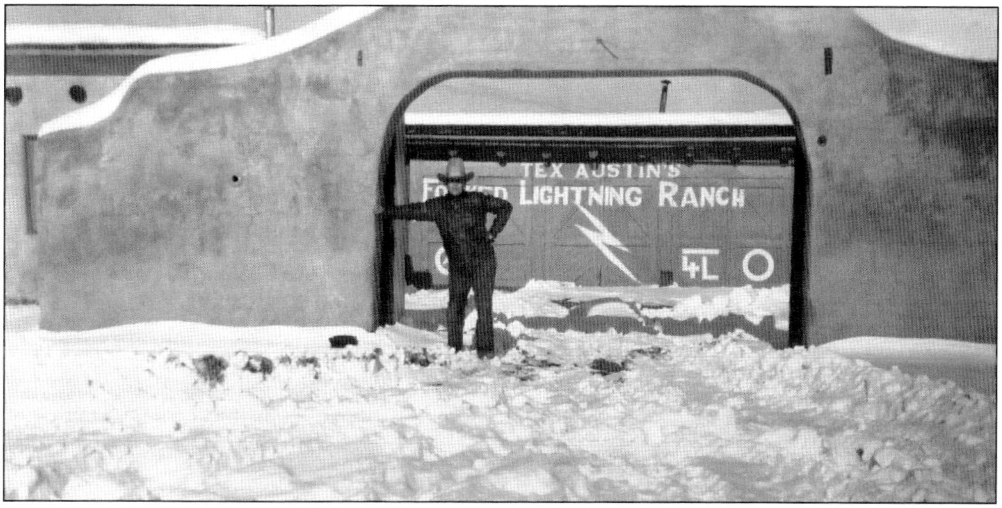

The two photographs on this page show the barns at Kozlowski's Ranch soon after it was purchased by Tex Austin in 1925. Austin converted the old buildings into his ranch headquarters, including a store to capture some of the expanding tourist trade. Even after he completed the new ranch house about a mile to the east, the Kozlowski buildings were used as a trading post and center for ranching operations. They continued as the ranch operations center during the Buddy Fogelson–Greer Garson years. (Both, NT.)

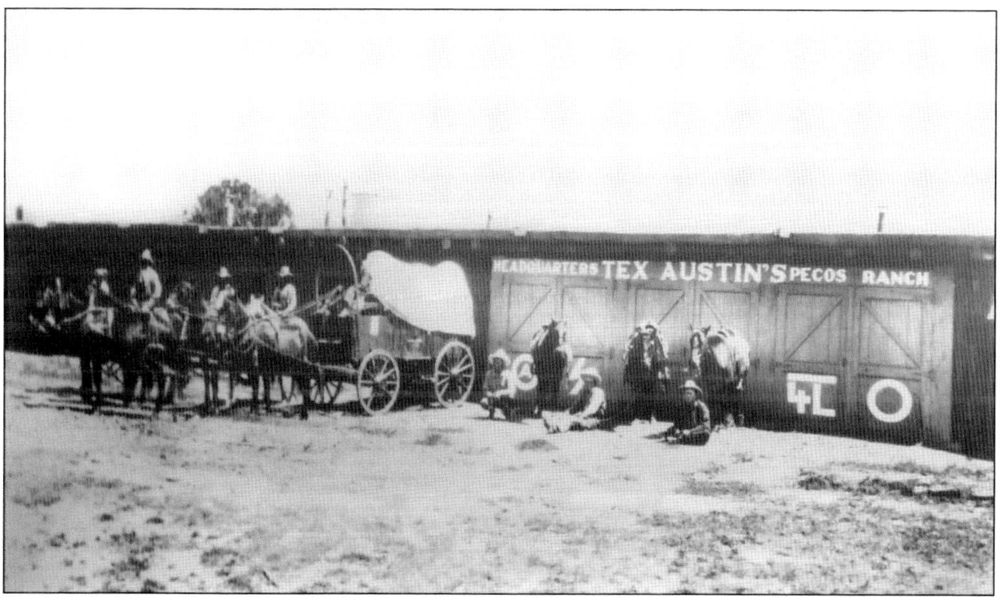

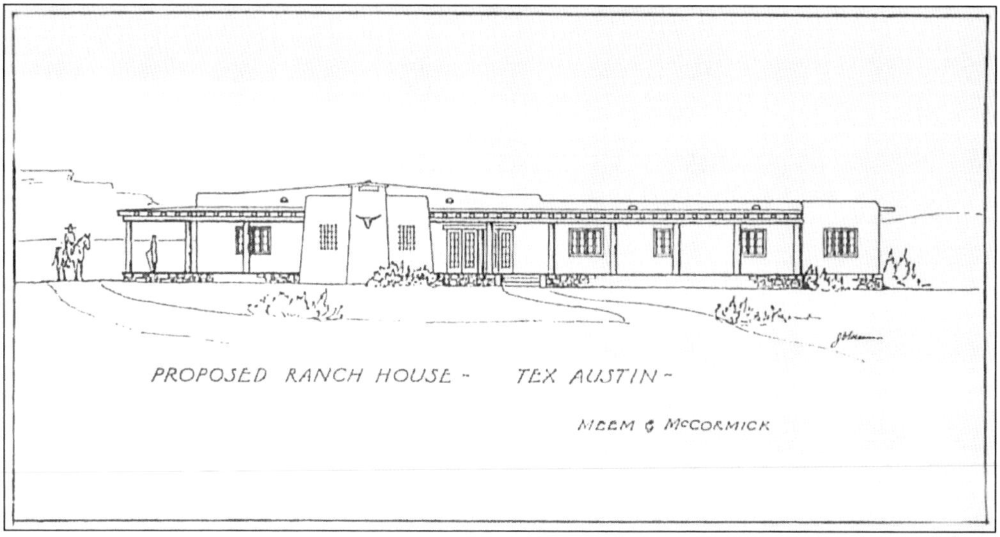

Within months of acquiring his Pecos ranch, Austin hired architect John Gaw Meem. The house that Meem designed for Austin is on a bluff overlooking the Pecos River valley, with vistas of pink sandstone outcroppings on Glorieta Mesa. It is a square, single-story structure with all rooms opening into the center courtyard. There is an expansive front porch from which to enjoy views down the Pecos Valley. (Both, CSWR, John Gaw Meem collection.)

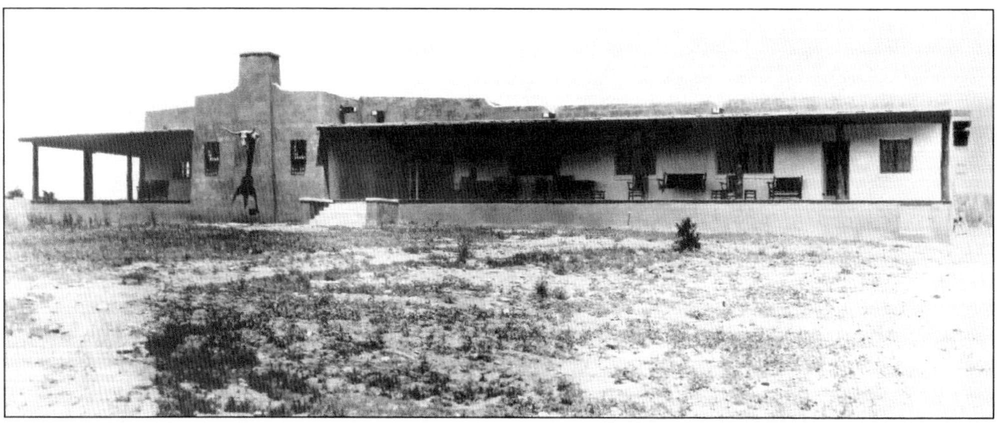

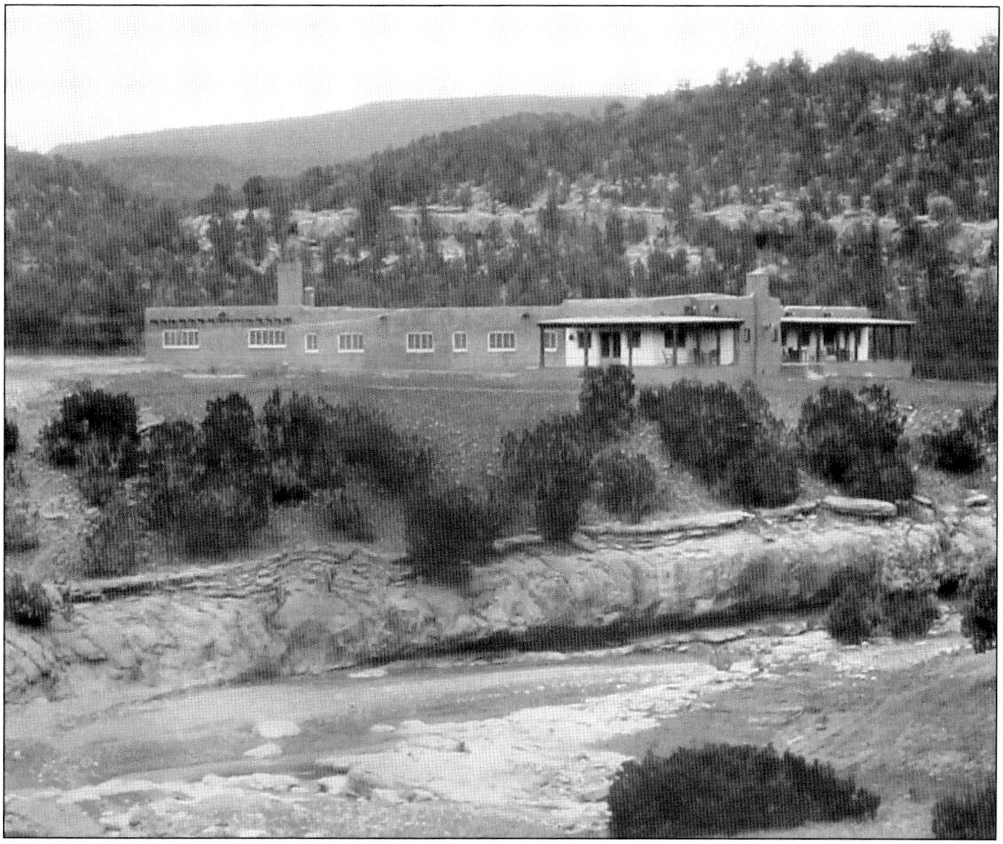

The photograph above shows the southern and eastern elevations of Meem's creation shortly after it was completed in 1926. Glorieta Creek is visible in the foreground, and the Pecos River is below a steep bank beyond the east side of the house. The house is actually more modest than it appears in photographs; the rooms are fairly small and the ceilings are low. Because it was designed to house guests, there is a very large kitchen and a separate dining room. Pecos can be quite snowy during the winter months, and the house was used little during the winter. (Above, CSWR, John Gaw Meem collection; below, PNHP No. 4720.)

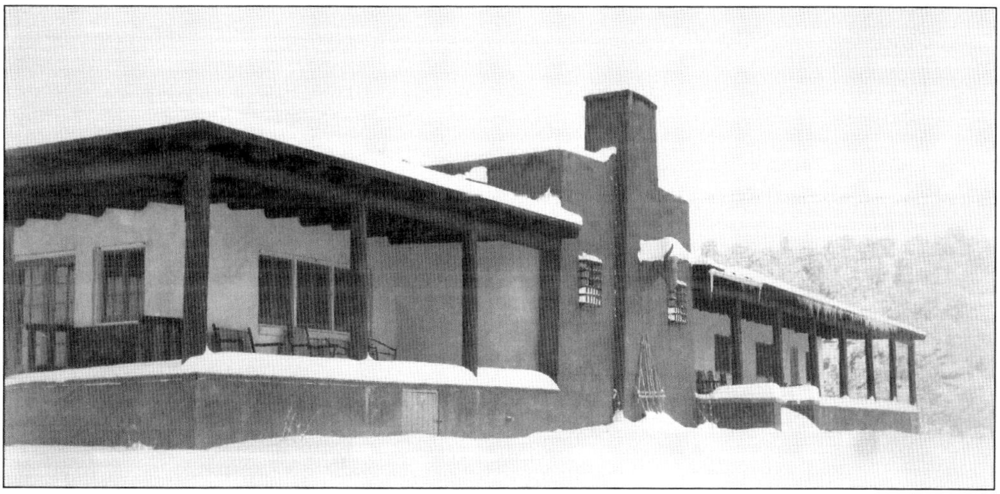

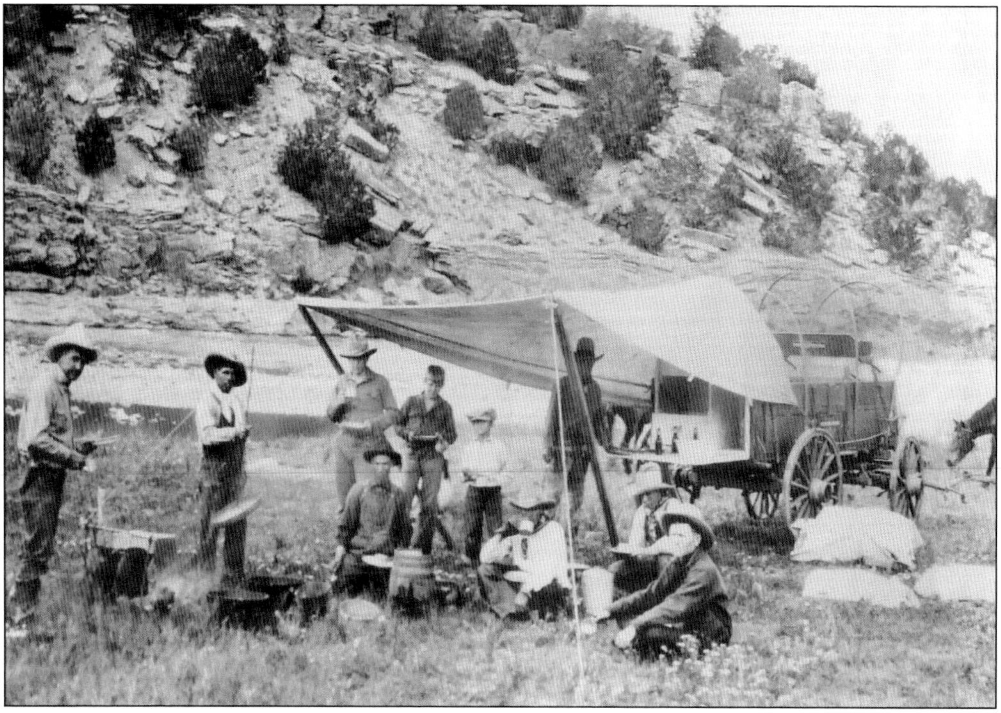

At the ranch, 18 guests shared 9 bedrooms for a weekly rate of $125 per person. Advertisements promised, "All proper service . . . to insure the comfort and friendly atmosphere of a country home . . . Feed—and how! . . . served ranch style . . . in big heaping dishes." Highlights for guests were camping trips into the high country and chuck wagon picnics, along with excursions to the nearby Spanish and Pueblo ruins, where guests were encouraged to dig for artifacts. (Above, PNHP No. 4780; below, No. 4781.)

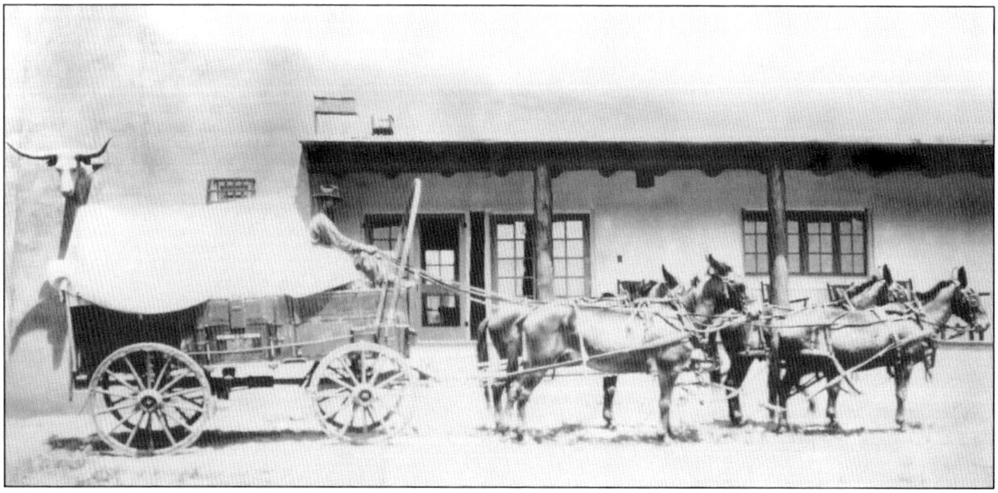

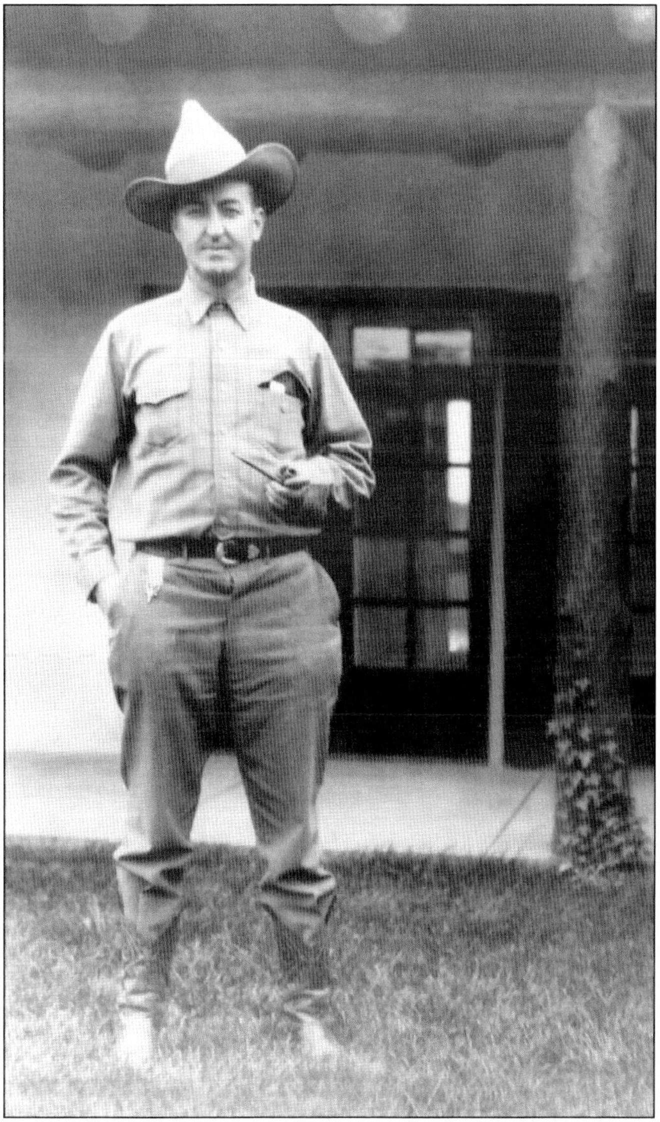

Austin often said that he ran several thousand head of cattle on 100,000 acres of leased grazing land. But then, he said a lot of things. The photograph at right shows Tex Austin at Forked Lightning. The photograph below shows a chuck wagon, along with cowboys, dudes, and horses. Unfortunately, the ranch only operated for seven years. Austin lost the property following the failure of a British rodeo promotion that was blocked by animal rights groups. He lost more than $20,000 in that one venture alone. The last paying guest stayed at Forked Lightning in May 1933. (Right, PNHP No. 4782; below, No. 5025.)

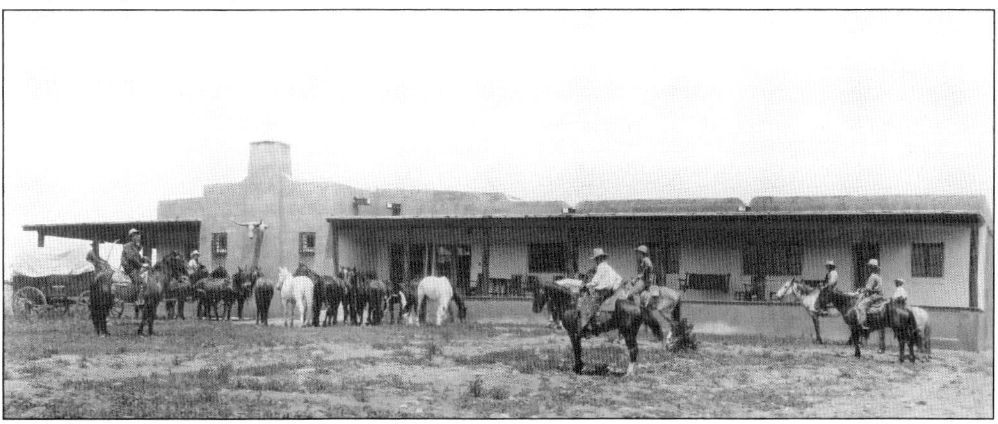

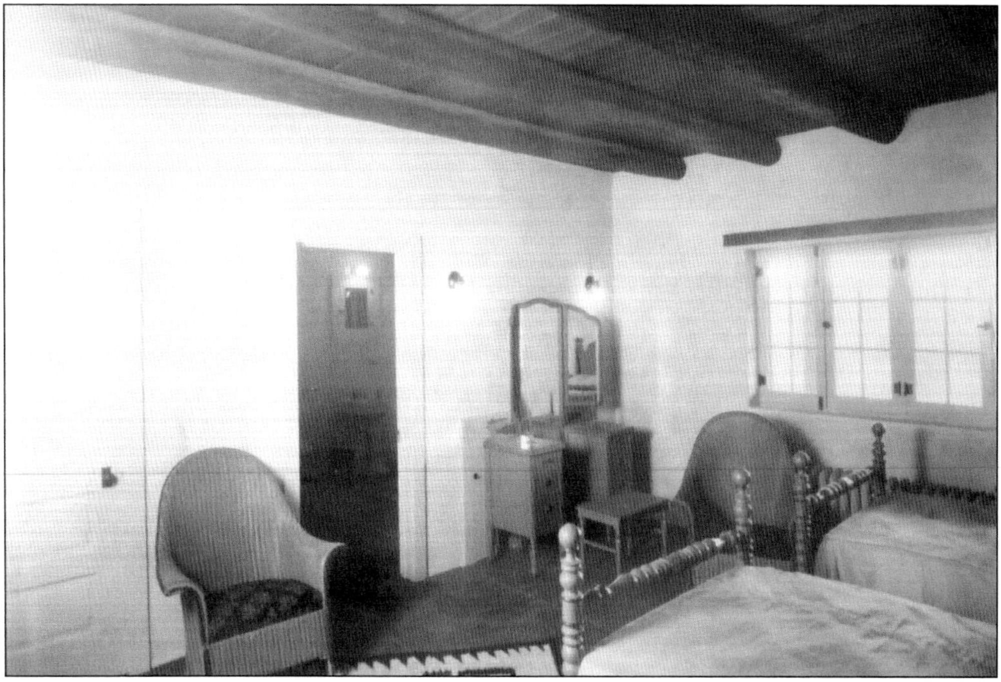

The photographs on this and the opposite page show the interior of the Meem-designed Forked Lightning ranch house in the late 1920s. It was little changed during the 50-year residency of Buddy Fogelson and his wife, Greer Garson, and it looks much the same under National Park Service stewardship today. The photograph above shows a typical guest bedroom. The photograph below shows the fireplace in the main living room. Above the fireplace is an early iteration of Tex Austin's cattle brand, before he created the Forked Lightning brand. Note the two pistols on the Navajo rug on the table in the foreground. (Both, CSWR, John Gaw Meem collection.)

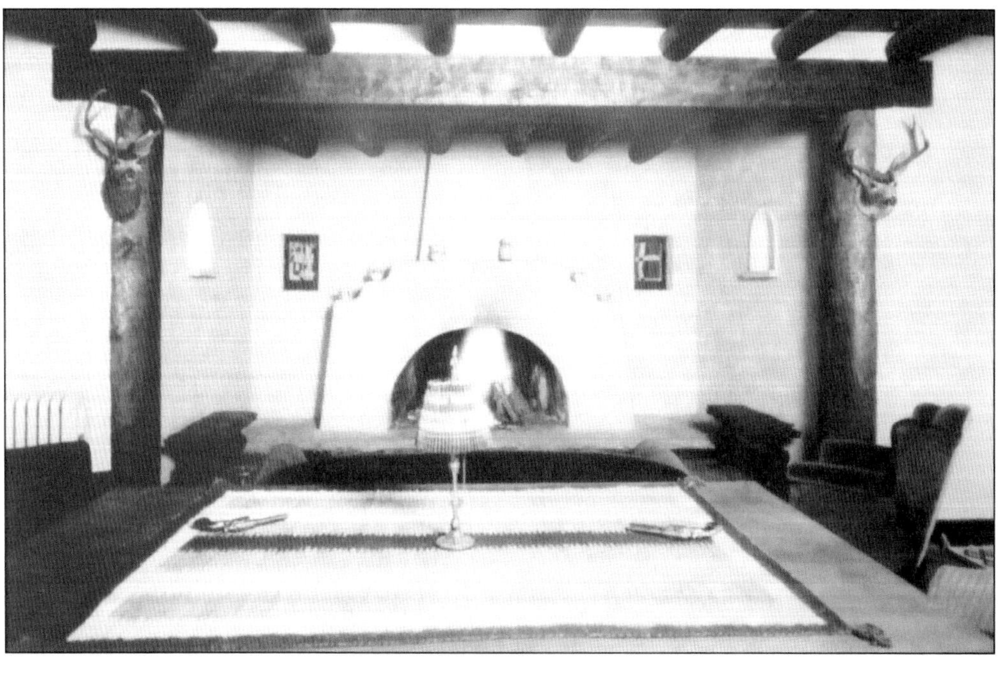

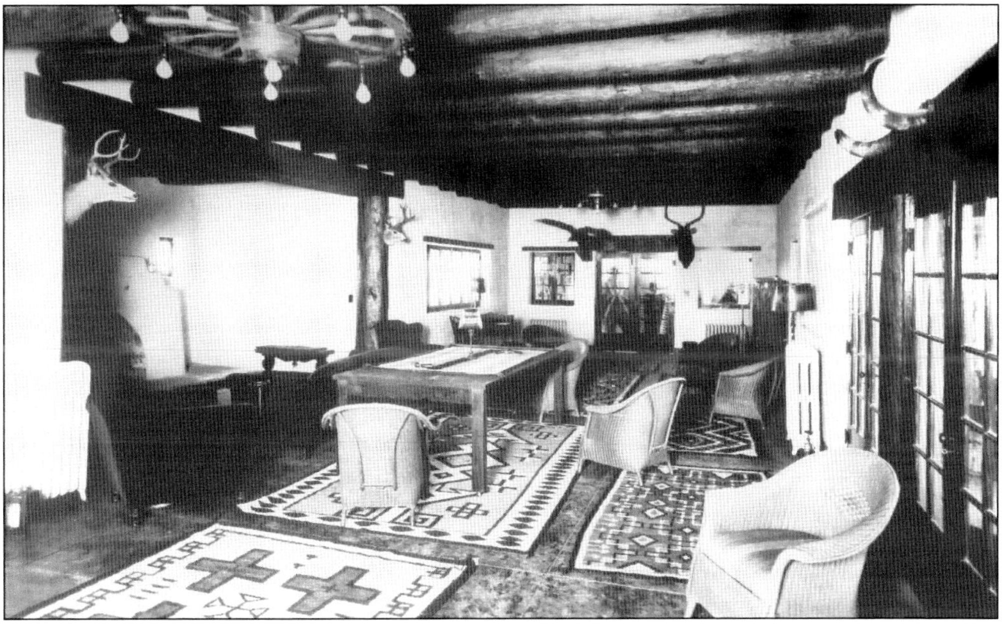

These photographs show the Forked Lightning ranch house's main living room. The photograph above is from the east side of the room looking to the west. The fireplace nook is to the left, and the french doors to the right opened into the interior courtyard. The doors at the end of the room led to a covered porch. Most of the house's rooms opened out to the inner courtyard. The view below is facing the opposite direction, with the fireplace nook to the right, beyond which are the front doors. The french doors on the left open to the inner courtyard. The door at the end of the room leads to Greer Garson's sitting room and bedroom. (Both, CSWR, John Gaw Meem collection.)

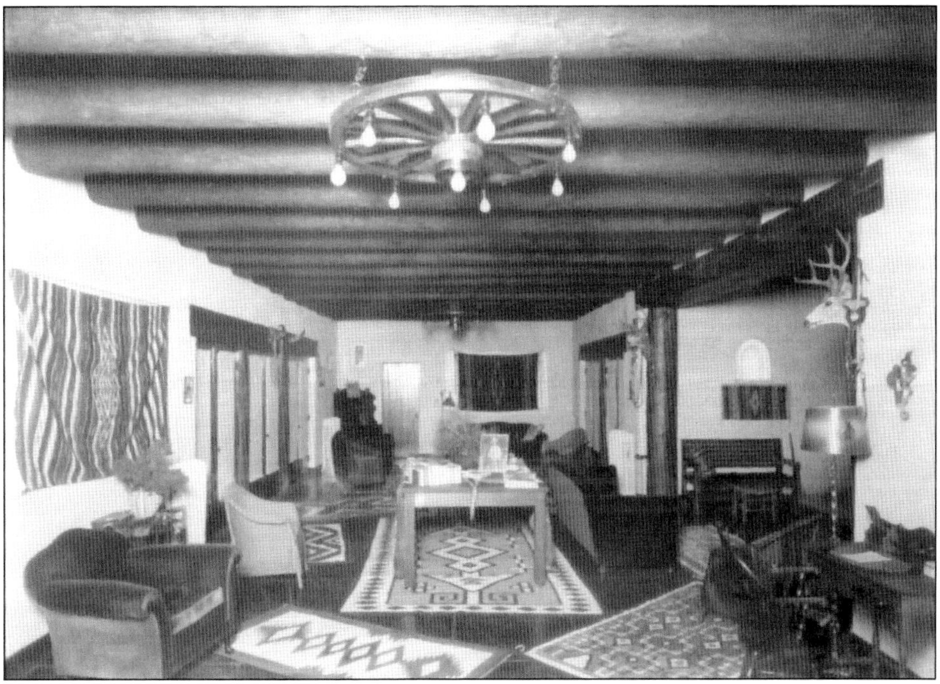

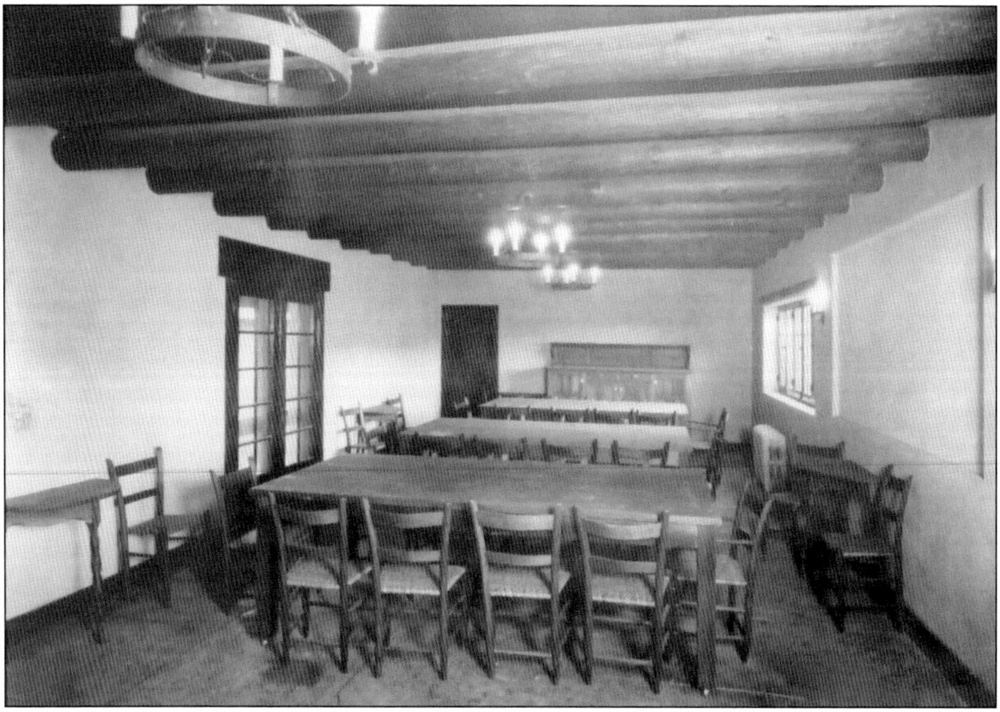

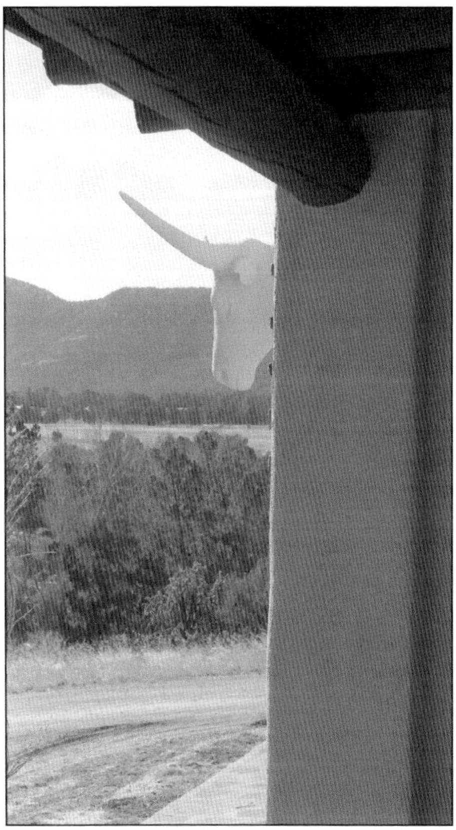

This photograph shows the dining room as it appeared in the Tex Austin days. Later, Greer Garson hosted dinners for many of Hollywood's elite in this room. The ceiling light fixtures and wall sconces, designed by John Gaw Meem, are still in place. The views from every room in the house either looked outside to magnificent scenery or into the shaded interior courtyard. (CSWR.)

The steer head mounted on the front of the house was sculpted by an East Coast artist who lived as a hermit in a nearby cave. Apparently, he put the horns on upside down, but when a furious Tex Austin saw the result, the sculptor refused to correct his "mistake." Austin was then forced to reorient them himself. In the background of this photograph is Glorieta Mesa, the pink sandstone outcropping of which inspired Greer Garson to paint the ranch house, outbuildings, and gates pink. (AC.)

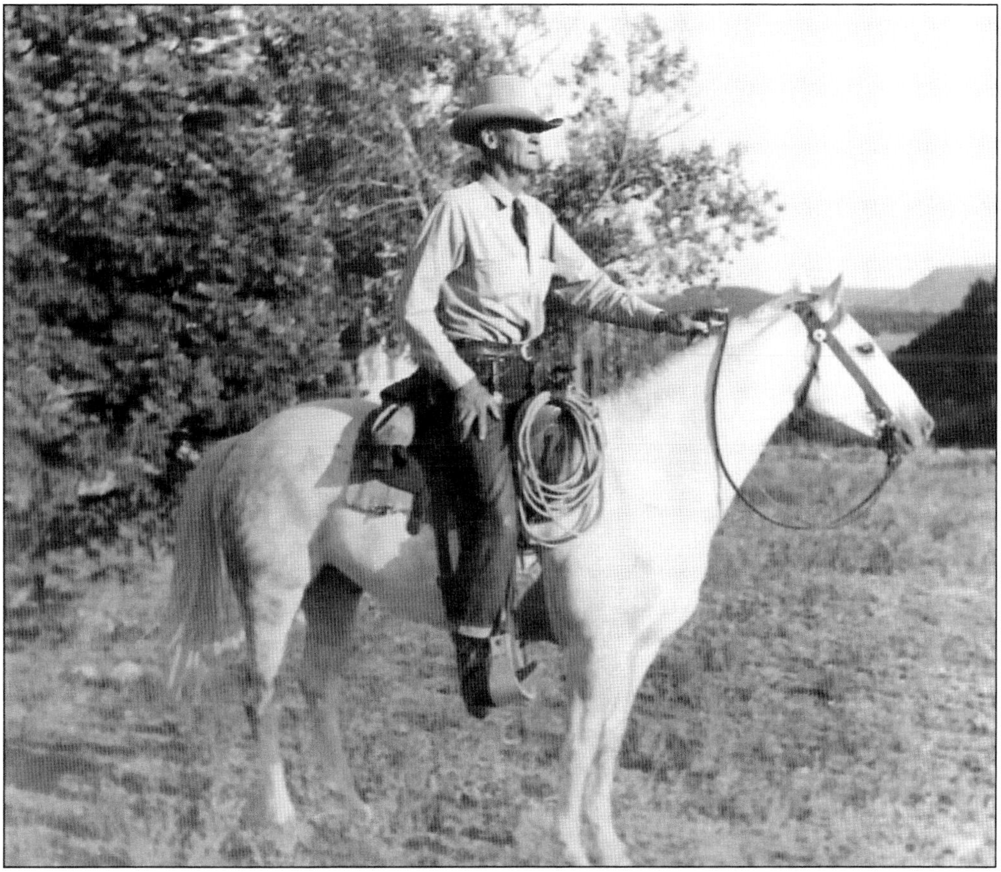

A.R. "Slim" Wasson was the ranch foreman for Forked Lightning during the time Greer Garson was in residence. Little is known about him other than that he was born in Texas in 1897 and was working as a ranch hand in Pecos in 1935. The photograph at right shows Greer Garson, in the black hat; Wasson, to her left; and two members of the Forked Lightning staff. The little girl is unidentified. Also in the image is one of Garson's beloved poodles, either Happy or Tiffany. (Above, PNHP No. 4721; right, No. 4737.)

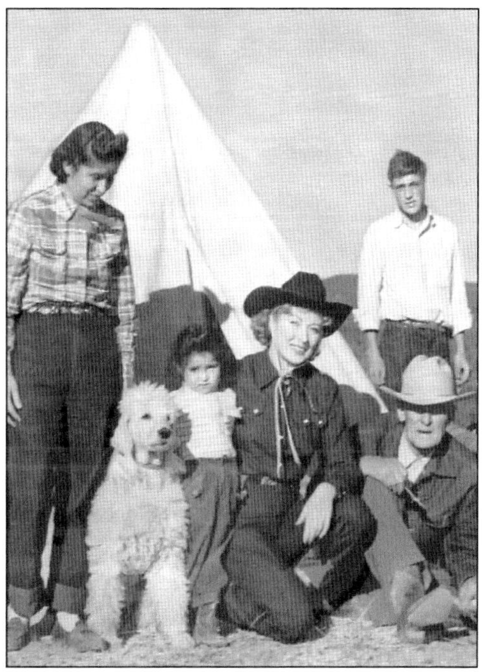

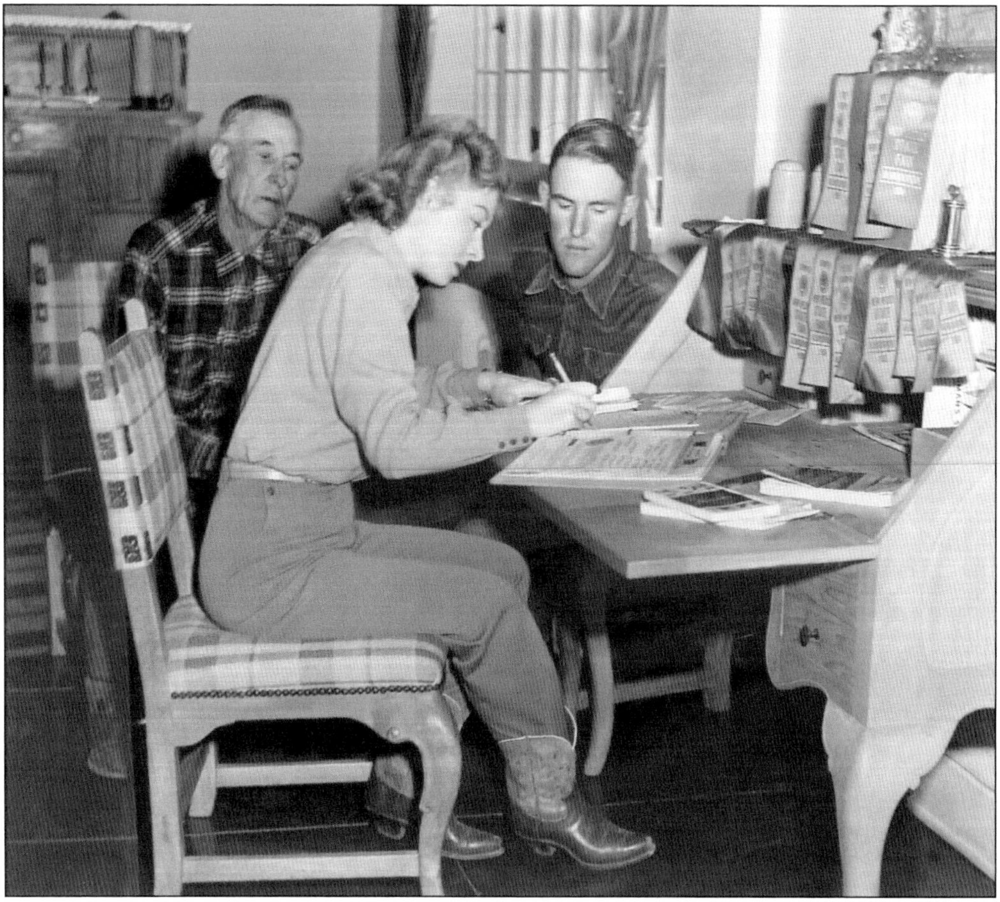

Greer Garson became enamored with the West immediately upon seeing Forked Lightning Ranch. She is seen here at her desk at the ranch, with ranch foreman Slim Wasson and ranch hand Vester Barnet, as she prepares applications to show cattle at the New Mexico State Fair. Note the first-place ribbons that line the top of the desk. Initially, she purchased a Scottish, all-white, Shorthorn herd that won top honors in its class at the 1952 New Mexico State Fair. The four yearlings shown here were offspring of champion herd sire Philorth White Knight. The man in the image is Vester Barnet, and the little boy is unidentified. These cattle proved unsuccessful and were phased out in the 1950s. (Above, PNHP No. 4726; below, No. 4545.)

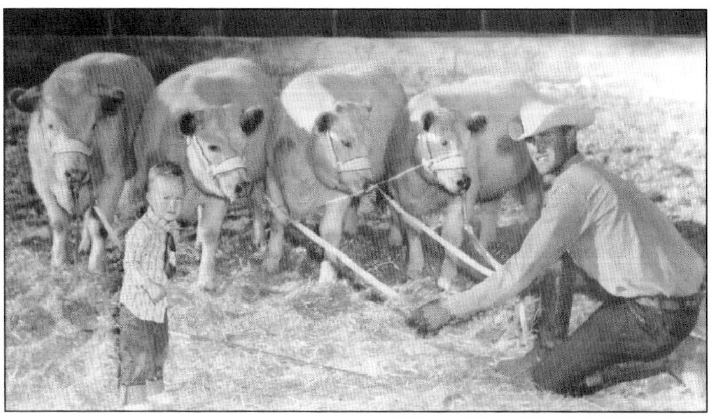

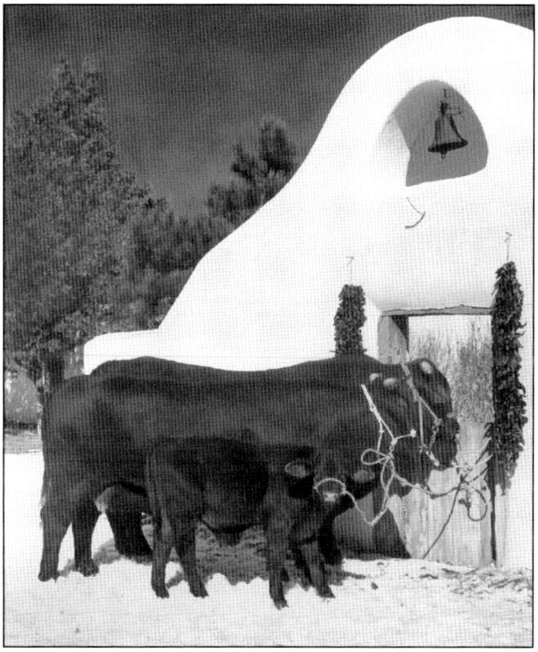

E.E. "Buddy" Fogelson, on a whim at a cattle auction in 1958, purchased a purebred Santa Gertrudis bull named Gee Gee, along with three heifers. They became the start of the famous Forked Lightning Santa Gertrudis herd. The breed, a cross between Shorthorn and Brahma, had been developed on the King Ranch in Texas and was the first recognized American cattle breed. The Fogelsons eventually stopped showing these cattle at the New Mexico State Fair to give others a chance to win prizes. The photograph at right shows Bertie and his calf in 1960 at the back gate to the ranch house. The photograph below shows two prize-winning bulls at Kozlowski's. (Right, PNHP No. 4748; below, No. 1743.)

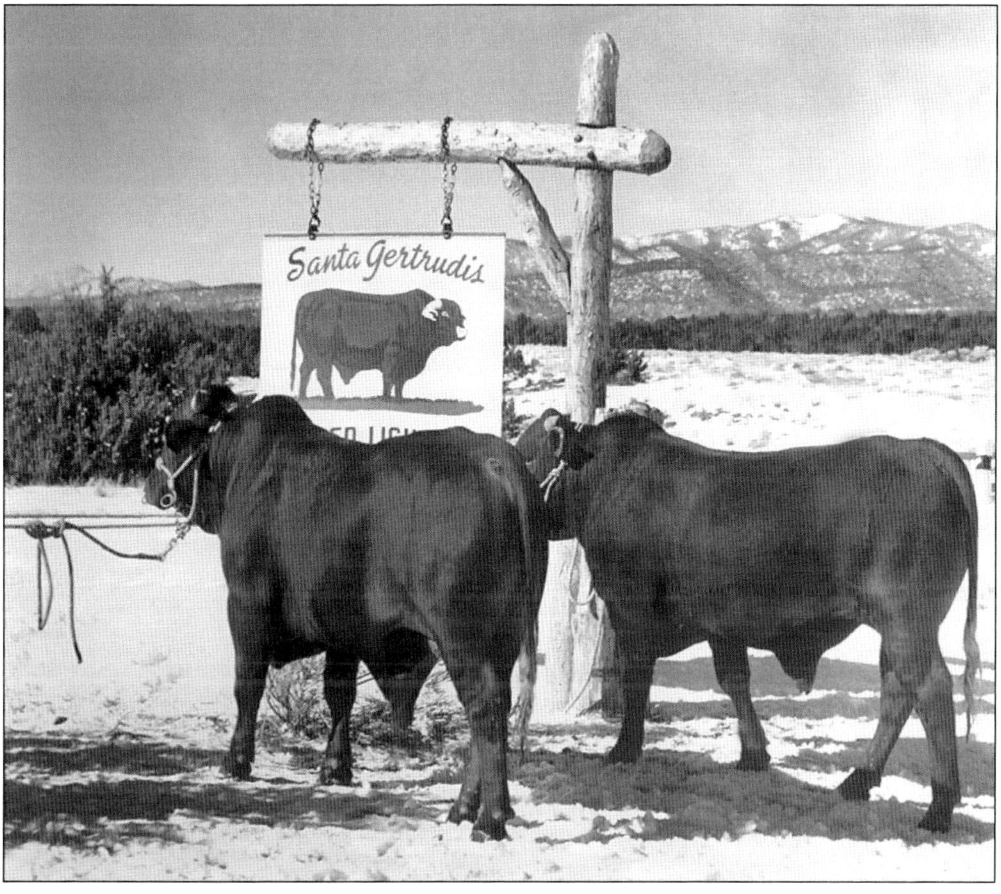

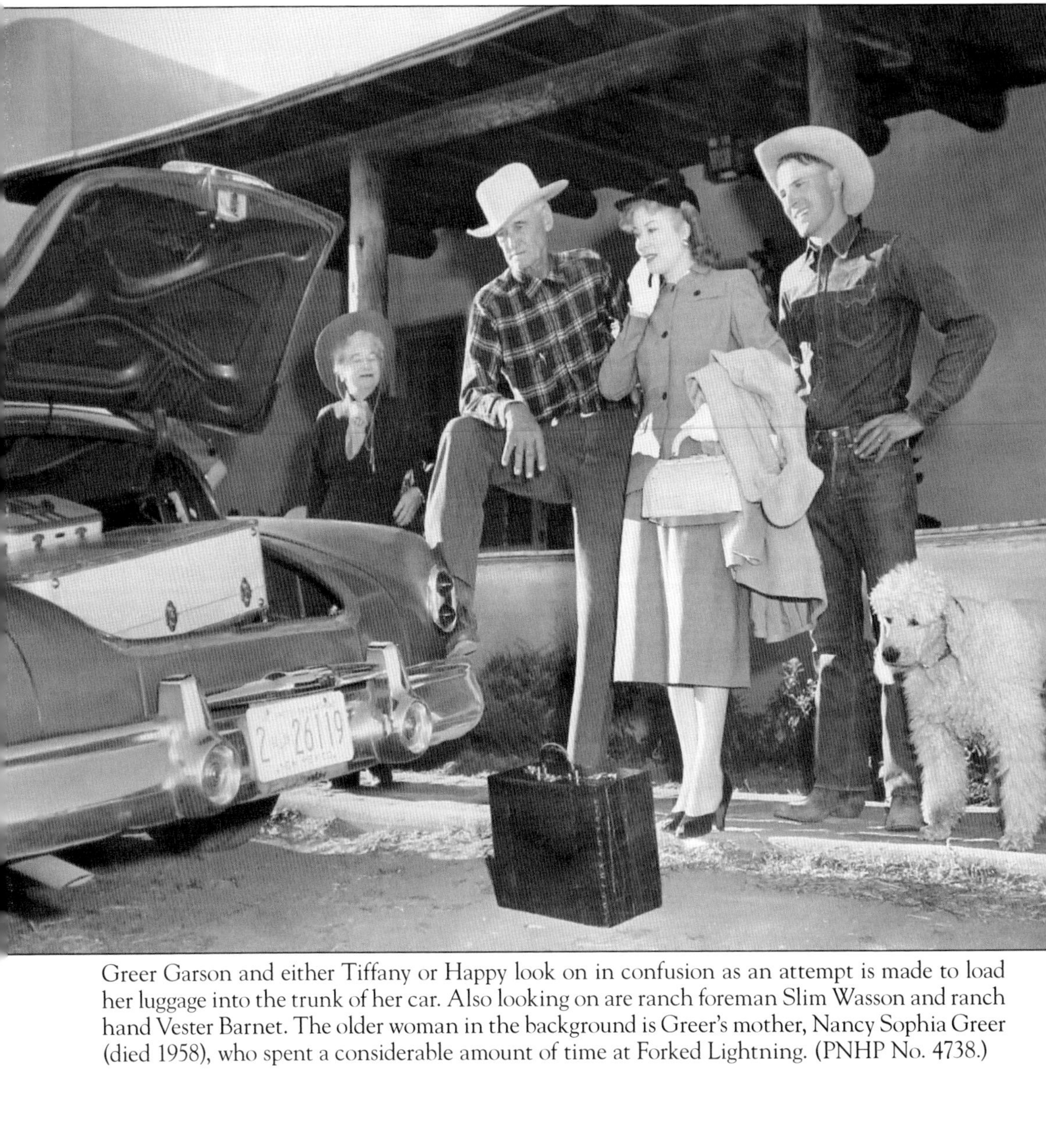

Greer Garson and either Tiffany or Happy look on in confusion as an attempt is made to load her luggage into the trunk of her car. Also looking on are ranch foreman Slim Wasson and ranch hand Vester Barnet. The older woman in the background is Greer's mother, Nancy Sophia Greer (died 1958), who spent a considerable amount of time at Forked Lightning. (PNHP No. 4738.)

Eight

An Indian Detour

The Indian Detour Transportation Company was created in 1925 by Maj. R. Hunter Clarkson after the Fred Harvey Company acquired a local tour operation. An Indian Detour was a trip to "terra incognita," "backstage" of the railroad tracks, with a stress on the "authentic."

Starting on May 15, 1926, for a price of $45 per person, passengers on the AT&SF between Chicago and Los Angeles could leave either from the Castaneda Hotel in Las Vegas, New Mexico (westbound), or the Alvarado Hotel in Albuquerque (eastbound), for a three-day, two-night Indian Detour in specially designed, thunderbird-emblazoned Packard buses or seven-person Packard touring cars. The "dudes," as guests were called, felt secure and protected by the experienced but taciturn "cowboy" drivers and were guided by charming, knowledgeable young female guides called "couriers." The dudes were soon to experience the romance of the Southwest: ancient mysterious ruins, peaceful "noble savages" living close to nature and turning out unique handicrafts, and descendants of Spanish conquistadors, all while surrounded by remote magnificent landscapes bathed in New Mexico's unique light.

The Pecos area was the focus of one day on the initial Indian Detour route. There was a stop at Pigeon's Ranch to see the Civil War battlefield and sights such as the "Oldest Well," a visit to the recently excavated ruins of Pecos Pueblo and its mission church and convento, lunch at the Valley Ranch Apache Inn, a drive by Kozlowski's old ranch and trading post with a look at the Santa Fe Trail, and a visit to the church and village of San Jose del Vado.

Following the writings of Charles Lummis (1859–1928), such as *Land of Poco Tiempo*, published in 1893, Fred Harvey exploited a "Disneyfication" of the Southwest. But, today, the ideal of multiple cultures living in harmony has, to a great extent, become a reality.

The reader is encouraged to read Chris Wilson's 1979 *The Myth of Santa Fe*, as well as the writings of Marta Wiegle, including her 1990 essay "Southwest Lures: Innocents Detoured, Incensed Determined" and her 1989 essay "From Desert to Disney World: The Santa Fe Railway and Fred Harvey Company Display the Indian Southwest," which are available on the Internet.

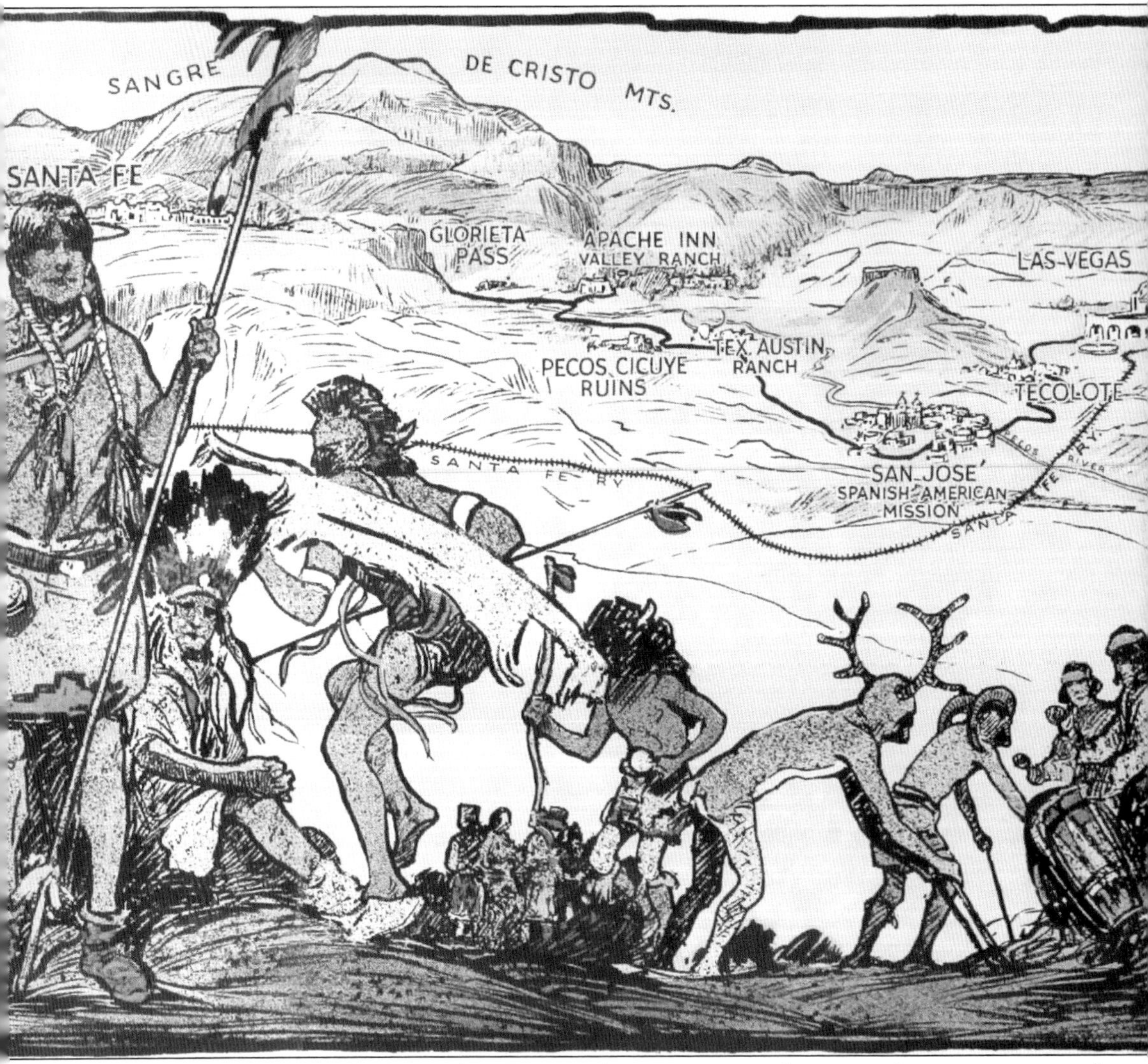

This map was used in the first Indian Detour advertising materials to introduce trip routes, and it shows many of the places found in this book. It is the work of Gerald Cassidy (1879–1934), who also did the large paintings hanging in the lobby of the La Fonda Hotel in Santa Fe. Detour founder Maj. R. Hunter Clarkson declared, "There is more of history, prehistory, human and scenic interest in New Mexico than in any other similar area of the world, not excepting India, Egypt, Europe or Asia; . . . the big idea is not only to let people know what is in Northern New Mexico but to tell them what it is when they see it." Pecos is at the very heart of this "big idea." (AC.)

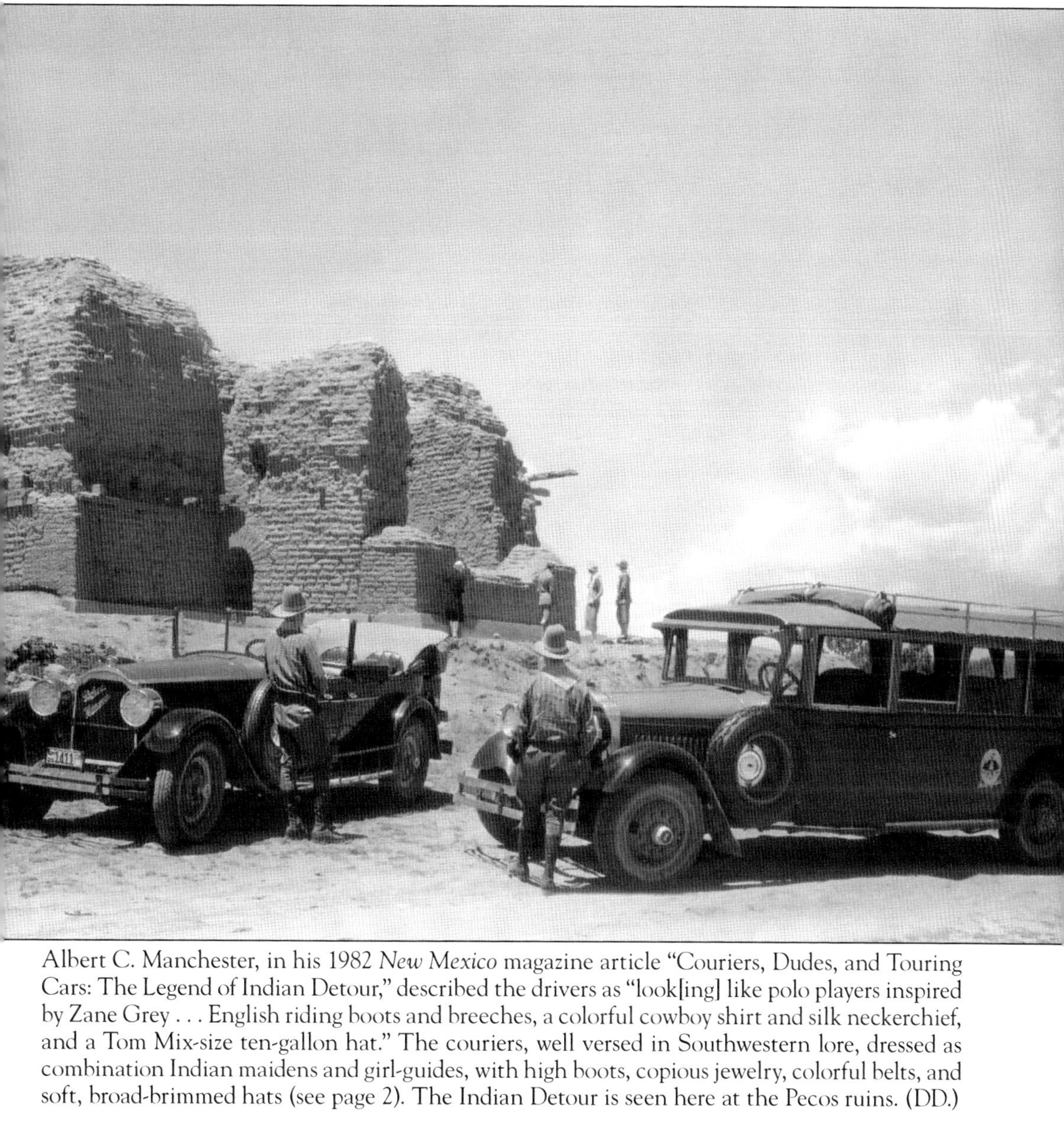

Albert C. Manchester, in his 1982 *New Mexico* magazine article "Couriers, Dudes, and Touring Cars: The Legend of Indian Detour," described the drivers as "look[ing] like polo players inspired by Zane Grey . . . English riding boots and breeches, a colorful cowboy shirt and silk neckerchief, and a Tom Mix-size ten-gallon hat." The couriers, well versed in Southwestern lore, dressed as combination Indian maidens and girl-guides, with high boots, copious jewelry, colorful belts, and soft, broad-brimmed hats (see page 2). The Indian Detour is seen here at the Pecos ruins. (DD.)

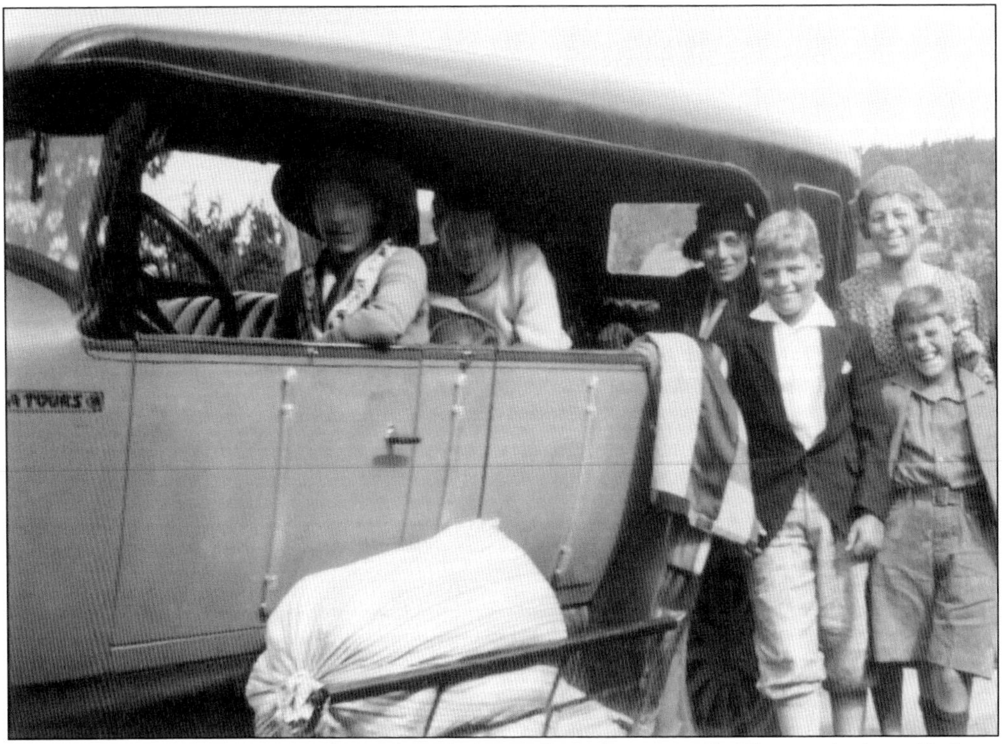

This 1925 Stanley Steamer is driven by Gladys Jenkyns (see page 2). This might be a Koshare Tours car or a car from another tour company, as the word "Tours" on the side of the car is plural, while "Indian Detour" is officially singular. Koshare Tours, founded in the early 1920s by future author Erna Fergusson, was bought out by Fred Harvey to become Indian Detour, with Fergusson hired on to train the couriers. (MH No. 1513.)

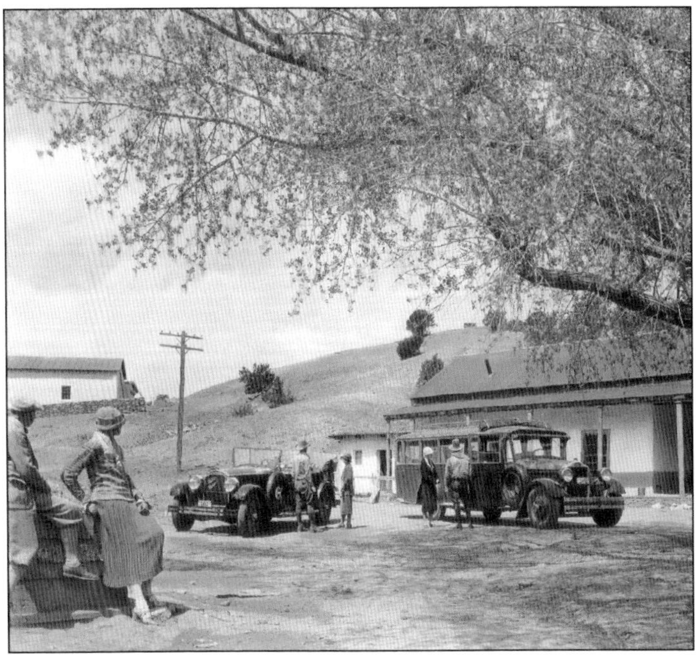

Here, an Indian Detour car and bus are stopped at Pigeon's Ranch, near Glorieta. The two dudes on the left are sitting on the "Oldest Well." The dudes toured key sites associated with the Civil War battle in the pass and were no doubt regaled with stories by Tom Greer. (DD.)

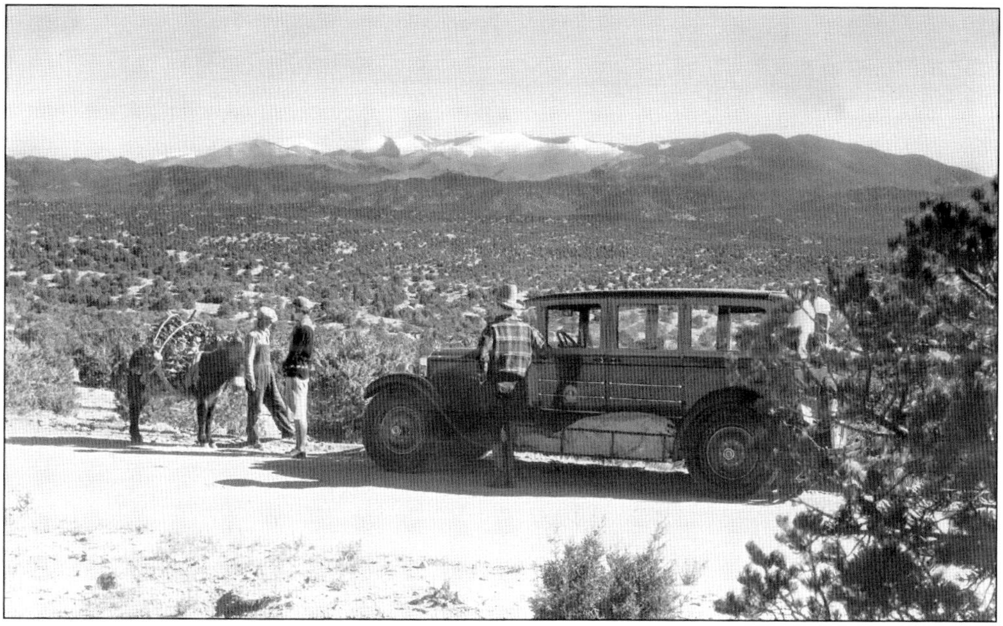

Harvey cars and buses were painted Tesuque brown, a color named for one of the pueblos they visited. The thunderbird, said to be a harbinger of good luck, was painted on a bright orange background and applied to the side of the vehicles. There is a fine example of an Indian Detour sign behind the concierge desk in the lobby of the La Fonda Hotel in Santa Fe. The thunderbird was the pastel coyote, or now the kokopelli (hunchback flute player), of its day. Above is an Indian Detour bus on the road to Pecos, and below is a car far up the Pecos River canyon. (Both, DD.)

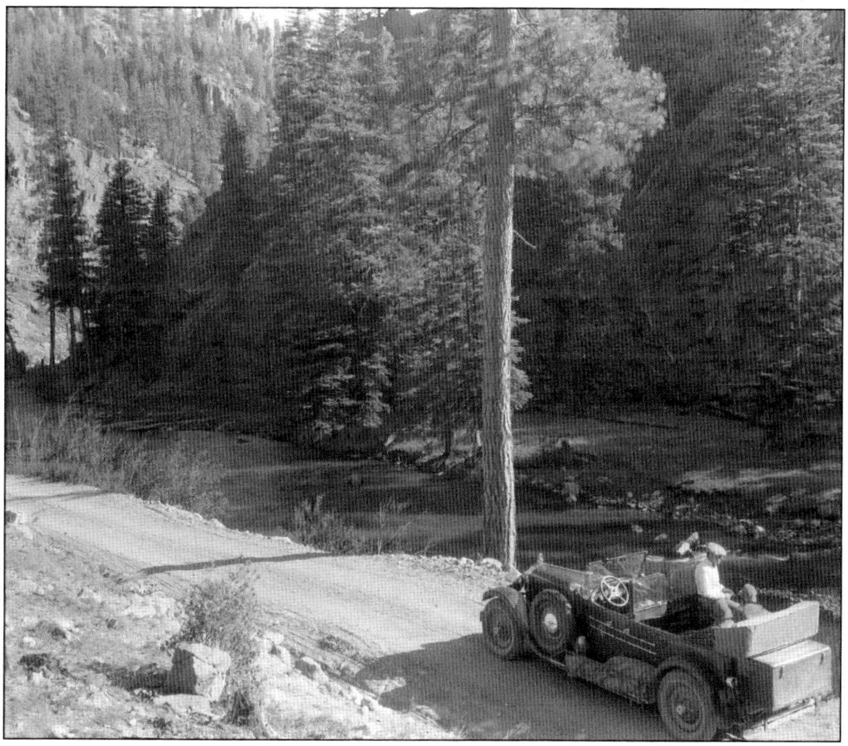

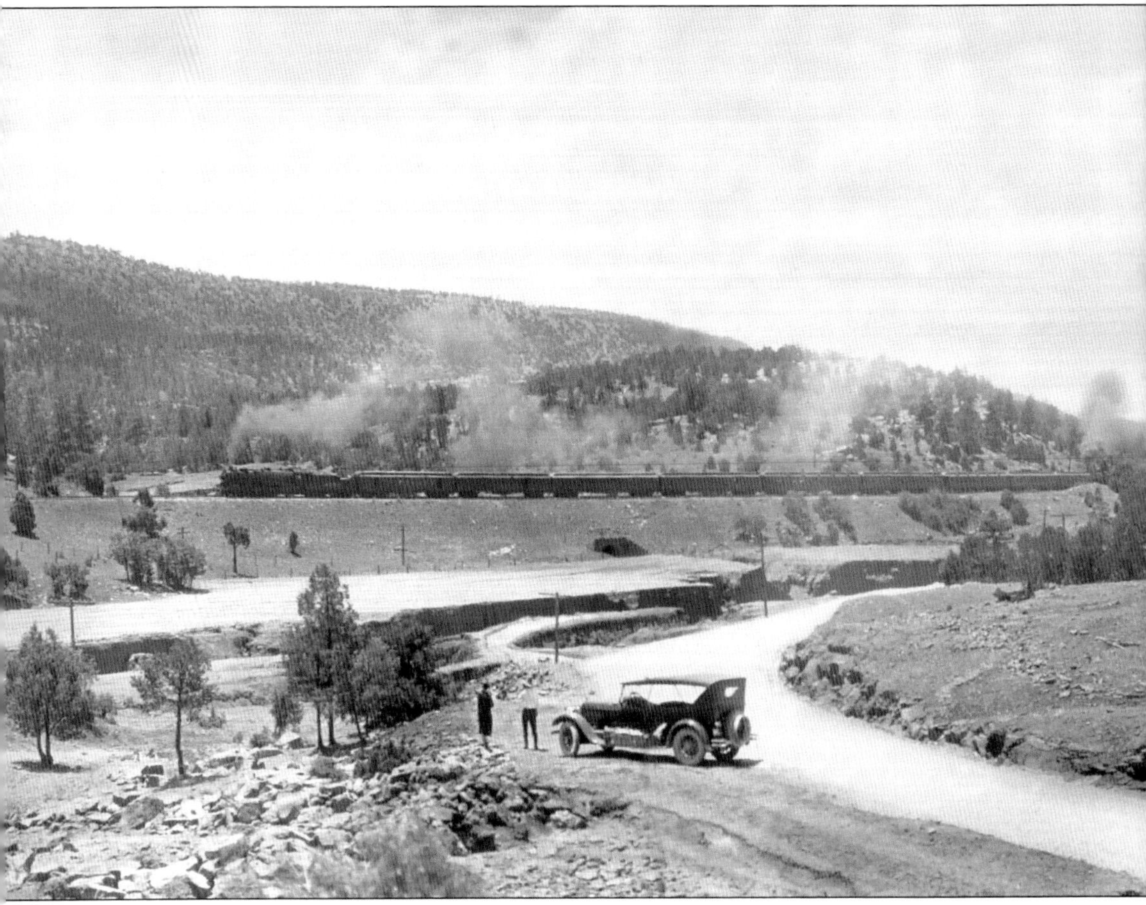

Will Rogers is quoted as saying, "Buffalo fed the west for years and they put it on a nickel. Fred Harvey took up where the buffalo left off." The Santa Fe's *Navajo*, *Chief*, and *Superchief* trains, along with the Harveycars (as the tour cars and buses were called), made it possible to enjoy the Southwest as if it were an amusement park attraction (in the late 19th century, there was a massive sign by the railroad tracks identifying Pecos), a trip on Disney's train through the Painted Desert and Grand Canyon, but here it was real. As many people view the Southwest out the car window and through stops at historical markers, visitor centers, and gift shops, the same still holds true today. But, if one looks a little closer, a clear vision comes into view. This photograph shows Glorieta. (DD.)

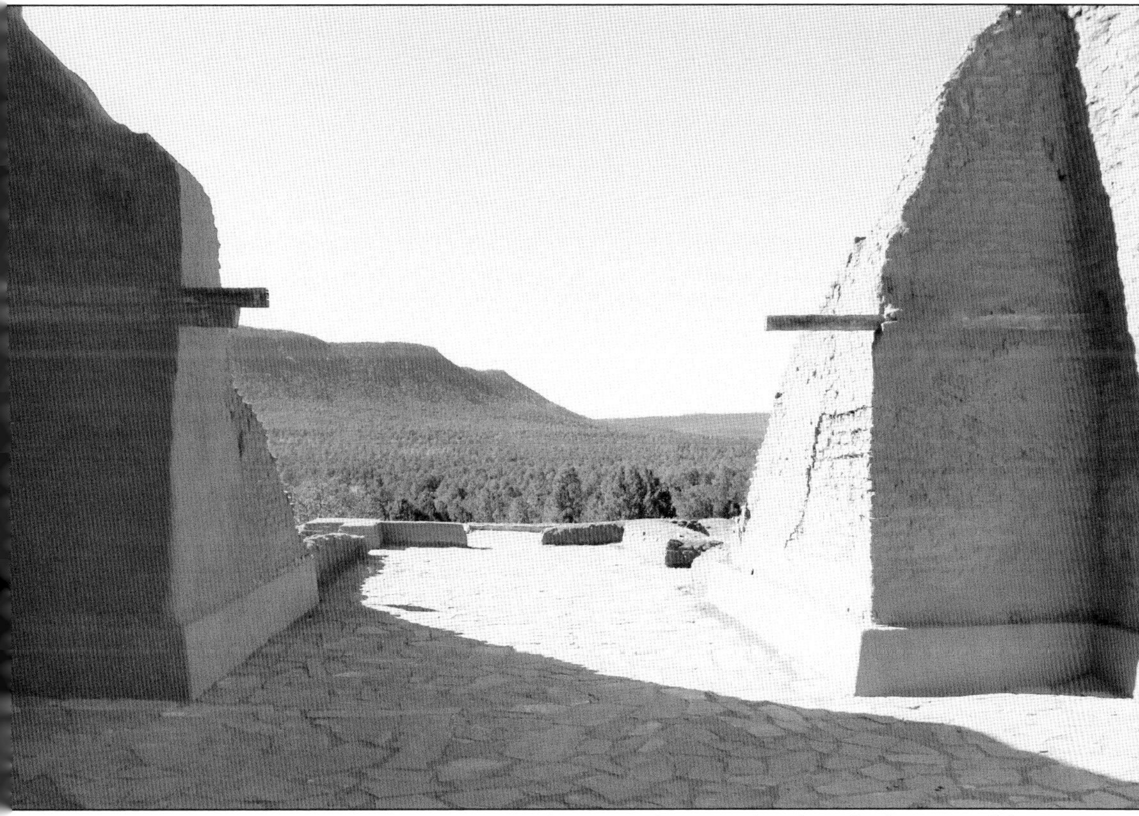

This photograph was taken from the interior of the restored Pecos Church at the location of the main altar. The view is to the west, showing Glorieta Mesa. Hidden in the middle-ground piñon/juniper vegetation is the Santa Fe Trail. There are also a number of buried archaeological sites, as well as the remains of Spanish and Mexican period homesteads. The Pecos River is out of the picture to the left (east). The vista from this spot is essentially the same today, as the area has been protected from development by the National Park Service. (AC.)

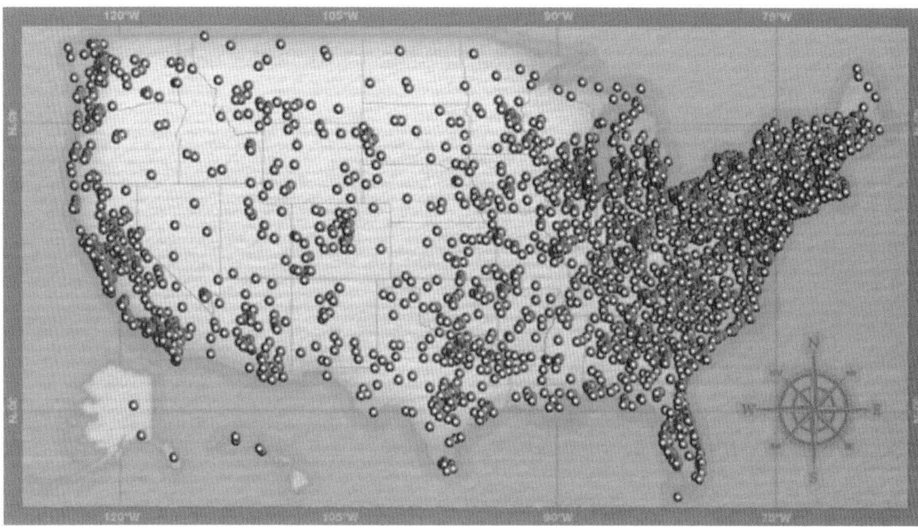

Consistent with our mission to preserve history on a local level, this book was printed in South Carolina on American-made paper and manufactured entirely in the United States. Products carrying the accredited Forest Stewardship Council (FSC) label are printed on 100 percent FSC-certified paper.

MADE IN THE USA